1

FINDING JESUS
THROUGH THE GOSPELS

History and Hermeneutics

Rene Latourelle, S.J.

Translated by Aloysius Owen, S.J.

ALBA · HOUSE   NEW · YORK

SOCIETY OF ST. PAUL, 2187 VICTORY BLVD., STATEN ISLAND, NEW YORK 10314

Library of Congress Cataloging in Publication Data

Latourelle, René.
    Finding Jesus through the Gospels.

    Translation of L'accés à Jésus par les Evangiles.
    Bibliography: p.
    Includes index.
    1. Jesus Christ—Historicity. 2. Bible. N.T.
Gospels—Criticism, interpretation, etc. 3. Bible. N.T.
Gospels—Hermeneutics. I. Title.
BT301.2.L2613   232   78-25732
ISBN: 0-8189-0379-1

Nihil Obstat:
Daniel V. Flynn, J.C.D.
Censor Librorum

Imprimatur:
Joseph T. O'Keefe
Vicar General, Archdiocese of New York
October 23, 1978

The Nihil Obstat and Imprimatur are
a declaration that a book or pamphlet is considered
to be free from doctrinal or moral error. It is not implied
that those who have granted the Nihil Obstat and
Imprimatur agree with the contents,
opinions or statements expressed.

Designed, printed and bound in the United States of
America by the Fathers and Brothers of the
Society of St. Paul, 2187 Victory Boulevard,
Staten Island, New York, 10314, as part of their
communications apostolate.

1 2 3 4 5 6 7 8 9 (Current Printing: first digit).

Also by the Author

Theology of Revelation (Alba House, 1966)
Theology: Science of Salvation (Alba House, 1969)
Christ & the Church: Signs of Salvation (Alba House, 1972)

TABLE OF CONTENTS

Part III. Outline of a Demonstration

INTRODUCTION

CHRISTIANITY AND CREDIBILITY

I. The Problem

The problem of credibility is due to the greatness of Christianity as well as to the radicalism of its demands.

Indeed, Christianity appears as something scandalous. In the first Epistle to the Corinthians, Paul speaks of the preaching of a "Christ crucified—a stumbling block to Jews, and an absurdity to Gentiles." (1 Cor 1:23). On the contrary, for those who are "called," Jews or Greeks, this Christ is the might and wisdom of God. Salvation through the Incarnation, through death and through the cross, cannot appear as a scandal today as yesterday.

Typical, in regard to this, is Paul's preaching to the Athenians. They treat him as "a magpie," a "promoter of foreign gods" (Ac 17:18), as "introducing a subject unfamiliar to us" (Ac 17:20). So long as he speaks of God the Creator, they tolerate him. But as soon as he speaks of salvation in Jesus

Christ, risen from the dead and glorified, some mock him, while others say: "We must hear you on this topic some other time" (Ac 17:32). Some, however, did join him and became believers.

This account is, as it were, the paradigm of the responses of man to Christ and to Christianity. The Christian message is scandalous, provocative. Besides, it comes to us, not as a scientific fact, but as testimonies of personal and communitarian belief which indissolubly link events and their salvific import. Finally, this is not a neutral message. It is proclaimed at the core of a commitment. It is not offered as information, but as a call to conversion. Christ's word brings out the meaning not only of our personal existence but also the meaning of all human existence. Thenceforth there is not the correcting in detail of our view of the world but of re-orienting all being, of risking all for all, of being or not being. The option for Christ involves not only the transitoriness of the present but the whole of eternity. It is understandable that man, before committing himself thus "in life, in death" wants to know whether he is really acting as man.

Such is the double characteristic of Christian faith. On the one hand, faith as personal adherence to Christ is not a compelling conclusion, of an inductive nature (as from historical evidence), or of a deductive nature (as the conclusion of a syllogism), but is the surrender of man to God. It is a gift of the whole man to God who "gives Himself" wholly in Jesus Christ. As a gift it goes beyond the premises. On the other hand, if faith is the integral deliverance of man to God, it is not resignation to the subconscious, failure of reason, being driven into fideism, incapability of establishing the human correctness of option. It is necessary to know, *before* believing and *for* believing. At its root faith is an act of the intellect. It expresses not only choice of Christ, but also lucidity. The man who commits himself to Christ must have sound reasons for so doing. These reasons can if necessary be made explicit in a coherent discourse. The believer can "test" the reliability of the reasons for his commitment (Lk 1:4). Most of the time, the most simple believer would not know how to detail them. But it belongs to the theologian, as a servant of Christ and of the community of the faithful, to show that the option of faith has sense, that it is *reasonable*.

The theologian should be able to establish that Jesus, not only belongs to the reality of human history, but also that He deciphers the human condition in all dimensions and accomplishes it beyond all that was foreseen. The theologian should be able to prove, not only that Jesus was a great prophet among men, but that there are also, in His life, in His death and in His resurrection, signs of His identity with God among us. This theological research does not command belief, but renders it possible, gives it a foundation, for, on proposing Christianity as "believable," it makes the option of faith appear "reasonable."

To confront the problem of the *credibility* of Christianity, is then to reach the "focal" point of fundamental theology, for the problem lies at the junction of the question of man and of the question of God in Jesus Christ.

II. Three Approaches to the Problem

The problem of the credibility of Christianity cannot be eluded, but today it is posed in a different way, compared to the perspective of the last centuries. In the 19th century and still at the beginning of the 20th, the testimony of revelation was looked on almost exclusively from the viewpoint of the *object*. There was concern to establish solidly the divine origin of the Christian message by "proofs," "arguments," "divine acts," sometimes called "signs." These arguments, in the anti-rationalist context of Vatican I, are above all miracles and prophecies. Historic sensitiveness is weak as well as attentiveness to the conditions for acceptance of revelation and signs on the part of man. Apologetic preoccupation is everywhere dominant.

For responding to the expectations of modern man, but above all, for being faithful to the facts of the problem itself, theological reflection on the credibility of Christianity should, it seems to us, admit of three *moments* or three equally indispensable *approaches*: a historical and hermeneutical moment, a philosophical moment and a theological or semiological moment.

1) A *historical* and *hermeneutical* moment. Historicity is the fundamental and decisive characteristic of Christian revelation. In contrast with oriental philosophies, with Greek thinking and Hellenic mysteries which allow no room for history or have little concern for it, Christian belief is essentially confronted with events "which have occurred." Scripture retraces acts, presents persons, describes institutions. Briefly, it refers to a certain number of events which are relevant to history. In Jesus Christ this principle of historicity has even greater depth. God, in fact, enters it on taking on the corporality of man. Consequently, the whole human existence of Christ (words, actions, examples, attitude, behavior) is subject to "questioning" by history and it could not be avoided.[1]

If then Christianity presents itself as God's intervention in history, which culminates in Jesus Christ, it is of supreme importance to know whether, how and in what measure we can attain this event. It follows that the problem of finding Jesus through the Gospels, is primordial in a reflection on Christian credibility. If, indeed, we cannot determine the relationship which unites history and kerygma, history and Christianity, or, more concretely, Jesus of Nazareth and the Christ of the Gospels, further research is useless, for the original event which is at the beginning of Christianity is inaccessible. If it is impossible, through the Gospels, to find Jesus and to know that His project, His message, His miracles, His passion and death are "events which truly happened"; what is left of Christianity? A superior gnosis, perhaps, but nothing else. It is not the *inter-vention*, the unique event of history; God among us.

2) The second moment of theological reflection on the credibility of Christianity, is a *philosophical* moment, philosophy becoming an auxiliary discipline in relation to theology.

Man is from the first, an inquiry about himself and the ultimate meaning of his existence. Who am I and why? What is my future? Man could not ignore this question without renouncing living. If Christian revelation is to interest man, above all, the man of today, conscious of his advances in the order of technology and thinking, solicitous to conserve his autonomy and his freedom, it does not suffice to show that, through the Gospels, we have found Jesus of Nazareth. There must still be shown that the Christian message concerns man and the fundamental question which he poses, that there is an intimate bond between the mystery of Christ and the mystery of man, and that both mysteries are destined to meet with each other and mutually clarify each other. This demand of contemporaneous man is expressed in diverse terms, but it is clear and insistent: he awaits to be shown that Christ responds to the capital problem of the meaning of human existence.

In fact, this preoccupation is central in the thinking and works of numerous authors, theologians as well as philosophers. It suffices to mention Pascal, R Guardini, M. Blondel, Teilhard de Chardin, K. Rahner, G. Marcel and H. Urs von Balthasar. Long ago, Pascal, in his *Pensees* sought to awaken in man an acute awareness of his paradoxical condition of misery and yet one marked with grandeur. Man is an abyss which God alone can fill and which Christ alone can explain. Teilhard de Chardin presents the same problem, but starting out from the human phenomenon, viewed in its totality, and under an evolutionary aspect. *L'Action* of Blondel seeks the meeting point between the mystery of man and the mystery of Christian revelation in the dynamics of human action. Karl Rahner follows the same procedure, but starting out from the dynamics of human knowledge. Each one has his own perspective and his own language, but all seek a common goal: to show that man could not learn to understand nor to realize himself fully if he does not open himself up to a transcendant action not his own. Man is himself an enigma, which Christ alone can clarify and decipher.

3) This brings us to the third moment of our reflection on Christian credibility, that is, the *theological* moment. There is

in fact the identifying Him whom we reach through the Gospels and who appears so closely bound to the mystery of man that man could not explain himself without this other mystery. For, neither history nor philosophical reflection will ever be able to deduce Christ as a conclusion of these researches. The analysis of the human condition, with its aspirations and demands, will never be able to deduce the open and troubling initiative of God, neither in its form of God incarnate in Jesus Christ, nor in its extreme of charity up to the point of the abyss of death on the cross, nor in its claims to credibility. Christ presents Himself as God among us and He bears in Him the *signs* of His own identity and credibility. These signs can be known and communicated in an intelligible language.

Such, in fact, is one of the characteristics most strongly underlined by revelation. Revelation does not present itself under the form of a knowledge to be uncovered, communicated by a more intelligent being, but as an absolute beginning. Its point of departure is an initiative of the living God, whose act, creative of the cosmos, does not exhaust infinite freedom. This time, there is the event of a new creation, a new status of humanity which makes of man a son of God and, of humanity, the Body of Christ. Such an initiative is beyond every exigency and every compulsion of man.

On the other hand, if history affects revelation, and if Christ is God present among men, manifesting Himself in the works and words of the man Jesus, there must be therein unequivocal signs, "very certain" signs (Vatican I) which enable us to discern this event, identify this person among the events and persons of ordinary history, and to recognize in the Gospels the "word of God." (1 Th 2:13), the "message of salvation" (Ac 13:26).

The signs of God are directed to man in his concrete condition of spatio-temporal being, matter and spirit, individual and social. This is why God, to "signify" to man His gratuitous and salvific intervention in history addresses to him, in Jesus Christ, signs in the cosmos, miracles; in history, prophecy; in man himself, testimony of life according to the Spirit. The transfiguration of nature through miracles, of history through prophecy, of man through holiness, is the visible trace of the coming of the Word into the world, the reflection of the glory of Christ present among us, as Word of God. This glory, which belongs to Christ as Son of the Father, not only is declared by His message, but it casts on the gravest problems of the human condition (labor, liberty, suffering, death, sin) a light which is itself a sign of God's presence among us. For Christ is the Light which enlightens all men, not by an illumination which would be extraneous to him, but in the very act by which He reveals to us the mystery of His union with the Father in the Spirit.

The study of the signs directed to man by God for helping him identify Christ as Son of God, constitutes the formally theological moment of our approach to Christian credibility.[2]

III. Three Actual Urgencies

The three approaches to the problem of Christian credibility, such as we have just described them, are not a simple construction of the mind. They respond to three questions posed by reality itself.

1) Through the Gospels, have we truly found Jesus of Nazareth? This question, of a historical and hermeneutical character, arises from literary and historical criticism and calls upon the sciences of language.

2) Is it true that the message of Jesus responds to the capital meaning of human existence, that is explains the human condition? Even more, the light which it sheds on man's problems is it at this point penetrating so that it causes the question to come up of the identity of the one who is inviting him to make a decision of faith? It is the philosophical question, which is already a question directed to theology.

3) Finally, the signs which emanate from Jesus, illumined by His behavior and His declarations, and above all, by His death, His resurrection and the centuries old religious movement to which He gave birth, are they of such a dimension that they enable us to identify Him as God-among-

us? It is the formally theological moment.

Strictly speaking, these three moments pertain to theology, inasmuch as they are a reflection on faith. Theological understanding, in fact, is applied here to comprehend this characteristic of the Christian message which is its *credibility*. That this reflection, due to the objective it pursues, ought to make use of history and of philosophy as auxiliary sciences, takes nothing away from its essential objective which is to comprehend the object of faith.

This is why the three questions posed have always been at the heart of fundamental theology. What is new, however, is the urgency of the first two questions: historical and philosophical. Contemporaneous criticism, in fact, after it has perceived the hermeneutical distance which separates the Gospel of Jesus, must face up to the new demands for verification of the historical authenticity of the Gospels. Besides, the present day sensitivity of man to the problems of man, gives a fresh relief to the philosophical insistence that nothing has been done to interest man in Christianity as long as it has not been shown him that Christ is the key to the human cryptogram.

What is equally new, is the handling of the problems addressed. In this regard, the studies of the first half of the 20th century, are already outmoded. There must be taken up again with renewed techniques, especially in matters of literary and historical criticism, the questions of ancient apologetics. This the more so, since the problem of Christian credibility is at the juncture of history, philosophy, exegetics and theology. Now, for a long time, these disciplines have followed parallel lines, those engaged in them having but rare contacts among themselves. Quite fortunately, now a more alive awareness of the status of the fundamental as a discipline with borders, has brought together men and disciplines. From now on there has come about that the professor of fundamentals works in close collaboration with his colleagues who are engaged in exegetics and the human sciences.

Finally, let us add that, in the context of our times, these questions are the ones which preoccupy an ever growing number of men who are sincere and seeking to find out the meaning of their existence. The study of these problems will not always bring them into full light right away. Bit by bit, however, if they do not stop trying, they will discover in Jesus the one who gives meaning and consistency to all human reality.

The present work appertains to the *first* moment of Christian credibility, namely, the possibility of historically finding Jesus of Nazareth through the Gospels. If it is true that this problem has indefinitely been taken up again by exegetics and theology of the last decades, under the form of monographs and methodological considerations,[3] it is equally true that it has rarely been the object of a systematic and complete consideration, articulated in all its stages.[4] Now, in this kind of problem, synthesis is today of more importance, in a sense, than detailed analyses. It is the task of systematization which we have undertaken.

We address ourselves first to the specialized public of professors and students of theology or of religious sciences, but also to the more numerous public of the faithful who want to reflect on the bases of their faith. We hope, in the following works, to take up the other two moments of Christian credibility: the philosophical and the theological.

Footnotes for Introduction

1. R. Latourelle, "La specificite de la Revelation chretienne," in : *Revelation Studia missionalia* XX (Rome, 1971), 45-53; R. Marle, *La singularite chretienne* (Paris, 1970), 123-124.
2. The subject of the resurrection as a sign, is of such importance that it calls for a special treatment.
3. The collective works published by K. Kertelge, *Ruckfrage nach Jesus* (Freiburg, 1974) and by J. Dupont, *Jesus aux origines de la christologie* (Gembloux, 1975), present the problem excellently.
4. For instance, the excellent studies of X. Leon-Dufour, *Les Evangiles et l'histoire de Jesus,* (Paris, 1963) and of J. Caba, *De los Evangelios al Jesus historico* (Madrid, 1970).

FINDING JESUS THROUGH THE GOSPELS

Chapter I

THE HISTORICAL APPROACH TO JESUS

The first moment of Christian credibility concerns history and hermeneutics. First, history. If Jesus was truly a man, whose existence could not seriously be held in doubt[1], it follows that His *dicta et gesta,* after having been, in his lifetime, the object of an experiential knowledge, have become after his death, an object of historical knowledge. Rightly, the research on Him as a subject is set in the same terms as for every person of the past. Actually, however, it soon became recognized that the historical approach, in the present case, runs into a hermeneutical problem. Now, if we conceive of the hermeneutical problem as the one of the levels of reality which we can reach in the reading of a document, we can say that the problem of access to the reality of Jesus, by way of the Gospels, is the first and the most serious problem of hermeneutics posed by Christianity.

I. A Real Problem

We do not know Jesus directly, by His writings, but by the movement He inaugurated in the first century of our era. The point of departure of our knowledge of Jesus is the first Christian community, witness of what Jesus said and did. Now the speech of this community is a speech of believers, and the evangelists who are members of it, pursue a religious finality: they testify to the event of salvation in Jesus Christ. They testify, with the entire primitive Church, that Jesus of Nazareth is the Messiah, the Lord, the Son of God and, so, the object of faith, worship, adoration. There is no doubt, the Gospels are neither chronicles, nor biographies, but documents of faith. The only Jesus we reach through them is a Jesus professed as Christ and Lord. A historical critical examination into the interior of the intention of the Evangelists' belief remains then as the point of departure for knowing the earthly Jesus.

Now if we visualize the image of Christ according to the Evangelists, we have the impression—with John especially, but also with Matthew and with Mark—of a considerable hieratization in relation to what the earthly Jesus has been. Christ is so divine that His earthly career resembles a sort of interlude between His descent among men and His ascent to the celestial world. If this is so, ought it not be concluded that the original image of Jesus is in some way hidden from us, or that Jesus has been at this point "transfigured" by the Christ of the confession of faith so that the historical contours of His life and of His person have become evanescent under the dazzling light of the Pasch?[2] Is it still possible to approach the reality of His passage among men?

We know, besides, that the Gospels, such as they are actually presented, are the result of a long process of reflection inaugurated by the Church on the eve of Pentecost. During many decades, the matter of the Gospels served for catechesis, worship, polemics, mission and, consequently bears the imprint of the primitive Church making it relevant and interpreting the text. We know, finally, that the evangelists, if they took over the prior tradition, did not simply reproduce it, but rethought and rewrote it following the theological and literary perspective peculiar to each of them.

But the question comes up anew. Can we be certain that the interpretation of the apostles, then of the Church, and finally, of the evangelists, has not altered or deformed the figure and the message of Jesus? Is it still possible to find out, under the multiple layers of primitive interpretation, the authentic acts, the "truly given" facts, and to understand the message of Jesus in its original freshness? The difference is so great, for instance, between the speech of Jesus in the Synoptics and in the Gospel of St. John. The liberty taken by the evangelists resembles a sort of license in regard to the real. In these conditions is there still hope of arriving, if not at *ipsissima verba Jesu* (a dream abandoned after a long time) at least at the essential content of His teaching, at this nucleus which nourished later reflection, and at the granite bloc of His most important actions? Can we finally establish the precise and strict criteria which give us the certainty of knowing the itinerant rabbi who troubled Palestine and threw into confusion the history of humanity? It is a basic question posed to Christianity. What is its relationship to the earthly reaty of Jesus? What is the link between history and kerygma, between text and event?

Theology cannot dispense itself from reflecting on this relationship of faith to history, for if Jesus did not exist, or if He did in such a way that it cannot base the interpretation of what faith has given of it, but another that is quite different, or wholly different, Christianity collapses in its first pretention. Christian faith implies a bond of continuity between the phenomenon Jesus and the interpetation which the primitive Church gave of it. This is so, for it is in the earthly life of Jesus that God manifested Himself, and it is this faith which authorizes the Christian interpretation of this life as the only one that is authentic and true. If the apostles could profess Jesus as Christ and Lord, it must be that he performed deeds, behaved in such a way, had such attitudes, spoke in such a way as to authorize such an interpretation. Theology must then be able to establish, through the Gospels, what justifies the Christian interpretation of the phenomenon Jesus, in his earthly condition.

II. Responses of Criticism

The responses of criticism to the problem of the possibility of finding Jesus, through the Gospels, have been multiple and quite bizarre. For example:

1) An acritical response, and one fully confident, which has dominated exegetics up to the 18th century. During a long time, in fact, the problem of the historical authenticity of the Gospels has coincided with that of the authenticity of their author. Based on the testimony of tradition, exegetics attributes the Gospels to the apostles (Matthew and John) or to the disciples of apostles (Mark and Luke). Since the Gospels emanate, directly or indirectly, from eye witnesses, it follows that all they narrate puts us in the presence of Jesus Himself. The texts are clear as crystal and historical authenticity is no longer a problem.

2) Response of historical scepticism, baited by Reimarus, elaborated by Strauss, Kahler, Wrede, and radicalized by Bultmann. The latter acknowledges a material or chronological succession between Jesus and apostolic preaching, but he declares there is an essential hiatus between Jesus of Nazareth, of whom practically nothing is known, and the kerygma of the Gospels. This historical scepticism runs up against a dogmatic principle: faith has nothing to do with the results of history. The encounter of the Word of God in faith is that of two subjectivities, beyond objective data. A parallel situation can afflict the historian but not the believer, nor the theologian.

3) A more moderate response by Bultmann's disciples, notably by Kasemann, Bornkamm, and the "New Hermeneutic," with Fuchs, Ebeling and Robinson. All regard as exaggerated the master's scepticism, and endeavor to find an essential continuity between the Jesus of history and the Christ of the Gospels. The present generation of Protestant theologians, represented by Pannenberg and Moltmann, affirms in turn, stolidly, the primacy of history. "Faith is first of all concerned with what Jesus *was*. It is starting out from there alone that we

know what He is for us today and how it is possible to announce Him today."[3]

4) Finally a response of contemporaneous Catholic exegetics, convinced that it is possible, by way of the kerygma of the Gospels to arrive at Jesus of Nazareth, but at the same time much more critical, since it is more aware of the difficulties of the enterprise. This new position can be formulated in the following terms. It goes without saying that, in Catholic thinking, the Paschal Christ is the same concrete person as Jesus of Nazareth. There could not be disjunction nor opposition between the earthly Jesus and the Christ of the Gospels, but unity and continuity. There is ever question of the same Jesus, but from now on identified as Messiah and Lord, following upon the resurrection. The present glorified one is the one crucified before. The conditions have changed, but the person is the same. It is the resurrection which has been as it were the catalyzer or, if it be wished, the illumination which has enabled Jesus of Nazareth to be fully understood and identified. To separate Jesus from the kerygma, would be to fall into gnosticism; to speak only of the Jesus of history would be to renounce understanding Him, even in his earthly condition. This is why the Church, upon projecting her new knowledge of the identity of Jesus on His terrestrial existence, is convinced of her fidelity. Her language is even the only one which is truly faithful to Jesus, since it reveals His true nature.

This the Lord whom the Church adores as Jesus of Nazareth; the Son of God is of Joseph and Mary. The destiny of this person is the historical destiny of a man of his times. There is not here question of the eternal happening of a myth, but of a history which is not repeated; not of an idea, nor of a symbol, but of an account; not a religious play but a serious fact of history; not something metaphysical but a happening. This concrete identity however, does not imply that Christ has been reunited as Jesus had been. Christ is no other than Jesus, but still in a sense Jesus *became* Christ. To deny Jesus is a myth, does not mean to close the eyes just the same to progressive procedures of reflection and awareness on the part of the Church. We, in fact, know that the *re-reading* about the event, Jesus, and about his earthly existence, from the resurrection, has set in march a whole procedure of interpretations inscribed in the very fabric of our Gospels. Between Jesus and the present text, there are many densities and many interpolations which, undoubtedly, enrich our knowledge and understanding of Jesus, but at the same time widen the hermeneutic distance which separates us from it. It is this distance and this process of organic growth which exegetics endeavors to find out and appreciate. What became the image of Jesus of Nazareth, as perceived by His disciples, from the moment when the image of Christ, Messiah and Lord, is imposed on them? By way of today's perception, is it still possible to retrace that of the past. The problem of finding Jesus through the Gospels has become a problem of hermeneutics.

III. The problem in the history of Christian Hermeneutics

In order to be better understood, the hermeneutical problem of the Gospels is helped by setting it in the much wider context of Christian hermeneutics. Viewed as a study of the Scripture-word-event relationship, the hermeneutical problem is not something new created by the 20th century. It is coextensive with the history of Christianity. From the beginning, in fact, Christians have interpreted the sacred text in order to know and understand the event of salvation. The problem, however, has been posed differently in the course of centuries. Certain characteristics of the hermeneutical situation of Christianity have not even been perceived save in our days. It is these characteristics which make finding Jesus through the Gospels an original problem.

To grasp this characteristic of originality, there can be distinguished, in the history of Christian hermeneutics, three stages or moments, corresponding to three aspects of Christian reality. The distinction of these three moments is already a systematization, for the three aspects brought out by this history, are all contemporaneous, that is to say, they all belong to the objective reality of Christianity. On the other hand, these three aspects not having bloomed in Christian consciousness save progressively, in the course of history, it is legitimate to speak of stages.

Originally, the Christians of the first generations applied themselves to grasp the relationship between the Old and the New Testaments. After having become an object of interpretation (our present hermeneutical problem), the New Testament has been a norm and key of interpretation of the Old. Christ, in fact, did not come to abolish, but to accomplish the Old Testament. The first task of Christian hermeneutics is then to find out the relationship between the Scripture of the Old Testament and the event of Christ, between the letter, the history of the Old Testament (persons, institutions, events) and the fulness of meaning revealed in Jesus Christ.

In this first stage, hermeneutics is presented first as a rereading of the Old Testament in the light of Christ. The Christic event itself acquires all at once "a temporal density," for it appears as the fulfillment of promises and of the whole history of the Old Testament. "The event becomes a coming; upon taking on time, it takes on meaning."[4] Christ thus becomes the exegetics and the exegete of the Old Testament: He is in person the key to the Scriptures (Lk 24:25-27).

Christian hermeneutics, then, in its first phase has been the solving, the spiritual understanding of the Old Testament through the New. St. Paul and the first Fathers of the Church (Justin, Clement of Alexandria, Origen and Augustine) practiced this first form of hermeneutics.

In the second stage, represented by St. Paul, by all medieval exegetics and, more recently by Bultmann, Scripture is viewed as a key to the interpretation of human existence and, in particular, of human action. St. Paul, for instance, invites the Christian to find the meanings of the movement of his existence in the light of the passion and resurrection of Christ. Interpretation of Scripture and interpretation of life mutually clarify each other. The middle ages, with its theory of the four meanings of Scripture, opened up a wide area for this type of hermeneutics.[5] In the global content of Scripture, the interpreter discerns first a *history* which is the base of all the rest. But this history does not reach the man of today save through the triple meaning it bears. The *allegorical* meaning, or the typical, or the Christological, finds in Scripture the mystery of Christ prepared for, announced, accomplished, and finally, prolonged in the Church. The *anagogical* meaning or the eschatological reads Scripture in the perspective of final hope. Finally, the *tropological* meaning or the moral serves to find the meaning of the human condition and of human problems in the light of Scripture. The meaning is nothing else but the point of impact of Scripture on the life of man, its relevance to daily existence: the word of God being addressed to each one *hic et nunc* as well as to the Church, and telling each one that which is of concern to his life.

Finally, in a third stage, which corresponds to the present day period, the hermeneutic proceeding has as its object the text itself of the New Testament, and the relationship existing between it and the event. This moment arises from the impact of Scripture on modern disciplines: criticism, philosophy, and history.

For the Fathers of the Church and for the middle ages, there was neither distance nor tension between the text and the event. This is no longer so today. From now on we know, thanks to *Form Criticism (Formgeschichte)* and to *Redaction Criticism (Redaktionsgeschichte)*, that the Gospels are not chronicles, but testimonies, born in a community of faith and of worship. We likewise know, that, between the actual text and the event there intervenes a period of several decades (from 30 to 100), in the course of which the matter of the Gospels was the object of rereadings and, consequently, of interpreting, making relevant, and constant deepening of knowledge. As a result of this the New Testament, after having been the key of interpretation in regard to the Old Testament, has need itself of being interpreted.

This need for an interpretation holds for the very nature of the Gospels (professions of faith) and also for the *distance*, minimal, but real, which exists between the words and deeds of

Jesus, and the written text; between the historical situation in the time of Jesus, and the situation of the Church at the moment of putting the Gospels in writing. During a long time, this distance, with all its implication, passed unnoticed: it is modern criticism which has brought it out.

To interpret the Gospels is then to discern the precise relationship existing between the text and the event itself (deeds and words of Jesus); it is to determine the respective contribution of Jesus, of the primitive community, of the evangelists. Modern hermeneutics shows the unique situation of the Gospels.

IV. The Problem and its Theological Implications

To succeed in making evident the gravity of the problem with which we are grappling, let us point out several of its theological implications. In a word, it is the existence and the very nature of Christianity which are at stake.

1) Historicity is the first characteristic of the originality and specificity of Christian revelation. Christianity, in fact, is not a gnosis parachuted from the sky, nor the sole vertical encounter of God with man, in the interiority of faith. It proceeds from a gratuitous intervention of God in History. Already, in the Old Testament, to make Himself known to Israel, God chose to make use of particular historical events of which the prophetic word is the interpreter and the echo. Whoever wants to understand the word of God then must take seriously the historical events to which the texts of the Old Testament give testimony. The faith which responds to this word itself takes the form of a narration, a profession of faith: the narration of the events which manifest the salvific design of God. The same structure is found in the New Testament. Apostolic kerygma is at the same time predication of an event and of its bearing on salvation: "Christ died (the event of the death on the cross) for our sins" (the meaning). The New Testament, like the Old, included the horizontal of the event and the vertical of the meaning. The synthesis inscribed in the

very title of Jesus Christ: the man of Nazareth, who declared Himself before the Sanhedrim Son of man with power to judge men at the end of time and, on account of this, was crucified and put to death, is from then on identified as Messiah and Son of God.

If Christianity presents itself as an intervention of God in history and if Christ is the most compact point, the decisive point of this intervention, it is of the utmost importance to know whether, how, and in what measure we can attain this epiphany of God, at the very least in its historical consistency accessible to human consciousness. It is true that God's revelation is not acknowledged as such save by faith, and not by historical knowledge; and, yet, it is not faith without it. For Christianity has a content of historicity and makes history part of its credibility. If it must be established that Christianity was born out of primitive faith alone, and that Christ is not responsible for the message attributed to Him, what would remain of Christianity, a pure doctrine, or perhaps an illusion? It is essential to verify that the apostolic kerygma is founded on the life, the deeds, the message of Jesus Himself, and that the formula *Jesus Christ* expresses a real unity and continuity. Now, we repeat, there is no other way to find Jesus than through the Gospels.

2) The question posed appears particularly grave, when we enter directly into the field of Christology. Dogmatic research, as a matter of fact, cannot abstract from certain facts we have about Jesus. Who is Jesus? What did He say? In what terms did He speak of Himself and of His mission, of His relation of God? Did Jesus have a theology? Is this theology truly accessible and is it different from the theology of the Church about Jesus? Let us illustrate this by an example.

One of the problems most discussed by contemporaneous research is that of the knowledge of Jesus. In the past, it was said: the faith of the disciples rests on knowledge of Jesus. Now Jesus knew He was the Son of God: He revealed it to His disciples and proved it on rising. Thus, from the knowledge of Jesus to the faith of Christians the passage is made through declarations of the Gospels, in which Jesus is explained in regard to His person and His work. We have a certain critique (*radical criticism* at the very least) which puts in doubt that Jesus had knowledge He was the Son of God, or quite simply Messiah.

If it is true, after attempts, which ran into some obstacles, of the Liberal School, to show that it is impossible to draw up a life of Jesus from the Gospels (since such was not the concern of the evangelists), equally we cannot arrive at knowledge of Jesus, at the very least as a living consciousness, in His spontaneous expression, that is to say: in His attitudes, His behavior, His style of action and speaking, in His manner of acting and reacting to the values of the environment (religion, authority, institutions), in His interpersonal relations with God, with social groups, with individuals, in the titles claimed or at least accepted? If, on all these points, we know nothing, the being of Jesus escapes us, His identity is dissolved. It is true that the mystery of His person was not fully unveiled save through the resurection. But, on the other hand, if nothing, in the action and the speech of Jesus, allows the theme of His Messiahship and of His divine filiation, to germinate, to ripen and to fructify in post-paschal faith and in the christological titles which express it, this faith itself is threatened and risks being naught but an illusion.

3) The problem of the possibility of finding Jesus through the Gospels, finally, shows its importance in the field of exegetics. In fact, the exegetical task is presented quite differently according to whether the response to the question posed is negative or positive.

If Bultmann's position be adopted, exegesis consists in searching in the actual account for the purity of the original kerygma, without being concerned about the underlying historical reality of the account, and to find out the meaning with which it is vested for the understanding of our human condition of pardoned sinners. On the contrary there can, in the perspective of historical positivism, be sought to reconstruct the event of the past, in its pure materiality, without concern for the interpretation it has received since its origin, nor for resonances it has taken on throughout a long tradition. Exegesis, finally, can seek to reach the event, but in the unity it constitutes with the meaning it received from Jesus and from primitive tradition. An exegesis which wishes to be complete does not separate the event from its interpretation, even if it distinguishes them. None of these two poles—event and interpretation—may be neglected. It is just as wrong to underestimate the event in order only to retain its meaning, as to be hypnotized by the event in order to sacrifice the meaning to it. In the New Testament, as in the Old, the text, precisely because it is testimony, never supplants the event, but assumes it, for the meaning attested is that of the event.

Before going into the arguments which enable the problem posed to be given a qualified response, two preliminary procedures are required.The first consists in examining the evolution of evangelical criticism, after about two centuries; the second, of a methodological order, consists in defining realities constantly implied in the discussion: that is the Gospel "literary genre" as also the nature, the objective and the limits of historical research. The whole procedure is developed in three periods: a period of history, a period of method, a period of properly called demonstration.

The demonstration is applied especially to the synoptic Gospels. It is also of value for the entire Joannine tradition, keeping in mind, however, the particular conditions of its formation and of its composition. The Gospel of the infancy constitutes an instance of a type which requires a special treatment.

Footnotes for Chapter I

1. Bultmann justly writes: "The fact of doubting that Jesus truly existed has no foundation and does not even deserve to be refuted. It is indisputable that Jesus is at the origin of the historical movement of which the primitive Palestinian community represents the first tangible stage." R. Bultmann, *Jesus Mythologie et demythologisation* (Paris, 1968), p. 38.
2. A. Descamps, "Portee christologique de la recherche historique sur Jesus, in J. Dupont, *Jesus aux origines de la christologie* (Gembloux, 1975), pp. 39-41.
3. W. Pannenberg, *Grundzuge der Christologie* (Gutersloh, 1964).
4. P. Ricoeur, Preface to R. Bultmann, Jesus, *Mythologie et demythologisation*, pp. 9-28.
5. H. de Lubac, *Exegese medievale* vol. I, (Paris, 1959), pp. 23-24; P. Grelot, Que penser de l'interpretation existentiale? *Ephemerides Theologicae Lovanienses*, XLIII (1967) 427-428.

Part I

THE EVOLUTION OF CRITICISM

To retrace the history of evangelical criticism, does not bring about yet a definitive response to the problem posed. However it does place research in a climate of either confidence or doubt. Indeed, it is not without importance that criticism, after a period of radical scepticism, of which Bultmann is the principal representative, became more moderate, and was characterized by an attitude of confidence in regard to the Gospels as source of knowledge of Jesus and of His history. It is no longer of no concern to underline that this return to confidence came about through researches carried out on diverse levels: the literary *level, with the methods of the School of Forms,* (Formgeschichte), *Form Criticism, and of Redaction Criticism; the* theological *level, by representatives of the "New Hermeneutic" (Robinson, Fuchs, Ebeling) and men of the present generation (Pannenberg, Moltmann); the formal* historical *level, by authors concerned with establishing valuable criteria for finding Jesus of Nazareth (Kasemann, Jeremias, Schurmann, Perrin, Lehmann, Calvert, McArthur, Cerfaux, de la Potterie, Lambiasi, etc). All these works came to the same conclusion: finding Jesus through the Gospels, long thought impossible by historical positivism and by the holders of the theology of the kerygma, now may be acknowledged as a necessary and possible enterprise.*

Such a conclusion, the fruit of two centuries of research, constitutes, if not the proof itself, at least a solid presumption in favor of the position it represents. If so many researchers, among which a certain number at first were partisans of the teachers of distrust, credit the Gospels as being a path to finding Jesus, it can legitimately be believed that the truth lies in this direction. Before giving full credit to the conclusions of criticism, without doubt there must be proven the solidity of the arguments it invokes. But this argument of authority, based itself on the internal criticism of the Gospels, constitutes even now a major part of the demonstration.

This history of criticism, even if it seems to us winding and slow in its course, has nonetheless its positive aspects: apart from that it familiarizes us with the facts of the problem and its implications, it already constructs an inventory of most of the arguments which we will subsequently encounter. It shows us how the historical finding of Jesus through the Gospels has been perceived more and more as a problem of hermeneutics and of speech. What is certain, without the knowledge of this history, the present works of the Gospels remain closed fountains. Finally, it clears the terrain of a certain number of objections that have no consistency. So now there is room for grappling with the real difficulties and the real arguments.

Chapter II

RADICALIZATION PHASE

Up to the 18th century, the problem of the historical authenticity of the Gospels is not posed. Protestants and Catholics esteem that our Gospels merit full confidence and that they present us with a faithful and authentic image of Jesus. Exegesis explains the content of the Gospels without over concern for their literary genre, and still less for the process of their formation. The idea of an opposition between the Jesus of history and the Christ of the Gospels, is wholly alien to the patristic and medieval mentality. The difficulties which are met concern less the historicity than the harmonization of the four texts. A preoccupation which arose with the *Diatessaron* of Tatian (in the 2nd century), in the *De consensu evangelistarum libri quattuor* of Augustine (toward 400), which endeavors to establish that the contradictions of the Gospels are but apparent, and in the medieval work of Gerson, *le Monotessaron*, which presents one single Gospel through four forms.

Today, it is not possible to speak of the problem of the relation of the Gospels to Jesus of Nazareth, without immediately evoking the name and enterprise of Bultmann. Actually, however, the problem of the Jesus of history has been the object of discussions which go back more than a century and a half before Bultmann. In fact the *"critical"* attitude in the face of the Gospels dates from the 18th century. In the areas dominated by rationalism and liberal Protestantism, inspiration is practically rejected, and Scripture itself is desecrated.

There is no intention here to draw up a list of the names of those who make up this history of criticism, but to discern (in relation to the problem with which we are concerned) rather the periods of this history when this critique was strongest and to mention the leaders. In the pre-Bultmann period, we will retain four most important names: those of Reimarus, Strauss, Kuhler and Wrede. We shall see that all the elements of Bultmann's position find their historical antecedent with these authors.

I. The Pre-Bultmannians

1) H.S. Reimarus (1694-1768) represents the attitude of radical rationalism toward the Gospels. Professor of oriental languages at Hamburg, Reimarus wrote a manuscript of four thousand pages: a sort of apologia of natural religion, in line with and in the spirit of English deism. G.E. Lessing discovered the manuscript and published it in seven tracts (1774-1778). Reimarus appears in this work as the promoter of a natural and philosophical religion. He distinguishes, in the Gospels, the project of Jesus and the aim of His disciples. For His part, Jesus did not wish to found a new religion; He performed no miracles; He spoke neither of His death nor of His resurrection. He was a political Messiah who dreamed of establishing a temporal kingdom and liberating the Jews from the foreign yoke. His enterprise, unfortunately, was a failure. Deceived, the disciples created the figure of Jesus which the Gospels transmitted to us. They invented the message of the resurrection and presented Jesus as the apocalyptic Messiah of Daniel. Reimarus thus introduces the distinction between the teaching of Jesus and that of the apostles. He does not eliminate the Gospels, but he does empty them of their supernatural and historical content.

2) David Friedrich Strauss (1808-1874) published in 1837 his life of Jesus *(Das Leben Jesu)*. The key element, for understanding the Gospels, he says, is the category of *myth*: a term he had to define immediately. The New Testament myth, in Strauss' thinking, is nothing else but the transposition and representation, in terms of history, of the religious ideal of the first Christians. This representation came about under the creative pressure of legend and was concretized in the historical person of Jesus. The Christ of the Gospels, professed by the Christians as God incarnate is a "mythical" Jesus, starting from elements borrowed from Judaism, from Hellenism and from Christian experience. All that precedes the baptism of Jesus derives from myth. The theophany of baptism, the temptation in the desert, the transfiguration, the miracles, the exorcisms, the resurrection are just so many instances exemplary of the processes of "mythologization." There cannot ze denied, consequently, that there exists, in the Gospels, a historical substratum. However, there subsists an unsurmountable hiatus between Jesus of Nazareth and the Christ of the Gospels, as a result of the pervasive action of the myth. A life of Jesus is then an unrealizable enterprise. The value of the evangelical accounts is before all of a theological order, in this sense that they give us access to Christian faith. Strauss' position, if it be compared with that of Bultmann, is astonishingly similar.

3) Contrary to Strauss, the liberal school of research on the life of Jesus *(Leben-Jesus-Forschung)*, represented by H.J. Holtzmann, K.H. Weisacker, K. Hase, B. Weiss, D. Schenkel, A. Harnack, E. Renan (and others), is convinced that it is possible, starting out from "pure historical" sources, that is to say, the Gospel of Mark and the Source *(Quelle*: theory proposed by Ch. H. Weiss and Ch. G. Wilke), to write a life of Jesus and even retrace His psychological itinerary. Basically, this research had as its object to free the image of the historical Jesus from the retouches given it by christological dogmas and, before that, by the kerygma of the primitive Church.[1] There was no longer belief in the Christ of dogmas, but in Jesus of Galilee who was venerated. There was the question then of

discovering the *man* Jesus, such as he was really and originally, His life and His religion before having an exemplary signification for Christians of the present times. In 1906, Albert Schweitzer showed that this attempt, indisputably the most considerable historical criticism of the 19th century, was seriously checked. This for many reasons.

First, because there was demanded of the Gospels what they manifestly do not intend to present, that is, a life of Jesus (even though they are rich in historical data). Furthermore, Jesus objectively researched reflects disturbingly the humanitarian, social and religious ideal of those who intend to reconstruct faithfully His traits and His career. This Jesus soon is a teacher of the century of Lights, truly teaching about God, virtue and immortality; a religious genius of romanticism; a friend of the poor and a champion of social ideas. In sum, the Liberal School let itself be distracted from its initial project. It rejected the dogmatic interpretations of Jesus, but it replaced them by its philosophical and sociological assumptions. Finally, the school ran into insurmountable difficulties concerning the sources themselves. There, where it saw "historically pure" sources (notably Mark), it found out that there were still testimonials of faith.

The Liberal School has been justly criticized. Its first initiative, however, is still worthwhile: to know that the historical person of Jesus is the foundation of Christianity and that it would not be possible to have access to Jesus, from the viewpoint of hermeneutics and apologetics, except by way of history. Christology must face the inevitable problem of research and of historical method; if not it stumbles against unbelief and fideism. The mistake of the Liberal School was changing the dogmatic teachings for philosophical ones and reducing Christ to the man Jesus, a fully accomplished religious man in the image of an ideal which it had forged.

4) In the same period, Martin Kahler rises up against the pretension of the *Leben-Jesus-Forschung* (Quest of the Historical Jesus). In his booklet on the "so-called Jesus of history" and the Christ of the Bible,"[3] published in 1892, he endeavors to show that the historical Jesus of modern writers

conceals from us the living Christ of the Bible. Now the only real Jesus, is the Christ of preaching and of faith, and not the Jesus of the past. He thus introduces a distinction, which will be widely accepted, between the Jesus of history and the Christ of the kerygma.[4] Our interest lies in the Christ of apostolic preaching, professed in faith, and not in the Jesus of history, about whom besides we know little, at least with a scientific certitude. Kahlet does not deny the Gospels have a minimal historical substratum, but he esteems vain and futile the research of the Liberal School on the life of Jesus.

5) To the names of Reimarus, Strauss, Kahler, we add that of Wilhelm Wrede who put an end to the illusion of the Quest of the Historical Jesus by the publication, in 1901, of his thesis on the messianic secret in the Gospel of Mark.[5] Wrede esteems that the Gospel of Mark, on which the Liberal School bases its reconstruction of the history of Jesus, is not a book of history, but an account elaborated under the influence of theological motives. Mark is not a historian, but a theologian. Thus, according to Wrede, the theme of the messianic secret is a creation of the primitive Church. During His public life, Jesus was unaware He was the Messiah, and never expressed such a pretension. It is the apostles, and the primitive Church which, in order to explain the differentiation between the real life of Jesus and the worship rendered the risen Lord, imagined the idea of a "secret" hidden by Jesus during His public life. If Jesus did not speak of His dignity of Messiah in the course of His ministry, it is because he wanted to defer its divulgation until the day of the resurrection.[9] Wrede says: "Considered in its ensemble the Gospel of Mark does not offer a historical image of the real life of Jesus. Only some pale vestiges have been preserved in his narrative, which reflects a metahistorical theological concept of Jesus. In this sense, the Gospel of Mark, considered up to now as the most faithful witness of Jesus, reveals itself also as a document of faith. The primitive community imagined, in the life of Jesus, something which was not found there. This "creative force" of the primitive community became, consequently, in the Form Criticism school, an indisputable axiom.

6) If we bring together the elements collected up to now, we verify that most of the positions taken by Bultmann, existed already among his predecessors, or had been prepared by them, that is: a) the impossibility of reaching the Jesus of history and of knowing His life and His personality (Strauss, Kahler);—b) the category of myth for explaining a good part of the evangelical material (Strauss);—c) the distinction between the Jesus of history and the Christ of the kerygma (Kahler);— d) the importance of the role of creator played by the primitive community (Reimarus, Wrede);—e) the devaluating of the historical element as foundation of Christian faith (Kahler).

7) The critique of the 20th century, henceforth aware that our Gospels are the terminal of a complex process of formation, which spread out over a period of more than thirty years, endeavors to retrace the stages of this formation. In this research, there can be distinguished, on an exegetical level, two great movements: the first, which is between the two world wars, from 1920 to 1945 (Form Criticism); the second, which dates from the post-war period (Redaction Criticism). The two movements make concrete the two forces which contributed to the formation of the evangelical tradition. Form Criticism has recognized for oral tradition a function neglected by the critique of written sources; while Redaction Criticism, reacting against the excesses of the form school, has recognized, for composers, for evangelists, an importance which the form school denied. The figure which dominates the first epoch is that of Rudolf Bultmann.

II. Bultmann and the theology of the kerygma

Bultmann took up the positions of Strauss, Kahler and Wrede, but radicalized them. For Bultmann, indeed, Christianity began with the *preached Christ*, that is, with the kerygma of the primitive Church. This kerygma assumes doubtless the historical existence of Jesus, but it shows no interest for the chronicle of this life. What interests it, is the fact itself (the *Dass*, the *thatness*) of the existence of Jesus, as the seat of the efficacious response of God to the question of man about the meaning of his existence. That Jesus was born, that He lived, that He was crucified, that He died, is no longer needed for Christian faith: the *Dass*, the fact itself of existence is the sole historical substratum for the event of salvation. The *Was*, that is, the moral personality of Jesus, and the *Wie*, that is, His teaching, His message, His action, are of no theological interest. "What went on in the heart of Jesus," says Bultmann, "I do not know, and I have no wish to know."[8]

Bultmann surely does not deny a material, chronological continuity between Jesus of Nazareth and the Christ of the kerygma, but he holds there is a real hiatus, an essential theological discontinuity between Jesus and the Christ of faith. He sees the indications of this hiatus in the following facts: a) in place of Jesus, the kerygma proposes the mythological figure of the Son of God; b) while the preaching of Jesus proclaims the imminent coming of the Kingdom, the primitive Church preaches Christ dead for our sins and risen: the preacher is now the preached; c) while Jesus speaks of unconditional obedience to the Father, the kerygma speaks now of obedience to the Church.

For Bultmann, Jesus still belongs to Judaism. What bond thenceforth, exists between Jesus and the Church? Bultmann deems that the kerygma was not born of the life of Jesus and does not seek its support in this life. The Synoptics do not seek to legitimize the kerygma by history, but rather, on the contrary, to legitimize history by the kerygma: it is the latter which clarifies everything and gives meaning to everything. Christian faith begins with the kerygma which takes the place of the historical Jesus. It begins when He who preached is announced as the eschatological action of God. St. Paul, did he not construct his theology without referring to the concrete history of Jesus? In the failure of the prophet of Nazareth, the kerygma sees the response of God to the question of man: in the crucified, God pronounces a judgment of condemnation on the sufficiency of man and proclaims His will of pardon and of authentic life for whoever accepts to die to himself.[9]

Simplifying it, it may be said that what Bultmann says

about Jesus is expressed in two times: first, a radical critique, declaring that a historiographic research on Jesus is an impossible enterprise, or an illegitimate one; next, a moment which wishes to be positive and creative, seeking to substitute for historiography a theology and a hermeneutic of the kerygma.

1) For Bultmann, it is chimerical to wish to describe a life of Jesus: not only because Jesus wrote nothing, but above all because the Gospels are first of all professions of faith. Furthermore, the image they present of Jesus is for the most part "mythologized" by the primitive community. That Jesus existed is beyond doubt; He exercised His ministry as Rabbi and He died under Pontius Pilate. But the Gospels combine in so inextricable a manner historical elements and mythical elements that it is impossible to find a consistent nucleus of historical truth and a trustworthy succession of events. The Synoptics present us Christ as Son of God through the image of Grecian divinity. Bultmann says, "I think that we can practically know nothing about the life and personality of Jesus, because the Christian sources we possess, very fragmentary and colored by legend, have shown no interest on this point."[10] Further on he says: "If we only know little about the life and personality of Jesus we are sufficiently informed about His preaching for forming a coherent image of Him. Nevertheless, there too, the character of our sources obliges us to be most prudent. The sources offer us first of all the preaching of the community, which assuredly attributes the greatest part of it to Jesus. Naturally, this does not mean that every word it puts in the mouth of Jesus was really and truly spoken by Him. In a number of cases, it can even be proven that they only go back to the community. As for others, they modified them."[11] In summary, the Gospels were born of faith and have meaning because of faith. They are a kerygma, not a chronicle.

2) For Bultmann, faith has no other justification than faith itself. What is important, is the meaning of the existence of Jesus, made known through the kerygma, that is, that through his total surrender to God in faith, man is saved. What

is after or before the kerygma, is of little importance. Thus Bultmann personally declares he is convinced that Jesus never had any knowledge that He was the Messiah. But he adds right away that, of itself, the problem is unimportant, for the acknowledgement of Jesus as He in whom the Word of God was realized in a decisive manner, is a pure note of faith independent of the response given to the historical question of knowing whether Jesus is held to be the Messiah. Only the historian can answer this question, to the measure that any response is possible. Faith, as a personal decision, cannot depend on his work. Faith, as a commitment of the whole person, must be free from the precariousness of historical research.

3) The historian and the theologian, in Bultmann, then seem to co-exist and to ignore each other. On the one hand, in fact, Bultmann, in his *Jesus* and in his *History of the synoptic Tradition*, studies the preaching of Jesus and makes an effort to reconstruct it; on the other hand, as theologian he seems to make an abstraction from his historical researches. How is this kind of methodological dualism to be explained? Would not historical criticism's only purpose be to show the impossibility of basing historically the kerygma and of thus freeing faith from all human support?

Bultmann's indifference in regard to the history of Jesus is attributable, we think, to his theology of faith much more than to his historical scepticism. In fact, historical interest in the pre-Paschal Jesus is not of itself condemnable. The proof of this is that Bultmann himself has such a motive. But this interest must stay strictly within its order, that is the *historical*. As soon as there mingles therein a theological interest, that is, the desire to legitimize the kerygma of faith by historical procedures, the inquiry becomes suspect right away. Such concern to legitimize faith, annuls faith. All research about the kerygma, all inquiry about the past Jesus, as soon as it is inspired by an apologetic preoccupation, can be only sterile and disavowed by the believer. What endangers faith, is the historical certitude we can obtain about what Jesus said and did. Having acquired this, we fall into the temptation to invoke it and rely on it.

Genuine faith does not have anything to do with historical information, certain or probable. The kerygma bears in itself its own intelligibility: it suffices that it be addressed to us so that the possibility of faith be assured.

So it is that mainly in the name of the kerygma and of faith Bultmann is not interested in the historical Jesus. Salvation does not come from knowing objectively, scientifically, as if it were possible to usurp God, but comes from *faith alone*. Bultmann's theology is justly defined as a theology of the kerygma. Every event of revelation is concentrated in the kerygma and in the decision of faith in God who calls us.

4) The kerygma is primary. But there must immediately be added: on condition that it be itself subjected to a rigorous process of interpretation, for the world of the New Testament is a mythical universe. Demythization and the problem of Jesus are then intimately linked. Demythization poses the problem of the data of the language of the New Testament in relation to the kerygma which is expressed by way of these data: and this, so long as the problem of the historical Jesus is the problem of the historical data concerning Jesus in relation to the Christ professed in faith as the eschatological event of salvation.

The myth, in the Bultmanian sense, speaks of the supernatural, divine, transcendent world, in terms of our spatial and temporal world. It describes the action of God in terms of historical, cosmological, psychological causality. Bultmann states precisely that he understands myth in the sense it has in the history of religions: myth is every representation in which the non-cosmic appears cosmic, the divine appears human, and God Himself appears as a spatial background. This notion of myth is evidently not to be confused with the modern meaning of pure ideology.

For Bultmann, it is evident that the New Testament is a mythical universe, peopled with divine or demoniacal personages, overrun by mysterious forces, divided into spatial and temporal sectors. It describes Christ as a preexisting being, as the Son of God, incarnate in the womb of the Virgin Mary. When the New Testament speaks of the miracles of Jesus, of the transfiguration, of the resurrection, of Pentecost, it has recourse to mythical language. Such a manner of speaking, Bultmann explains, betrays the influence of Hellenism, of gnosticism and of Judaism. We must eliminate this manner of speaking, as did the rationalists. But above all we must reinterpret and reexpress the gospel terms in terms adapted to modern man, notably in terms of Heidegger's existential philosophy. In regard to this, what is of importance in the kerygma, are the elements which relate to our existence and to our interpersonal relationship with God. All else is myth.

Jesus has especially a value indicative of the salvation which comes to us through faith. He is a great prophet, but He is not the Savior: He is rather the chosen by God for letting us know about salvation. Thus, the account of the resurrection does not send us back to the historical event of a true corporal resurrection, but declares the historical meaning of the cross. The cross signifies the judgment, the condemnation of the world, while the resurrection signifies the possibility of a genuine life conferred on man through the obedience of faith. The resurrection is part of the kerygma, not by title of a historical event, which truly happened, as the cross, but as an announcement of our salvation. Bultmann says: "To speak of the resurrection of Christ can it be other than to express the signification of the cross? Does it say anything else but this: the death on the cross of Jesus is not to be viewed as a simple human death; it is God's judgment on the world . . . The cross and the resurrection are but one, for they are both but one single cosmic event, by which the world has been judged and we have been given the possibility of a genuine life. The resurrection of Jesus cannot be a miracle which causes faith, due to which those who seek it would be able in full sureness to believe in the Christ."[13]

The salvific act of God then does not pass through the free will of Jesus. God makes use of the sorrowful adventure of the prophet of Nazareth and of His death on the cross to make it the efficacious symbol of salvation: the intention of Jesus does not enter in as cause. Salvation is only brought about as a result of a vertical event bending down over our lives. This absolute event has been made known to us once for all in the historical event of Jesus of Nazareth. Information which is present first in the preaching of Jesus, but which took on a definitive form only in the apostolic kerygma. This kerygma remains ever relevant thanks to the preaching of the Church. The kerygma announces to us the mystery of God who, on the cross, opens our eyes to our sinful condition, but at the same time reveals to us His pardoning grace, and offers us henceforth the possibility of living from Him and in Him. Thus, Jesus is the instrument of God, in some way despite Himself. Outside of the meaning the kerygma confers on Him, the life and earthly existence of Jesus is of no interest.[14]

Footnotes for Chapter II

1. H.J. Holtzmann, in: *Die Synoptische Evangelien, ihr Ursprung und ihr geschithtlicher Charakter* (Leipzig, 1863), has well formulated the objective of the Leben—Jesu—Forschung: He says: "For us there is simply question of knowing whether it is as yet possible to reconstruct the historical figure of Him from whom Christianity derives not only its name but its existence, but whose person has become the center of a quite characteristic view of the world, in a way that satisfies all the just demands of historical criticism. There is question of knowing if it is possible or not to elucidate what was truly the founder of Christianity, utilizing all legitimate means of historical criticism." Quoted by W.G. Kummel, *Das Neue Testament. Geschichte der Erforschung seiner Probleme* (Munchen, 1958), p. 187. Our translation.

2. A. Schweitzer, *Geschichte der Leben—Jesu—Forschung* (Munchen, 1906).

3. M. Kahler, *Der sogenannte historische Jesus und der geschichtliche biblische Christus* (1892).

4. *History*, is the materiality of facts, accessible through the techniques and methods of history; *Geschichte*, are the facts understood as human events and of significance for the life of humanity. *Jesus*, for Kahle, designates the man of Nazareth, such as a biography of Jesus presents Him. *Christ* implies now a faith in the Savior proclaimed by the Church. Historical *(historisch)* signifies the material facts of the past; historical *(geschichtlich)* defines the meaning of the facts.

5. W. Wrede, *Das Messiasgeheimnis in den Evangelien, zugleich ein Beitrag zum Verstandnis des Markusevangeliums* (Gottingen, 1901).

6. C. Minette de Tillesse, *Le secret messianique dans l'Evangile de Marc* (Paris, 1968), p. 12.

7. W. Wrede, *Das Messiasgeheimnis*, p. 131.

8. R. Bultmann, *Glauben und Verstehen, I* (Tubingen, 1933), pp. 101 and 251.

9. On Bultmann's position concerning the relationship between the Christ of the kerygma and the Jesus of history, consult the capital text of Bultmann: *Das Verhaltnis der urchristlichen Christusbotschaft zum historischen Jesus* (Heidelberg, 1960). Text published immediately after in E. Dinkler, Exegetica. *Aufsatze zur Erforschung des Neuen Testaments* (Tubingen, 1967,), pp. 445-469). Brief resume in: H. Ristow—K. Matthiae, *Der historische Jesus und der kerygmatische Christus*, pp. 233-235.

10. R. Bultmann, *Jesus,* (Paris, 1968), p. 35.

11. *Ibid.* p. 37.

12. *Ibid.* p. 38.

13. R. Bultmann, "Nouveau Testament et mythologie," in: P. Laffoucriere, ed., R. Bultmann. *L'interpretation du Nouveau Testament* (Paris, 1955), pp. 177-178.

14. L. Malevez, "Jesus de l'histoire et interpretation du kerygme," *Nouvelle Revue theologique*, XCI (1969) 792-793.

Chapter III

PERIOD OF REACTION

As was to be expected, the radical positions of Bultmann stirred up strong reactions from all sides: from the left, from the right, from the center, with, however, varied intensity.

Many authors maintain in regard to the Gospels an unbreakable confidence. Thus, English exegetes, such as Taylor and Dodd, remain convinced that it is possible to find Jesus and understand His message. Taylor, on his part, judges inadmissible this sort of "intellectual paralysis" which takes over certain ones when there is question of the Jesus of history. Catholics, as a whole, esteem that the synoptic tradition is substantially faithful to the historical reality of Jesus, yet at the same time recognizing that the Gospels are testimonials of faith, and that the Church and the evangelists interpreted and made relevant the original facts.

In the Protestant world, the reaction to Bultmann unfolded in three successive waves: the first, represented by Jeremias, Kasemann and Borkamm; the second, by the New Hermeneutic, with Robinson, Fuchs, Ebeling; the third, finally, in the field of christology, by the present generation of theologians, such as Pannenberg and Moltmann.

I. Joachim Jeremias

Conservative Protestants, such as Stauffer, Kunneth and Jeremias accuse Bultmann of undermining Christian faith by his works. During this first phase, J. Jeremias is undoubtedly the one who has most vigorously aroused criticism against the excesses of Bultmann. His work on the historical problem of Jesus, which appeared in 1960[1], is, as it were, the program of the right wing in the discussion opened up by Bultmann about the historical Jesus and the Christ of the kerygma.

Jeremias' works on the Aramaic language and the Jewish environment and the parables and words of the institution of the eucharist, show he is a master of Literary Criticism, notably form criticism, of which he has acquired the best elements.[2] Jeremias acknowledges that Bultmann has had the merit of calling attention to the importance of the kerygma and the gratuity of salvation. He accuses him, however, of having emptied Christianity of the primordial fact, that is, of the Incarnation, and of having put Paul in place of Jesus. Bultmann has undervalued the initiative of God Savior and substituted the idea of the Christ for the person of Jesus, thereby returning to a sort of docetism. Jeremias thinks that we should return to the Jesus of history and of preaching, and this in order to be faithful to the *sources* and to the *kerygma* itself.

"The sources first of all forbid us to restrict ourselves to the kerygma of the primitive Church, and oblige us ceaselessly to pose the question of the Jesus of history and of His message. Each verse of the Gospel attests to us, in fact, the source of Christianity, that it is neither the kerygma, nor the paschal experience of the disciples, nor an ideal Christ: the coming on the scene of the man Jesus of Nazareth, who was crucified under Pontius Pilate, and His message, there, indeed, is the source of Christianity."[3]

We must return to the Jesus of history, not only to be faithful to the sources, but to the kerygma itself, which proclaims that God has saved humanity by an event of history. In fact, the central assertion of the kerygma: "died for our sins according to the Scripture," is the interpretation of a historical event. Now it is important to know whether this interpretation of the death of Jesus on the cross is arbitrarily ascribed to the facts, or on the contrary, whether in the events themselves there is something which justifies this interpretation. In other words, we must ask: "did Jesus speak of his imminent death, and what meaning did He give to it?"[4] The same question is posed a propos of the resurrection. The risen Christ whom the apostles announce, and whom the community invokes, has basic traits which the apostles well know: the traits which characterize the aspect and the being of the earthly Lord. The affirmations of the kerygma have their origin in Jesus and have been made clear through the primitive catechesis, but never has there been known a kerygma without Jesus.

Our research on Jesus must appear as a response to the truth of the Incarnation. "The Incarnation implies that the history of Jesus lends itself to historical investigation and to Historical Criticism, and even more, demands it. We must know who the Jesus of history was, and what His preaching was. We have not the right to set aside the scandal of the Incarnation . . . The Incarnation is the act by which God gives Himself over, that we must accept."[5] At the conclusion of his exposé, Jeremias underlines that revelation is linked to the Word made flesh, to Jesus and to His message, while apostolic preaching would represent in some way the response of the Church to revelation, but would not be revelation.

In summary, in Jeremias' eyes, Bultmann's enterprise is one of *dehistorization* of the New Testament, a practical denial of the historical character of the revelation constantly and throughout emphasized in Scripture. He accuses Bultmann of not taking seriously the *Verbum caro factum* with all its implications. Thereby, Jesus is found reduced to a pure fact of existence, without content. He is no longer a real person, inserted in the course of history, whose words and deeds have a decisive import. The most vulnerable point of Jeremias' position is to reduce revelation to the primitive image and message of Jesus of Nazareth, independently of apostolic interpretation. While Bultmann reduces revelation to the sole kerygma, Jeremias reduces it to the sole Jesus of history. Testimony yields to history.

II. Ernest Kasemann

But it is in the very field of Bultmann's disciples that the controversy over the Jesus of history was fiercest. For them, there was not question of returning to the lives of Jesus of the Liberal School, but of finding a middle way between the position of exaggerated historicity of the 19th century and the radical position of Bultmann. They questioned themselves as to the legitimacy and the meaning of a research on Jesus of Nazareth, His life and His message. The problem is set by the kerygma itself which refers us to Jesus. Now this Jesus, is He a symbol or a historical person? There is opposition to a separation, or even an antithesis between kerygma and history. There is rather to be carried on research as to the real continuity between the Jesus of history and the Christ of the Gospels. This term "continuity," accompanied by various qualifications, according to each one's tendencies, is without doubt that which best characterizes post-war exegetics. We shall explain at greater length Kasemann's position, since he is the one who of the generation of the disciples of Bultmann opened up the debate, and also since he discusses most of the problems we are studying.

Kasemann is a historian and an exegete of the New Testament. His center of interest is the question of the relation between history and truth. Kasemann's inquiry is developed counter to the unilateral accent of Bultmann on the kerygma of the primitive Church to the detriment of the earthly Jesus, on the Pasch to the detriment of the events which preceded, on the *fides qua creditur* to the detriment of the *fides quae creditur*.[6]

1) In a conference on the problem of the historical Jesus,[7] delivered at Marburg, in 1953, and which marks a turning point in the world of Protestant criticism, Kasemann declares he cannot absolutely subscribe to the radical positions of his master. In fact, his master shows no interest in the concrete existence of the Jesus of History; he is content to pass over this existence. To separate thus the Christ of the kerygma from the Christ of history is to run the risk of transforming the Christ into myth, reducing Him to an ideology without figure or

body. The truth is that the Church has never wanted to let myth take the place of history, nor to have a celestial being substitute for Jesus of Nazareth. In this regard, it is significant that "only the Gospels present the message of Christ in the framework of the history of the earthly life of Jesus."[8] Opposition to the Liberal School is not a reason for contesting what the evangelists resolutely maintain, that is, that the historical life of Jesus has a decisive import for faith. Kasemann shows that the primitive Church has always combatted two excesses: "she knows that it is not possible to understand the earthly Jesus if we do not start out from the Pasch . . . and inversely we cannot know adequately the meaning of the Pasch, if we set aside the earthly Jesus."[9] Further on, he explains: "We cannot suppress the identity of the risen Lord and of the earthly Lord without falling into docetism and depriving ourselves of the possibility of making the distinction between the faith of Pasch of the community and a myth. Inversely, neither our sources nor the knowledge previously acquired authorize us to substitute the historical Jesus for the risen Lord."[10]

In fact, Mark and Matthew, upon integrating history in the kerygma, have stressed the continuity which exists between Jesus and the Christ, and they have prevented the historical figure of Jesus from being shadowed in abstraction. Is it not strange that even "the Gospel of John speaks of the permanent presence of the risen Lord precisely in the framework of a history of the earthly Jesus?"[11] Luke, finally, underlines more than the others the earthly itinerary of Jesus, becoming thus "the first Christian historian . . . His Gospel is truly the first life of Jesus . . . The history of Jesus becomes something absolutely of the past, truly a History, the *initium christianismi*,[12] after which comes the history of the apostles.

The event of salvation is inseparable from this man of Nazareth, who lived in Palestine, at a definite period. Thus there stands out the gratuity of salvation as an act of God existing *before us*. "Because primitive christianity had experience of Jesus as *Kairos,* it wrote the Gospels, and it did not simply, after the Pasch, abandon the history of Jesus."[13] The paschal event is the basis for the kerygma and for faith, but it is not the first nor the sole event. Paschal faith itself professes that God acted before we became believers and "it attests to it including in its preaching the earthly history of Jesus."[14]

A research about Jesus is theologically legitimate. Furthermore, it is possible to do so utilizing the same method of the Form School, for many elements of synoptic tradition are incontestably authentic. It may be that Jesus did not openly declare He was the Messiah, but His manner of acting and of speaking, His attitude in regard to the prophets and to institutions (laws, the sabbath, rites) constitute an "explicit" christology which the kerygma has rendered "explicit."

We must then undertake a positive research on the Gospels. The object of this research is to verify the *real continuity* which exists between the preaching of Jesus and the apostolic kerygma. "The question of the historical Jesus is legitimately that of the continuity of the Gospel in the discontinuity of temporal moments and in the variety of the kerygma."[15] This text condenses Kasemann's thinking, such as expressed in his conference of 1953.

2) He returned to the offensive in an article which appeared in 1964.[16] This text does not modify his essential theses, but it formulates what seems to be his definitive position. This position is mid-way between those of Jeremias and of Bultmann,[17] and comes near that of Ebeling.

In the first part, Kasemann takes on Jeremias whom he fiercely attacks. He esteems that he is over optimistic when he claims to be able to find the *ipsissima verba Jesu*. Jeremias asserts that Jesus is at the origin of Christian faith. But the real problem is to know how and to what measure He is at the origin of Christianity. Finally, Jeremias renders faith too unilaterally dependent on historical research, hoping to offer to our adoration the genuine image of Jesus. Kasemann suspects that Jeremias wants to return to the concept of the *Leben-Jesu-Forschung*. Faith, observes Kasemann, is a response to the kerygma, and not to the discoveries of science. But, in the perspective of Jeremias, one gets the impression that history takes the place of apostolic kerygma.

In the second part, Kasemann goes on to the examination

of Bultmann's position, in order to get him to make a self-criticism. For Kasemann, there is involved in this more than a personal confrontation: there is involved the very understanding of primitive Christianity. Here are some of his reflections:

a) He begins by saying that Bultmann sets down false premises when he contrasts "material continuity" and "historical continuity," Jesus of history and Christ of the kerygma.[18] In fact, continuity could not be pure temporal "continuity." All continuity, in the field of history, implies certain changes, or hiatus or fresh interpretations, otherwise it is futile to speak of history and the historical process. To speak of history is always to speak of continuity in the midst of a certain discontinuity, inherent to history itself. So it is excessive to conclude consequently that there is a "radical" discontinuity."[19]

b) Bultmann, following closely upon Herbert Braun, asserts that the autocomprehension of the believer (that is the meaning of his new condition which faith gives) is the stable, permanent element which links the Gospel and the kerygma, while christology is the variable element. The factor of unity and of coordination of the New Testament would be of an anthropological character, while the diverse christologies would serve only to explain the diversity of speech and of ecclesial situations. Kasemann replies that such a position is false. In fact, nothing is more variable, from one generation to another than autocomprehension of self. Can it be held that children exactly follow in the traces of their parents, when circumstances change completely? No, continuity and discontinuity are in dialectical relation. The only stable, permanent element of Christianity is reference to and belonging to Christ. So Christianity cannot be reduced to a "variable" quantity. Continuity is a process which operates in the interior of a change in order to maintain, in the face of the pressures of discontinuity, a determined tendency. Pasch is the event which "forms the bridge" between apostolic preaching and Jesus Himself. The term "Gospel," which designates at the same time apostolic preaching and the history of Jesus, is the sign of this intimate relation which unites them. In regard to this, it is significant that the fourth Gospel, the most theological, the most kerygmatic of the writings of the New Testament, assumes the narrative form of a Gospel, indicating thus that its author was not indifferent to the history of Jesus.[20]

c) Kasemann next examines at length Bultmann's thesis according to which Paul and John had no interest in the Jesus of history: He was a Jew, not a Christian; His teaching does not belong to Christianity, but to its "prolegomena." This thesis, Kasemann replies, is quite simply unsustainable. In fact, it can be observed that not only Jesus, but Paul and John also were Jews. Must it be concluded that they were not Christians? Where are the frontiers to be fixed between Judaism and Christianity? Must He whom Paul presents as the end of the Law, as "the author and consummator of our faith" (Heb 12:1), must He be made subject to that Law? There is not question of knowing whether Jesus was a Jew or a "Christian: Jesus is the new Adam, the archetype of our obedience, the very bearer of the Good Tidings." Without Jesus' teaching, Ebeling rightly says, "the kerygma itself would not exist."[21] He is not the presupposition, nor the preface, but the heart of the New Testament.

d) Bultmann insists unilaterally on the *Dass*, that is, on the bare fact of the existence of Jesus, without concern for the details of this existence: I know that Jesus lived, but I do not know how. But then, observes Kasemann, we are threatened by another danger, not less grave: that of imposing the attribute "Christian" on a certain comprehension of God and man, in which Jesus is no more than an occasion, and Christ is no more than a mythical symbol. Christianity would be the messenger of a gnosis. In this perspective, it can be asked whether there exists a difference between the hymn in Ph 2, 5 and the myth of Hercules. Why could not Marxism, which exercises such a seduction on men of today, why could it not become the norm of human self-understanding, rather than the kerygma of Christ.[22] Kasemann is convinced: we must go beyond the simple *Dass* and accord a much greater importance to the earthly Jesus. It must be admitted that "the kerygma was already contained *in substance* in the words and deeds of

Jesus."[23]

e) A propos of this, Kasemann asks whether the New Testament considers the Jesus of history as the criterion of its own validity. He replies affirmatively. As a matter of fact, Paul, in his kerygma, refers to the historical Jesus, who truly suffered, who died for us, who is risen. His kerygma is inseparable from the historical Jesus. John places the kerygma on the lips of the earthly Jesus and adopts the narrative form of a Gospel, manifesting thus his intent of historization. The Synoptics, although they are not scientific works, do not preach but *relate*, and have recourse to the literary genre proper to history.[24] All are based on history. Kasemann asks whether, correlatively, the historical existence of Jesus (deeds, actions, words, suffering) contains the kerygma itself. He thinks that the kerygma is found "in germ" in the words and deeds of Jesus of Nazareth. In brief, the Gospels give to the fact, Jesus, definite and irreplaceable characteristics, which assure continuity in discontinuity, and prevent the kerygma from vaporizing into pure ideology.

f) Finally, Bultmann brings up the question: how to explain that Jesus, preacher of the Kingdom, became the object of the kerygma. Bultmann's explanation invokes paschal faith and the mythical language used by the kerygma to express its faith. We must still state, Kasemann observes, that the primitive Church, which began by preaching Christ as Savior, Son of God and Judge of the world, thought it well to write—and this after the epistles—the Gospels, which relate the deeds and words of the earthly Jesus. The Church felt the need of refreshing its memory of Jesus. Why this "anamnesia?" Due to the following: after the *Kurios* had been preached, for decades, the Christian community had to fight against some deviations of a spiritualist type which neglected the Christ *extra nos* to keep only the Christ *intra nos*. Faced with this danger, to which the epistles to the Corinthians allude, the Church had to find a norm of discernment. Who can recognize with certitude one who is truly inspired and truly speaks in the name of Christ? For the Spirit Himself can be manipulated, used as a tool. In order to protect the very purity of the kerygma, the Church calls back to mind the words and deeds of Jesus. This recalling of Jesus is not a temptation to historization, a sort of nostalgia for the past, but a necessity for assuring the rectitude of the kerygma itself. Without this going back to the past, for gaining support from it, christology is dissolved and becomes a pure ecclesiology, or a pure pneumatology, or a pure anthropology. The Gospel of the evangelists then protects the Gospel of the kerygma. The Jesus of history prevents the preached Christ from becoming a myth, a gnosis, an ideology. The references to Jesus protect the kerygma against the threat of subjectivism.

III. Gunther Bornkamm

Three years after Kasemann's first conference and thirty years after Bultmann's *Jesus*, another one of his disciples, G. Bornkamm, professor Heidelberg, published a work entitled: *Jesus von Nazareth,*[26] a concrete illustration of Kasemann's program.

Bornkamm, too, refuses to confine himself to the kerygma. He says that some think the interlacing of history and faith so inextricable in the Gospels that every attempt to reach the Jesus of history seems to them doomed to failure. Listening to them it would seem the chart of the history of Jesus must be replaced by a carte blanche. "I cannot share such scepticism."[27] It is quite clear, there is not a question of writing a life of Jesus; but nonetheless we cannot renounce historical research. "The Gospels and the tradition they communicate could not forbid us to pose the question of the historical Jesus not only do they allow this research, but they require it."[28] For the first time, a representative of the Form School writes, if not a biography of Jesus, at least a synthesis of all we can know about Jesus of Nazareth.

No one can deny that the evangelical tradition rests solidly on the pre-paschal history of Jesus. The Gospels proclaim that faith does not begin of itself, but lives from a history which preceeds it and of which it cannot speak save as in the past. The

Gospels do not authorize in any way at all "resignation and scepticism" ". . . They render us, on the contrary, sensitive to the historical person of Jesus, although in quite another manner than do chronicles or historical accounts . . . What the Gospels tell of the message, the acts and the history of Jesus, is characterized by an authenticity, a freshness, an originality which even the paschal faith of the community could not diminish. All this brings us back to the earthly person of Jesus."[29] It is historical criticism, well understood that opens up for us access to Jesus, ridding us of biographical obsession. "If the Gospels do not present the history of Jesus in all its stages, nor in its inner and outer evolution, they do nonetheless speak of history as a fact and an event . . . Primitive Christian tradition on Jesus is replete with history."[30]

Bornkamm then endeavors to bring together the most suitable elements for giving a first sketch of the figure and person of Jesus, bringing out that which "prior to all interpretation of faith, is offered to us unaltered and original."[31] He is interested not only in the teaching of Jesus, but also in His action and the impact of His personality on the milieu and men of His times. This is of prime concern for understanding the messianic question. If it is true, in fact, that Jesus did not declare directly He was the Messiah, He nonetheless manifested His dignity as Messiah by His acts, by His attitudes, by His manner of speech, by all His behavior.[32] We have no reason to dispute that Jesus, by His coming and His ministry, effectively aroused the messianic hope and the belief that He was the promised savior.

Bornkamm, finally, recognizes that the kerygma underlines more the "contemporaneity" of the Christ, that is, His living and actual presence in the Church as Kurios than the historical development of His earthly life, for the Gospels were written in the light of the Pasch. It is still true however, that this Jesus, seen in the light of the Pasch, is the Jesus of history. There is continuity in the person.

IV. Conclusions

There exists, among the post-Bultmanians, a basic accord on a certain number of points, which we can now list:

1) There can no longer be a return to the type of research on the history of Jesus, such as that conceived by the Liberal School of the *Leben-Jesu-Forschung.*

2) There is *historical* and *theological continuity* between the Jesus of historicity and the Christ of the kerygma. It is therefore legitimate and even necessary to pursue researches on the earthly existence of Jesus.

3) While Bultmann stresses the differences between the preaching of Jesus and the kerygma of the Church, the post-Bultmanians stress the common elements.

4) All agree on emphasizing the existential value of the kerygma for the man of today. And this leads us to study the position of the "New Hermeneutic."

Footnotes for Chapter III

1. J. Jeremias, *Das Problem des historischen Jesus* (1960).
2. J. Jeremias, *Theologie du Nouveau Testament.* I: *La predication de Jesus* (1973); *Id., Les paraboles de Jesus* (Paris, 1962); *Id., La derniere Cene. Les paroles de Jesus* (Paris, 1972); *Id., Le message central du Nouveau Testament* (Paris, 1966).
3. J. Jeremias, *Le probleme historique de Jesus*, pp. 36-42.
4. *Ibid.,* pp. 36-42.
5. *Ibid.,* pp. 36-42.
6. P. Gisel, "Ernst Kasemann ou la solidarite conflictuelle de l'histoire et de la verite," *Etudes theologiques et religieuses,* LI (1976), n. 1) 21-37; Id., *Verite et Histoire, La theologie dans la modernite: Ernst Kasemann,* (Paris - Geneve, 1977, pp. 29-38.
7. E. Kasemann, Das Problem des historischen Jesus, *Zeitschrift fur Theologie und Kirche,* LI (1954) 125-153. French translation: *Le probleme du Jesus historique in Essais exegetiques.*
8. E. Kasemann, *Le Probleme du Jesus historique,* p. 151
9. *Ibid.,* p. 154.
10. *Ibid.,* p. 162.
11. *Ibid.,* p. 160.
12. *Ibid.,* pp. 157-158.
13. *Ibid.,* p. 159.
14. *Ibid.,* p. 162
15. *Ibid.,* p. 172.
16. E. Kasemann, "Sackgassen im Streit um den historischen Jesus," in *Exegetische Versuche und Besinnungen,* II (Gottingen, 1965), pp. 31-38.
17. Kasemann responds to the two following texts: J. Jeremias, *Le probleme historique de Jesus* (Paris, 1968); R. Bultmann, *Das Verhaltnis der urchristlichen Christusbotschaft zum historischen Jesus* (Heidelberg, 1960).
18. E. Kasemann, *Blind Alleys in the Jesus of History Controversy,* p. 36.
19. *Ibid.,* p. 37.
20. *Ibid.,* pp. 39-40.
21. *Ibid.,* p. 42.
22. *Ibid.,* pp. 44-45.
23. *Ibid.,* p. 47.
24. *Ibid.,* pp. 48-50.
25. *Ibid.,* pp. 63-64.
26. G. Bornkamm, *Jesus von Nazareth* (Stuttgart, 1956).
27. *Ibid.,* p. 16 *Qui est Jesus de Nazareth* (Paris, 1973).
28. *Ibid.,* p. 30.
29. *Ibid.,* p. 32.
30. *Ibid.,* pp. 32-33, 63.
31. *Ibid.,* p. 63.
32. *Ibid.,* pp. 193-195.

Chapter IV

THE NEW HERMENEUTIC

In the movement of reaction to Bultmann, primed by Jeremias and Kasemann, the "New Hermeneutic" represents as it were a second wave. The School owes its name and its official existence to the work of James M. Robinson.[1] *The New Hermeneutic*, is a work which contains an important contribution by Robinson himself. On the other hand, the new School could not be understood without setting it in the current of modern hermeneutics represented by Schleiermacher, Dilthey, Bultmann, Heidegger and Gadamer. The originality of the position of E. Fuchs and of C. Ebeling will afterwards be better grasped.

1) The "New Research" on Jesus

James M. Robinson is himself considered one of the representatives of the "New Hermeneutic," If a "New Research" on Jesus is possible[2] he says, it is not that we have a propos of the Gospels, new sources or new ideas, but because, thanks to the works of Dilthey and of Heidegger, we have found out a new concept of history and of human existence. Positivist Historicism no longer has value as a criterion of historiography, and neither does the psychology of the Liberal

School, in the case of biographical material.

History is not a chronicle of material facts, faith fully registered, but the understanding the *ego* has of itself and of its course of existence, such as they are revealed in its decisions and its commitment. This new view of history and of human existence has had as first effect to bring to the attention of New Testament research the kerygma as an expression of history and of the person of Jesus. In fact, the material preserved, on account of its kerygmatic interest (without being substantially altered by the process of kerygmatization), is precisely that which corresponds to the exigencies of a research founded on the modern view of history. The primitive community preserved essentially intact as the *logia* and accounts in which Jesus expressed most clearly His intentions and His concept of existence. We are thinking especially of the parables, the antitheses of the *sermon on the mount*, and the *logia on the Kingdom*. These *logia* are more important historical sources, for knowing the history and the person of Jesus, than chronological and psychological material vainly researched through the *Leben—Jesu—Forschung*.

This basic agreement between the modern concept of history and the preoccupations of the kerygma, is a capital fact. It means that the actual sources authorize a new type of research on the "historical Jesus," that is, on Jesus such as He may be reached by the paths of modern historiography.

The New Research is distinguished from the ancient under many other aspects. The Liberal School wanted to free itself from dogmatic restraints and react against the interpretation of Strauss. The "New Research has also its own dymanic, that is the question man asks himself about the possibility of a more authentic existence, one that is more meaningful. The Liberal School, besides, wanted to disassociate the Jesus of history from the kerygma of faith, only to preserve the man Jesus. This was its mistake. For the kerygma, on the contrary, there is identity between Jesus humiliated and the Lord exalted. The Gospels do not present a historical Jesus apart from the kerygma,—they offer, rather, a kerygmatic image of the history of Jesus. Theology finds itself in the face of a kerygma which presents, as a place of the event of salvation, a historical person to whom we equally have access through the paths of historiography. If a new research must be undertaken, it is the kerygma itself that proclaims the decisive importance of the historical person of Jesus. This unbreakable bond of history and of the kerygma expresses the paradox of Him who, issued from God, lived, however, as the men of His time and of His milieu.

Following this renewed concept of history, what will be the objective of the New Research? Briefly, let us say that there is question of verifying whether the meaning of the existence which the kerygma attaches to the person of Jesus is in conformity with the meaning of the existence which historiography finds in the historical Jesus. History cannot establish that the kerygma is true, but that the existential decision in face of the kerygma is an existential decision in face of Jesus."[3] "The New Research," Robinson again underlines, "cannot support the truth of the kerygma, according to which this person lived really of the presence of God and has opened up to me effectively the coming of God in my historical existence. But it can verify whether this kerygmatic knowledge of the existence of Jesus corresponds to the comprehension of the existence implicitly contained in the history of Jesus. For we can recompose this understanding of the existence of Jesus, with the help of modern historiography." The problem "consists in deriving profit from accessible sources and from the present day historical method in such a way as to penetrate the reason for Jesus' actions, His concept of existence, to compare it with that contained in the kerygma."[4] Thus, after having compared some fragments of the preaching of Jesus (notably in the parables) with the kerygma of Paul, Robinson discovers, in two cases, the same dialectic, the same understanding of Himself, that is, life in death, glory in the cross, exaltation in humiliation. Once it is verified in this way that the concept of existence proposed by Jesus, such as known by history, is faithful to the concept of existence contained in the kerygma, then the meaning of human existence which is given us by the kerygma becomes for us a norm of the understanding of existence.

But the question comes up. If we can dialogue with the "historical Jesus," either by way of the kerygma, or by way of history, why does not the kerygma suffice. Precisely because there are a number of extant kerygmas: gnostic, doretist, Paulinian. The effort made by research has as its objective to discern, among these diverse kerygmas, that which allows us a true encounter and a true dialogue with Jesus. Thus, the Jesus known through history does not found the kerygma, but *verifies* it. While Kasemann seeks between Jesus and the kerygma a logical and theological continuity (a relation of the implicit and of the explicit), Robinson seeks rather an existential continuity.

The work of Robinson, wholly concerned that the fidelity of the kerygma to the "historical Jesus" be established, leaves the reader sceptical about the possibility of finding the authentic person of Jesus and of hearing His authentic message. In fact, in a subsequent article, Robinson no longer so strongly accents the encounter with Jesus by means of a historiography of existential style, but rather emphasizes parallelism, even more, the unity which exists between the message of Jesus (words and deeds) and the primitive kerygma.

II. Predecessors of the "New Hermeneutic"

The "New Hermeneutic" belongs to a current of thinking which goes back to Schleiermacher.

Hermeneutics is the science of the interpretation of texts which belong to a distant and different period than our own. When I read a novel which has just appeared, I understand it right away, because the speech and the milieu of the author are connatural to me. We belong to the same universe. It is not the same when there is question of a Babylonian text. Then the difficulties met do not concern merely the translation, but even more the inner meaning of the words and the reality of the cultural milieu which they impart and conceal at the same time. Exegetics has after a long time drawn up a certain number of rules of interpretation which are still worthwhile. Bultmann reduces these rules to five. They are: a) A literary work is to be analyzed as to its style and overall structure, the whole expressing the parts and the parts expressing the whole; b) In texts written in a foreign language, grammar and syntax merit special attention; c) Each word has the meaning given it by the author; a meaning found out by analysis of the whole work; d) A work is the better understood the more the personality and culture of the author are better known to us; e) Every document is the reflection of his milieu and his epoch. Consequently, the more one and the other are known, so much the more is the document understood.[6]

Even after having strictly applied these rules, we cannot expect, in every case, the text to become fully clear to us. Indeed all depends on what we mean by "understand" a text. At the beginning of the 18th century, when the method of the exact sciences dominated every form of knowledge, it was thought it possible to apply to history and literature the same principles of research which were current in the world of the natural sciences. Thus, there would be no difference, on the level of objectivity and of certitude of results, between chemical analysis of a substance and the interpretation of a text of Homer or of Plato. It is a question of method.

1) The first to react against this despotism of the natural sciences was Schleiermacher who, from the beginning of the 19th century, in his lessons on hermeneutics, demonstrated that the interpretation of a text could not abstract from the reader, who actively addressed himself to it, with his formation and his knowledge. Understanding a text consists in retracing the text to the author, in order to follow the author's itinerary in reverse to the text and to find the author's *intuition*. Interpretation and creative act correspond to two analogical moments. The mind of the reader, by a sort of "divining," takes up, in the moment of interpretation, what was produced at the creative moment. Schleiermacher's "psychological" theory tries to put itself within the creative process of the author, then to advance toward the understanding of his work, and finally toward the unity of his life and the ensemble of his works. In

this perspective, there could not be conceived a text the meaning of which would be independent of the author and apart from him. A hermeneutic circle is formed between reader and author, even though access to the text and to the author necessarily passes through the subject confronted with the text, who deciphers it actively, putting into it all that he is and all that he knows.[7]

2) Wilhelm Dilthey (1833-1911) sanctioned this position of Schleiermacher by distinguishing explicitly sciences of nature *(Naturwissenschaften)* and sciences of the spirit *(Geisteswissenschaften)*, that is those disciplines which express the interior life of man, such as history and literature. In the natural sciences, there is question of explaining, while in the human sciences there is question of communicating with an experience and of understanding it. Dilthey denounces the epistemological inconsistency of the German school of absolute historical objectivity. A textual approach which would intend to exclude every contribution or every intervention of the subject (that is, the reader), is illusory and utopian. The categories of value for the natural sciences, are no longer valid when applied to the interior world of man. In particular, the natural sciences ignore the dimension of historicity. The temporal is a congenital trait of human experience. It would be impossible to understand the present except on the horizon of the past and of the future. The objective of hermeneutics, according to Dilthey, would then be to find a method objectively worthwhile for interpreting the profound life of man, in its totality of lived experience.

This way of approaching the *experience* of another, cannot be but that of experience, since life possesses a richness which is beyond the rational process alone. Only life meets life. For understanding another person, we must, in some way, by affinity and communication, pass over ourselves to the heart of this person and find a common denominator with our own experience. A passing over which is only possible by virtue of a *pre-comprehension*, that is, of a similarity of a vital experience existing between reader and author. Literary works are, for Dilthey, the privileged place of hermeneutics, for, through the mediation of speech, they manifest not only the experience and the psychology of the author, but moreover his whole universe, that is, the historical-social reality which is expressed in them.[8]

The distinction made by Dilthey between natural and human sciences may be criticized, for, in every act of knowing, to explain and to understand are found in varying proportions. For instance, the historical phenomenon, in so far as "fact," enters into the explicative process; in so far as "significant," it is relevant to understanding. The hermeneutic movement unfolds in both directions. It may be equally doubted that it be necessary, for the reader, to recreate the author's experience for understanding his work. One thing is certain, these distinctions have been well used. Above all, Dilthey has contributed to widening the horizon of hermeneutics setting the problem of interpretation in the human sciences. It is no longer possible, from now on, for appreciating the historic authenticity of the Gospels, to apply to them the canons of historic positivism.

3) With M. Heidegger *(Sein and Zeit,* 1927), modern hermeneutics acquires an even more decisive influence, for, through R. Bultmann, it penetrates the field of New Testament criticism. Bultmann, in fact, admits that he found in Heidegger's philosophy a valuable model for speaking correctly of human existence and, consequently, of the existence of the believer.

The question which the message of the New Testament poses to man, is that of the existential decision he must make face to face with God: to believe or to reject faith. This decision is the supreme act of man's free will placed face to face with God in His word: an act which determines the meaning which each man gives to his own existence. The affinities are clear between Heidegger's philosophy and this focial point of the message of the New Testament. As a matter of fact, Heidegger tells us that the problem of existence is the central problem of philosophy and that man is a subject rising into existence and projecting himself toward the future in the decision in which his free will is asserted. It is a decision for an authentic life opening itself up to the future by the exercise of a free will ever renewed and ever creative, or a decision for an unauthentic life, which means relinquishing and wrecking free will. Man thus finds himself constantly confronted by a choice which involves his future.

History, therefore, is so much the more true as it goes to the heart of these decisions (or the possibilities of existence chosen among so many others) which have projected man toward the future and which have rendered his existence authentic or unauthentic. To question history does not signify, then, not to gather the events of an objectively constituted past, but to ask ourselves how the man of another epoch understood his existence, at the core of his decisions, and how in turn we can arrive at the understanding of our own existence. To question a text, especially a biblical one, means to ask the meaning that it gives of existence and the meaning it offers to existence. Such would have to be moreover the sole question addressed to a document: how to conceive existence. It is not otherwise in regard to the New Testament.

But a text could only constitute a meaning for existence if, previously, there was suspected at least something of the existential bearing of the text. This *Vorverstandnis* or precomprehension is not a prejudgment but the prior understanding, elementary and imperfect, of every reader who questions a text. How does one understand friendship, love, suffering, solitude, if one has no experience of their realities? Without a relationship to the life lived, how does one understand the life expressed by the text? This first understanding, doubtless, will be amended and enriched in contact with the text, without however being ever definitive. Let us add that, in order to be true, the understanding should open out on an existential decision. It is of the philosophy of Heidegger that Bultmann demands this prior understanding of existence which will be then clarified by the word of God.

Carrying out the hermeneutic, then, means to question a text on what it says *about* existence, and *through* existence, the two points of view being complementary and necessary, since a text cannot truly be significant for existence without a precomprehension of existence.

Bultmann takes up Heidegger's language to formulate his

own exegetical and theological principles. Thus we have the existential interpretation of Scripture. The New Testament can be interpreted by the reader from different viewpoints: historical, psychological, and theological. But the Church tells us the only point of view that is true, the one which responds to the profound view of Scripture, is the one which leads to the existential decision required by the Gospel. It is futile to pose a question to the New Testament which is alien to it.

What the Word of God, in the New Testament, unveils to us, is the structure of our being, distended between two modes of contradictory existence: unauthentic existence of sinful man, cut off from God, and authentic existence of man saved by grace. What philosophy shows us in the existential constitutive categories of our being, finds consistency in the message which the event of Christ contains for us. The task of the exegete is to try to deal with the sole problem which has a real importance, since it still concerns us today, that is, the understanding of our existence, face to face with the Word of God.

If then the New Testament does not speak of everything but only in an authentic manner of understanding our existence, it follows that the *Formkritik* should be accompanied by a *Sachkritik* which knows how to discern, in the material offered by the New Testament, the only elements having an existential import. Here is where there enters in demythologization, which is but an aspect of Bultmann's general hermeneutics and a practical means for bringing about an existential interpretation of Scripture.

To demythologize does not mean to set aside the mythical as rationalists did heretofore, but to interpret it and express it in a language accessible to the generation with the technique of the 20th century. The mythical language of the New Testament derives from diverse sources: Semitic, Hellenic, gnostic. It must be expressed in existential categories in order that the New Testament bring men to the decisive choice which the Gospel requires, today as at the origin of the Church. The event of salvation is brought about when, responding to the call of God, man decides to pass from the unauthentic existence of sin (the condition in which he wants to take into his own hands his future and declare himself master of his existence) and pass on to the authentic existence of faith, in the profession of the event of salvation in Jesus Christ. This act of faith is a leap in the dark, which has no other basis but itself. It has nothing to do with the arguments from history or from reason. Thus, the pre-understanding of existence proposed by Heidegger, set in dialogue with the New Testament, leads in faith and by faith, to the understanding of authentic existence.

4) While Bultmann develops these ideas from *Sein und Zeit*, Heidegger pursues his reflections, all centered henceforth on the nature of speech (*Unterwegs zur Sprache,* 1959). Now the creators of the New Hermeneutic refer especially to the Heidegger of this second period, without however renouncing the existential interpretation of Bultmann.

In the Heidegger of the second stage, speech is the primordial fact of human existence, the first experience which is born of contact with being. Taken in this sense, speech is not first the expression of ideas conceived by the mind, then expressed in words: this is already speech in its second stage. Speech is the very essence of man, in so far as it is communication with being and response to the call of being. Man is, as it were, the loudspeaker of the silent voice of being, and he is only truly man when he carries out that task. Man is born of speech and lives out of speech. It is less the man who speaks than the language which speaks.

There is authentic speech and unauthentic speech which is repetition or idle talk. Authentic speech is that which proceeds from the encounter with being. On that account, the poet is the creator of language, for he is the shepherd of being. He it is who welcomes, accepts and renders it present. A propos of authentic speech, two things are to be noted. First that speech is ever richer than the words it uses, for the being which is revealed in speech is pregnant with a wealth that is only partially expressed by way of words. Next, speech has for its objective to arouse in the listener an experience analogous to that which has been lived by the one who is speaking. Thus, each poet bears within him an intuition which his verses but imperfectly impart. To understand it is to try to find out this primordial intuition which dwells in the poet, for sharing in his original experience.

5) G. Gadamer, in *Wahrheit und Methode,* 1960, does not share this view, which is that also of Schleiermacher and Dilthey. The objective of hermeneutics, in his eyes, is not to understand the author, but the text. What is especially important, is not the *one who* tells things, but rather *that which* is told. Understanding is not a mysterious communion of souls, but research into the *meaning* proposed by the text. Once produced, the text emancipates itself from its author, acquires a personality and a life of its own: that of a subject which is questioned, but who in turn questions the one who interprets it. The meaning of a text is then not first what the author wanted to say, but what the text says to the reader *hic et nunc.* It follows that a text has never found a definitive interpretation, for read and interpreted anew by each generation, it is susceptible to a growth of its indefinite meaning.

III. E. Fuchs and G. Ebeling

Directly, or as catalysts, all the elements we just described, exercised their influence on Fuchs and Ebeling.

Fuchs was born in 1903, Ebeling in 1912. Both professors at the University of Marburg, are in agreement on a certain number of points. Today they are regarded as the fathers of New Hermeneutic. Even if the works of Ricoeur, Pannenberg and Lapointe constitute a much more recent hermeneutics, the term *New Hermeneutic* has become a technical term reserved to designate the school represented by Fuchs, Ebeling, with whom the names of Herbert Braun and of James C. Robinson are to be associated.

The New Hermeneutic is not a new method of exegesis or explanation of classical texts. It has become a new theological system since its attention is set above all on the existential decision and on the communicability of revelation for the man of today. Its concept of man is related to that of Heidegger.

Man is not a static being. He is constructed to the measure that he conquers himself, in face of the future, and by way of the decisions he makes. His whole life is defined by "the hour," by "the time," and each hour calls for a decision, particularly grave when there is question of major events of existence.

In this perspective, what is the role of speech? On this point likewise, faithfull to Heidegger of the second phase, the New Hermeneutic attributes above all to speech a function of summons. It should incite and lead to a decision. For Heidegger, being and speech are linked parts and arise at the same time. For Ebeling and Fuchs, event and speech come as a pair. Fuchs speaks "of event of speech" *(Sprachereignis)*, and Ebeling, "of event of the word" *(Wortgeschehen)*, both are synonymous expressions. For Fuchs, speech is an event, not in the banal sense of a reality situated in space and time, but in this sense that it renders being *efficaciously* present in time. It permits being to be, truly. Thus, to call someone "brother," is to validate the purely biological bond which exists between two persons. For Ebeling, "the power of the event of the word consists in that this word is capable of transforming us when one man speaks to another and communicates to him something of his own existence, of his will, of his love, of his hope, of his joy, of his suffering, but also of his harshness, of his hate, of his baseness, of his malice, and thus gives him a share in it."[9] The word is man himself. "The essence of the word is not reached by questioning about the essence of its content, but by asking what the word operates, what it engenders, and what future it opens up."[10] The word of man is often deceitful. It does not carry out what it promises. Only the word of God can promise man a true future, that is, salvation. When the word of God comes, the world is changed. The true speech, "the event of speech" par excellence, is the word of salvation. Thus, the preaching of Christ is a *Sprachereignis*, that is, a speech generative of faith and love. In its turn, the teaching of the Church is a *Sprachereignis*: by it in fact, she is constituted the Church or the Body of Christ.[11] The word of God serves as the common speech, of men, but it is distinguished from it on the level of "effectiveness." Thanks to its divine office, human speech becomes suitable for leading to life rather than to death.

This concept of speech is of grave consequence for the interpretation of the New Testament:

1) While, for Bultmann, it is existence that interprets the text, and this interpretation leads to the demythologization of the New Testament, for Fuchs and Ebeling, it is the text which interprets existence, and this interpretation ought to lead to conversion. "The first phenomenon, in the domain of understanding, Ebeling stresses, is not understanding speech, but understanding by way of speech."[12] The New Hermeneutic is less an effort for understanding the text than for deciphering the meaning of existence by means of speech. Text and interpreter ever constitute the two poles of hermeneutics, but the relationship is changed. It is the text which interprets us, and the text itself sends us back to the event of the word or of speech which gave it origin. The reason for this new relationship is found in the theory of Heidegger, according to which it is not man who engenders speech, but rather speech which engenders man. Now the text is precisely an event of speech, engendered by it. In the perspective of Bultmann, it is man, decidedly, who judges the text; for the New Hermeneutic, on the contrary, it is the sacred text which judges human existence. The hermeneutic relationship passes necessarily through the Word of God.

2) The task of hermeneutics is to transform the word of the past, embodied in a text, into a living, actual word, which never ceases to call out. It applies itself to find the event of the word to the native state, "the source." It must then eliminate all the elements which overload or limit the text (mythical elements, elements related to an epoch) in order to return it to its first function which is to bring the reader to the experience which engendered it.

3) Authentic speech has value for summons rather than for information. Consequently, the interpretation of a text does not aim at it bringing out teachings, but at discovering the understanding of existence it proposes. A text, then, cannot be approached with indifference. The interpretation is not achieved so long as the text has not become an invitation to

take seriously the event of speech which has aroused it and to bring about a decision which involves the very meaning of our existence. If the text is religious, the event of speech from which it originates, is faith. Consequently, the interpretation of the text is not complete as long as the reader-listener does not reproduce in his life the faith which is at the origin of the text.

In what spirit, thenceforth, should the text of the Gospels be approached? The preaching of Jesus was an "event of speech"; a summons inviting his listeners to conversion, that is, to changing their understanding of the world and of life. To read the Gospels in order to find therein objective information on Jesus, would then be an error of perspective: a sin against authentic speech. For dialoguing with the Gospels, it is necessary to approach them from an existential viewpoint, in order to find their first end, which is to bring man to the decision of faith. We must consider the Gospels above all as a kerygma. There is question of knowing how Jesus understood His own existence, face to face with God. Every other non-existential interpretation is sterile. Even more, it constitutes a perversion of the text.

The decision of faith is important, for only the Word of God expresses the truth of man. Only it confers on human reality its consistency, and saves it from the absurd, from void, from the insignificance into which the sin of man plunged it. Left to himself, man is but an illusion and a lie. Faith alone frees him. Now this faith is not adherence to a sum of articles and propositions; it is not a new object offered to intelligence, but rather a *light* which illuminates all reality and transforms the attitude of man. Faith is a new being face to face with God, with men and the world.

Our faith is authentic, if it is an echo of the faith of Jesus until His death. The life of Jesus, in fact, is the authentic interpretation of existence. His faith until His death is the supreme example of the man who renounces himself and his own future to open himself up to the future of God. This general principle becomes the very norm which enables the recognition of the authenticity of the words of Jesus. All that contradicts this principle is unauthentic. The attitude of Jesus is expressed in the christological hymn of Ph 2:6-11: because He was obedient unto death, God has exalted Him. If Jesus had not lived, we would never have known what is true faith, nor true life.

Henceforth, the position of Fuchs and of Ebeling in regard to the problem of Jesus is better understood. For Bultmann, the only thing that concerned him about the Jesus of history is the fact of His existence and of His death on the cross, that is the *Dass*, and not the *Was* and the *Wie*. Kasemann contradicted this thesis maintaining that it was also important to know the modalities of the existence of Jesus. The New Hermeneutic equally maintains that the kerygma is in continuity with the preaching of Jesus. It is what announced that the "time," the "hour" of the Kingdom is "now." Jesus Himself belonged to this Kingdom and His attitude is exemplary. Fuchs writes, "If previously we interpreted the historical Jesus with the help of the primitive Christian kerygma, today, we interpret this kerygma with the help of the historical Jesus; both directions of the interpretation are complementary."[13] Research on Jesus is not only possible, but necessary. There is, indeed, question of discovering the authentic faith of Jesus in the purification of ulterior interpretations which could contaminate or deform it. Jesus thus becomes not only the witness, but the foundation of our faith." To believe, is to accept the faith of Jesus and reproduce it in us."

Now the faith of Jesus becomes event in His speech. The history of Jesus is the history of His speech. The gift of Himself to men is the gift of His word. This speech of Jesus is found principally in the parables of the Kingdom; Fuchs, Ebeling and Robinson have also been attracted by them. The parables, however, are not definitions of the Kingdom, but a new manner of viewing life. They demand to be read, not as by spectators but by actors. Each one of us, on reading them, should feel summoned, constrained to an existential decision, invited to choose between the view of the world proposed by Jesus, or the self-sufficiency of the ancient world. Each must decide, in the light of his own situation, in what measure the parables relate to him.

If the parables are chosen as the highest form of gospel language, the miracles, on the contrary, are deprecated, being considered as mythological accounts. The resurrection, on being considered demythologized, possesses with the cross, an incomparable existential import. The true message of the resurrection is the proclamation of the scandal of the cross, which we must constantly surmount. Each time that, in our lives, following the example of Jesus, we surmount this scandal, the resurrection is proclaimed.

Jesus represents a decisive turning point in the history of human self-knowledge. In Him, man recognizes God as the bounds of his own ego and abandons himself to the future of God. The apostles in turn have transmitted to us the faith of Jesus through the language of the kerygma and of the text of the New Testament, which calls us to become an "event of speech" in the decision of faith in our lives.

IV. Conclusions

1) With Fuchs and Ebeling, the objective of hermeneutics underwent a decisive transformation; it is not only we who interpret the text, it is the text which interprets us, that is, clarifies and judges our existence. On other points, the New Hermeneutic is still inspired by Bultmann's positions: recognition of existential philosophy, preoccupation with demythologization (notably of miracles and of the resurrection), devaluation of the history of salvation, counter to Cullmann and Pannenberg.

2) On the problem of the historical Jesus, the New Hermeneutic is part of the anti-Bultmann current. In disagreement with Bultmann for whom the historical person of Jesus is without importance, Ebeling esteems that this person is the legitimization and foundation of the kerygma. In a christological perspective, nothing can be asserted about Jesus which is not based on the historical Jesus Himself. The understanding of the human existence which the speech of

Jesus reveals to us, being the sole authentic speech, the kerygma, still today, has need of Jesus as authentic witness of the faith.

3) Heidegger, Fuchs, Ebeling have had the merit of bringing out the value of an important aspect of speech, too often neglected, that is, its function of summons. But they have exaggerated by reducing unilaterally speech to this dimension. If it should be affirmed that the only authentic speech is that which leads to an existential decision, it would have to be concluded that all speech of an objective type (in philosophy, in science, in history, in daily affairs), is unauthentic. The Gospels also have as objective to inform us about Jesus, (his life, message, passion, death, resurrection), and on the event of salvation accomplished in Him, even if we must admit that this information tended finally to conversion and to the decision of faith. On this point the New Hermeneutic has much to teach us. However, faith is no less an assent than a decision. A religious option would not be able to be made without previous consideration of a great number of objective facts, especiallly when the whole of life is at stake. Without the content of the Christian message about the salvific act of God in Jesus Christ, how would we be able to make a decision about it? The Church must then verify the soundness of the kerygma starting out from the teaching of Jesus.

4) Another weak point of the New Hermeneutic is the depreciation of the sacraments as an occasion of actual, personal encounter with the glorified Christ and with the objective event of salvation which is in Him. In the perspective of Fuchs and Ebeling, Jesus makes God present to us through His speech. But it seems that our faith wears itself out in this speech-event which is the decision of faith. There is wanting to the New Hermeneutic a theology of sacrament: it keeps unilaterally centered on word and speech. This identification of word and salvation is typically Protestant, and the Bultmannian School only brought the Lutheran doctrine to its ultimate consequences.

Footnotes for Chapter IV

1. James M. Robinson and J.B. Cobb, ed., *The New Hermeneutic* (New York, 1964).

2. James M. Robinson, *A New Quest of the Historical Jesus* (London, 1959). *Le kerygme de l'Eglise.*

3. *Ibid.*, p. 86.

4. *Ibid.*, p. 88.

5. James M. Robinson, "The Recent Debate on the New Quest," *Journal of Bible and Religion,* XXX (1962) 198-208. This text constitutes one of the three contributions of a symposium on the work of Robinson. The other two texts are by M.S. Enslin, *The Meaning of the Historical Jesus for Faith,* JBR (XXX (1962) 219-223; and by S.M. Ogden, *Bultmann and the New Quest,* JBR (XXX (1962) 209-218.

6. P. Grech, "La Nuova Ermeneutica: Fuchs ed Ebling," in *Esegesi ed Ermeneutica,* Atti della XXI Settimana biblica dell'Associazione biblica italiana (Brescia, 1972), pp. 35-69; R. Bultmann, "Das Problem der Hermeneutik," in *Glauben und Verstehen* II (1952), pp. 212-213.

7. R.E. Palmer, *Hermeneutics. Interpretation Theory in Schleiermacher, Dilthey, Heidegger and Gadamer* (Evanston, 1969), pp. 84-97.

8. R.E. Palmer, *Hermeneutics. Interpretation Theory in Schleiermacher, Dilthey, Heidegger and Gadamer,* pp. 98-123.

9. G. Ebeling, *L'essence de la foi chretienne* (Paris, 1970), p. 216. Translation of *Das Wesen des Christlichen Glaubens,* (Tubingen, 1959).

10. *Ibid.*, p. 217.

11. *Sprachereignis, Wortgeschehen* correspond to *Heilsereignis* and *Heilgeschehen* of Bultmann.

12. G. Ebeling, *Word and Faith,* (London, 1963), p. 318. German original: *Wort und Glaube,* I, (Tubingen, 1960).

13. E. Fuchs, *Zur Frage nach dem historischen Jesus,* (Tubingen, 1965), p. 7.

Chapter V

THE GENERATION OF THEOLOGIANS

The last decade there appeared a "third generation" of researchers (after Bultmann and after the generation of disciples reacting against their master). This time there are theologians. It is significant that a good number of the major works published by these authors are christologies. The authors are Protestants and Catholics. The Protestant authors are, for instance, O. Cullmann, W. Pannenberg, Moltmann, H. Braun, E. Stauffer; the Catholic authors are, W. Kasper, H. Kung, von Balthasar, P. Schoonenberg, E. Schillebeeckx, K. Rahner, J. Alfaro, Ch. Duquoc, J. Galot, L. Bouyer etc. These christologies have led their authors to take a position on the problem of the historical finding of Jesus through the Gospels, sometimes under the form of a *status quaestionis* and promises, for giving a solid basis for a deeper understanding, sometimes, too, under the form of a lengthy, elaborated discussion. Obviously we cannot expound the thinking of each one. Among the Protestant authors we shall study more thoroughly the positions of the two most representative, namely, Pannenberg and Moltmann; among the Catholic authors, positions of Duquoc and Schillebeeckx, and more briefly, of Kasper and Kung, will be discussed.

I. Christology Among the Protestants

1) Already, in *Offenbarung als Geschichte*,[1] Pannenberg reacting against Bultmann for whom revelation hardly touches on history, identifies revelation with the course of events and the meaning which emerges from it, for the events are themselves bearers of meaning. God's revelation is indirect, that is, by way of the events of history, and universal, that is, offered to the eyes of all. But each particular event provides only a limited knowledge of God, so history must be developed in its entirety in order that God's revelation be knowledgeable and known. On the other hand, the resurrection of Jesus, being the anticipated expression of the end of this history, is what enables the meaning of universal history to be deciphered from this moment. Christ becomes thus the hermeneutic key of history as God's revelation.

So it is important to know Him. All christology, Pannenberg asserts, must begin with Jesus.[2] "The Jesus preached today is none other than He who of old lived in Palestine and was crucified under Pilate, and the inverse is true.[3] After the works of the *Formgeschichte*, we know without doubt that it is no longer possible to consider the Gospels as a chronology of the life of Jesus, but that does not solve the problem of knowledge of Jesus. We must still explain how the destiny of Jesus could raise up the preaching of Christ among the first Christians. "It is possible to go back, beyond the apostolic kerygma, to the historical Jesus. Not only possible, but also necessary."[4] In the context of the renewal of research on Jesus (with Kasemann, Fuchs, Bornkamm especially), Bultmann can no longer be followed by considering as accessory that Jesus is the true author of the message transmitted by the Gospels. Henceforth it is acknowledged that faith must have its base on Jesus. "And this is the Jesus such as our historical inquiry reveals Him."[5] So the "legitimization" of the kerygma by Jesus Himself is to be taken seriously.

Beyond the texts, it is necessary to go back again to Jesus, for it is only in this manner that the unity of the New Testament appears. Indeed, the unity of the assertions of New Testament witnesses "is in Jesus alone, to whom they relate all of them, and that unity is not found save in going back beyond the kerygma of the apostles."[6] This unity becomes perceptible when the writings of the New Testament are regarded as a "historical source" and not only as a "text of preaching." "As a historical source, they in fact do not say only what was believed formerly, but they at the same time make known something about Jesus Himself, in whom the Christian believes."[7] If it was not possible to show that Christian faith relies on the historical Jesus Himself, it would be necessary to conclude that preaching concerning Jesus is a product of faith.

But in what manner is the Jesus of old the foundation of the kerygma? The response cannot be provided save through deep reflection on the Jesus of old and on the real relation of the primitive message with Him. Without doubt the foundation of our faith must be able to be verified by our present experience of reality, "but it consists itself entirely in what happened of old."[8] The New Testament teaches us that, by His exaltation, Jesus was taken away from the earth and from His disciples, but "it is only through what happened of old, that we know Jesus living in glory, and not by virtue of our actual experiences . . . No one now has an experience of it, at any rate an experience that can be distinguished with certainty from an illusion . . . So, even in what concers the certitude of the present life of the Glorified, we rely wholly on what happened of old . . . We must say, counter to Althaus: 'What concerns faith, is first what Jesus was.' That alone enables us to know what He is for us today and how it is possible to preach Him today." Pannenberg concluded his exposition on the problem of Jesus: "The task of christology is then to base on the history of Jesus the true knowledge of His significance."[10]

2) J. Moltmann, as did Pannenberg, reacted against Bultmann. In his recent work, *Le Dieu crucifie*[11] he has a chapter entitled: *Les questions sur Jesus.*

Moltmann says, christology is found at the center of Christian theology. But who was Jesus of Nazareth? Often, Christians and non-Christians, have made of Jesus an image corresponding to their desires: a teacher of morality, a Galilean rebel, a prophet. "Who was Jesus Himself and what does He Himself mean today? Do we know Jesus and who is He truly for us today?"[12] Within the very interior of Christianity, Jesus has been an object of discussion. Moltmann recalls the long debate of modern criticism over "jesuology" and "christology:" Where is Jesus in His reality: in the earthly Jesus who appeared in Palestine in the reign of Tiberius and was crucified under Pontius Pilate, or in the risen Christ, preached and believed in the apostolic primitive community? Faith assumes that the profession of Jesus as Christ, is reality and not illusion.

The central question of Christianity and of christology is: "What is the relation of the primitive Christian message on Christ to the historical Jesus? By what right did the community announce Jesus as Christ after His public death on the cross?... Every Christian should ask himself whether his faith in Jesus Christ is true and conformed to Jesus Himself, or whether the Christian tradition has given him or has been given something else instead, an idea, a spirit, or a phantom. The retrospective auto-criticism of faith in Jesus and in His history is born of faith itself."[13]

Moltman assigns to Christian theology a twofold task. It must first show the true view of the profession "Jesus Christ." It must shed light on the internal basis and justification of christology in the person and history of Jesus.[14] In other terms, Jesus and His history (life, teaching, death, resurrection) do they demand a christology? "It is the question of the intrinsic truth of faith and of the Chruch, and of their right to appeal to it in the name of Him whom they believe and of whom they speak. This question does not come from outside, but from faith itself, which is eager for knowledge and reason. "Is the kerygma in conformity with Jesus, or rather does it put something else in His place? "Faith in Christ, does it proceed with interior necessity from the apprehension of the person and the history of Jesus, or rather do the assertions about Him derive from arbitrariness of faith and are they personal judgments of worth?"[15]*M*

Moltmann esteems that the denial made by Bultmann to

the question of the internal legitimation of the message of Christ in relation to Jesus and to His history, is a position unjustified, but determined by a dogmatic notion of the kerygma.[16]

A second stage of christology, Moltmann continues, is showing that the profession of Jesus manifests His pertinence for the understanding of the reality of today: God, justice of man and of the world. Indeed, by christological titles faith is not only expressing who Jesus was in person; it opens out on the future, and expresses its meaning in relation to God, to men and to the world.

"The first task of christology is then the critical verification of Christian faith in its origin in Jesus and in His history. The second is the critical verification of Christian faith in its consequences for the present and future. To the first may be given the name of hermeneutic of origin, and to the second that of hermeneutic of effects and its consequences."[17] Both tasks are equally indispensable. A hermeneutic of origin only, despite its fidelity to Scripture, remains sterile. A hermeneutic which is unilaterally concerned about the effects of christology in Christianity and in the history of the world, readily loses sight of the internal justification and authority of faith. Both approaches must be united constantly.

In the profession of Christ, a name, *Jesus*, is joined to the titles which express His dignity and His functions: Christ, Son of Man, Lord, Son of God, Logos. By these titles, faith expresses what Jesus is for it, what it believes, awaits and hopes of Him.[18] The titles could vary with linguistic and cultural worlds: the historical beginning and the variability of the titles have, however, a fixed point and criterion. "They are specified by the proper name of Jesus and by His history, which ended in His crucifixion and His resurrection." If it is wished to say who is Christ, the Son of man, the Son of God, the Logos, there must be pronounced the name of Jesus and there must be related His history. This name is irreplaceable by the name of any other person: His history is irreplaceable by any other history.

As is seen, Pannenberg and Moltmann maintain an

unbreakable link between faith and history, between Jesus and the Christ. There is here the same person in newness of conditions: Jesus crucified and glorified. Pannenberg, by the primacy of the historical reality of Jesus of Nazareth, over the interpretation he derives from it; Moltmann indissolubly joins faith, and the event, in their historical consistency, and the signification which dwells in it.

II. Christology among Catholics

A christology would have to handle a certain number of problems concerning the relationship of Christianity to history. Nonetheless the treatment of these problems, in contemporaneous christologies, as well as the amount of space given them, vary from one author to another. With some, there is a preliminary statement to be made; with others, there is question of a problem to be discussed.

1) In *Jesus der Christus*,[19] Walter Kasper devotes a chapter to the historical question of Jesus. After having retraced the great lines of the history of criticism, of the 18th century to our days, Kasper stresses the growing reaction to Bultmann's position, especially starting out from Kasemann, in 1953. The conflict between Jesus of Nazareth and the preached Christ no longer is maintained. The objective of present day research is rather to understand Jesus in the light of ecclesial faith and, reciprocally, to interpret ecclesial faith in the light of Jesus. Christology and Historical Criticism are reconciled. The starting out point of christology is the profession of faith of the primitive community; but this faith finds its content and its norm in the history and destiny of Jesus. Consequently, the whole christology of Kasper is divided into two parts: I) The history and destiny of Jesus; II) The mystery of Jesus-Christ. The focal point of christology, according to Kasper, is the cross and the resurrection of Jesus. Here, indeed, is carried out the passage of the Jesus of history to the glorious Christ of faith.

2) In *Christ sein*[2] Hans Kung, addressing himself to a large

public, refrains from going into too technical explanations. However, his position on the possibility of access to the Jesus of history, through the Gospels, is firm and clear. He says that we more perhaps than any Christian generation, with the exception of the first, are prepared to know the authentic Jesus of history, thanks to the researches and the results of the historical method. A return to Jesus is possible, legitimate and necessary. The theology of pure kerygma, of the Bultmann type, "has had its day:" on this point the French, German and Anglo-Saxon schools are in agreement. The kerygma of the primitive Christian community is incomprehensible without a concrete link to Jesus of Nazareth. The alternative "kerygma" or "history" is a false alternative. There must be acknowledged the historical interest of the evangelists in the words, actions and destiny of Jesus. This general assertion must evidently take into consideration the respective contribution, recorded in the actual text, of the evangelists and of the primitive community. This task of discernment is a difficult undertaking, but there could never be opposition between the Jesus of history and the Christ of faith: there is always question of one and the same person.

3) A interval of four years separates the two volumes of Ch. Duquoc's *Christologie*.[21] While the second volume is in dialogue with the post-Bultmannian theologians (Ebeling, Fuchs, Pannenberg, Moltmann), the first is in dialogue with the American theology of the "death of God." Also, the problem of the historical Jesus is rather touched on lightly than thoroughly treated. Duquoc briefly retraces the history of criticism[22] then concludes his exposition by taking a position: "Every separation between the Christ of faith and the Christ of history weakens the singular situation of Jesus and of His unicity. . . The Christ of faith takes on greater meaning from the singularity of the Christ of history."[23] Consequently, theological research cannot abstract from the concrete figure of Jesus.

In the second volume, the problem of the relationships between the Christ of the Gospels and Jesus of Nazareth is clearly primary, and that from the very pages of the introduction, where Duquoc refers explicitly to the works of Pannenberg and Moltmann, and to their anti-Bultmannian attitude. Having to treat of the passion and of the resurrection, he is led to make precise the relationship he perceives between the history of Jesus and its postpaschal interpretation. Though acknowledging that Bultmann's demythologizing enterprise has been, as a whole, a beneficial incentive for theological reflection, Duquoc esteems "The Bultmannian influence has been overturned."[24] Pannenberg and Moltmann are correct in rejecting the hiatus between *fact* and *meaning* which demythologization implies. The cross and the resurrection cannot be reduced to symbols of God's wrath and forgiveness. "The Risen is the one who, on account of His word, of His action, of His attitude, of His historical conflict, was officially condemned."[25] Duquoc emphasizes, "If we insist so much on the historical attitude of Jesus, it is that, through the experience of the theologies of demythologization, we are aware of the danger of methods which do not take seriously the relationship which is indestructible between the man Jesus of Nazareth and the risen Christ."[26] He energetically rejects the opinion which suggests that the tracing back of the kerygma to the Jesus of history is doomed to failure. The texts of the New Testament, in fact, are not only witnesses of the faith of the primitive Church: they are also, in the judgment of a good number of Catholic critics, witnesses of "faithful memories which enable a reciprocal clarification to be established between the expressions of faith and the events which played a role in their elaboration."[27] The Christ of faith evokes the Jesus of history.

Duquoc underlines in particular that the evangelists never abstract from what effectively brought Jesus to death and to resurrection, that is His confrontation with the religious and political powers of the epoch. To snatch Jesus out of this history, is to renounce thinking of the universal meaning of the resurrection. Thus, the discourse of Peter, on the day of Pentecost, shows to what point *what happened to Jesus* is necessary for understanding *what comes.* "This Jesus whom Peter proclaims risen and donor of the Spirit, is none other

than the prophet followed by crowds and, on account of His
free speech and attitude, rejected and condemned by the
representatives of the established religious order."[28] If the
resurrection projects a fresh light on the historical existence of
Jesus, it does not invent, it does not distort the public events
which were well-known to Peter's listeners. What they do not
know, is the *meaning* of this earthly existence. His failure is
only apparent. In His words, His deeds, His actions as prophet
Jesus, the Kingdom of God, object of the messianic
expectation, He truly matured. "The light of the Pasch was
reflected on the earthly life of Jesus, not to suppress it, as if of
no importance, but on the contrary, to establish it in its
truth."[29] The resurrection does not "inject" a meaning into
what has none: this meaning is present from the beginning.
"The resurrection is not a coup de force, it is the meaning of the
history of Jesus."[30] The re-reading of Jesus in the light of the
resurrection is not a betrayal but on the contrary the unveiling
of what is already present in the historical Jesus, but could not
yet be perceived. The wish of the evangelists is never to separate
the announcement of the Risen One from His historical
existence, for "it is the man Jesus who is the Lord."[31] The
Savior is one who has shared our condition. Deprived of their
historical dimension, death and resurrection became
categories, symbols, without anchorage in our world.

4) E. Schillebeeckx devotes the entire first part of his
christology[32] to the question of the believer's access to Jesus of
Nazareth.

From the historical point of view, we have access to Jesus
only through the first Christian communities, in direct contact
with Jesus or the "memory" of Jesus. These communities,
doubtless, made a choice among the sayings and deeds of
Jesus, but the *event of Jesus* is at the origin of their testimony.
Likewise, all that the centuries have been able to say about
Jesus and about what He represents, must be appreciated,
judged, corrected starting out from one sole norm: what was
Jesus truly in history. The question of the historical truth about
Jesus is vested with an extreme importance.

In the Jesus of Nazareth there is something ineffable and

inaccessible to the purely historical method, that is, the living person of Jesus offered to the direct and intimate experience of the apostles and first disciples. This experience comes down to us indirectly by way of the testimonies of primitive faith. On the other hand, recourse to the historical method is a question of life or death for Christianity. If Jesus, for instance, did not exist or was someone else completely different from what faith asserts about Him, the kerygma would be properly un-believeable. A radical hiatus between the knowledge of faith and historical knowledge of Jesus is unsupportable. Such a dualism leads invevitablly to the rejection of one of the two poles.

Post-Bultmannian exegetics has rightly shown the inconsistency of the opposition held to exist between Jesus of Nazareth and the Christ of the Church. Rather than discontinuity, there is said to be continuity between the historical Jesus and the Christ of the announcement, of catechesis, of exhortation to virtue and of the liturgy of the primitive churches and it is also thought that the Jesus presented by the Gospels corresponds, if not literally, at least substantially to historical reality. It can be maintained that the beginnings of the tradition on Jesus are found in the life of communion Jesus had with His apostles, that is, with those who were fascinated by His personality, His message and His behavior. These memories, and also the experiences happening unexpectedly after the death of Jesus, are as it were the matrix of Christian faith. Consequently, the kerygma, by virtue of its "formal auto-comprehension," manifests an intent of reference to the *event Jesus*. There is a constant reaction between the memory of Jesus and the post-paschal experience. For it is only after the death of Jesus that His disciples, in the light of the new experiences which clarified the memories of the past, penetrated the meaning of His life as a definitive reality of salvation, and could identify Him as the Messiah and the Son of God. If Jesus of Nazareth is the norm and criterion of what believers say about Him, then a historical research about Jesus has a *theological import*. If the paschal kerygma was the sole basis for knowing and understanding salvation, for what would the Gospels and a tradition of Jesus serve?

What may be the result of historical research on Jesus? It may show the continuity between the self-understanding of Jesus and the understanding of Jesus in the Church. It may provide faith with a concrete content. It may show that the Christian interpretation of Jesus is coherent with the historically present direction in the life and message of Jesus. It cannot, however, force admittance of this interpretation. To profess this interpretation as truth, is already an act of faith. But historical research is also necessary for understanding that the question of life posed by Jesus could not receive a definitive response save after His death. That is why a modern christology could not do without historical research on Jesus.

Schillebeeckx concludes thus. A kerygma without Jesus may still be attractive, but Christianity loses its historical foundation and becomes a purely casual phenomenon in the life of humanity: it could also disappear as quickly as it appeared. One may believe indefinitely in ideas, even if these abstract ideas are "existentially" replete (as in Bultmann's kerygma). Christianity loses then the right to speak of the salvific action of God in history. The world would be governed by a history of ideas. Too often men are victims of ideas which become ideologies.

Schillebeeckx continues that, for him, Christian faith implies not only the personal and living presence of the glorified Jesus, but a link with His earthly life. For him a Christianity or a kerygma without historical Jesus of Nazareth is, definitively, deprived of content, and no longer Christianity. If the nucleus of Christian faith consists in the affirmation of the salvific action of God in history, it becomes decisive in the history of the life of Jesus of Nazareth, for the liberation of man, then the personal history of this Jesus cannot go up in smoke: otherwise, our discourse of faith degenerates into ideology.

In Chapter I of the first part, Schillebeeckx studies the criteria of historical authenticity which enable access to the historical Jesus. He esteems in fact that the use of such criteria is necessary for a critical verification of Christian faith. This usage, however, to be worthwhile, should operate by way of "convergence."

Among the positive and valid criteria, he retains the following:

1) A *historico-redactional* criterion, that is, one of opposing traditions. While an evangelist preserves some elements which are in contrast to the perspective of his Gospel, it may be thought that it is the weight of fidelity to tradition which induces him to preserve these elements. This redactional criterion could not be employed separately.

2) A *critico-formal* criterion, that is the principle of the double irreducibility of an element to the concept of ancient Judaism or to that of the primitive Church. It is the classical criterion of discontinuity.

3) A *historico-traditional* criterion, that is the principle of the transversal section. It is the criterion of multiple attestation.

4) A criterion of *coherence of content.* There is involved the establishing of conformity or consistency of the details of the Gospel with the whole image which results from traits pertaining to Jesus. The convergent usage of these criteria has as its effect the establishing that the Gospels are effectively faithful to Jesus of Nazareth.[33]

III. Conclusions and lessons of a history

The history of the long debate has agitated Protestant criticism, especially in the German world. It enables us to bring out a certain number of points of major relief, and also to make a certain number of conclusions:

1) The method of the Form School is universally accepted and practiced.

2) The principle of a demythologization, more or less radical, is generally accepted as a demand for existential interpretation. The miracles and the resurrection[34] of Jesus cause difficulties; for most of the critics, they do not enter into the field of historical reality.

3) All recognize the difficulty of reconstituting the image of the earthly Jesus. A compact group, however, recruited from among the disciples of Bultmann, protests the master's radical scepticism. Kasemann and the representatives of the New Hermeneutic (Robinson, Fuchs, Ebeling) endeavor to show the continuity which exists between the message of Jesus and the primitive kerygma: that which was implicit in one became explicit in the other.

4) Criticism remains centered on the existential interpretation of Jesus. In the history of Jesus, there is researched less information than a significance for human existence.

5) Recent historians, such as Cullmann, Pannenberg, Moltmann, bring back the value of the history of salvation. "What concerns faith," Pannenberg underlines, "is first what Jesus was." Moltmann declares that christology should verify that Christian faith takes its origin from Jesus and in history.

6) These last positions are close to Catholic ones, even to the point of coinciding with them. Designedly, we have expounded, in one and the same chapter, the most recent contributions of Protestant thinking and Catholic thinking in the matter of christology. On the precise point which occupies us, that is, the necessity and possibility of a historical finding of Jesus of Nazareth through the Gospels, Pannenberg, Moltmann, Kasper, Kung, Duquoc, Schillebeeckx have given a unanimous answer. There is no christology without a knowledge of what Jesus of Nazareth was. On the other hand, this knowledge, in the present state of historical criticism, is a feasible enterprise, which leads to certain and substantial results.

7) And so, after two centuries of history, criticism has *made a full turn.* We find ourselves, at the end of the venture, before the same initial affirmation: through the Gospels we truly know Jesus of Nazareth (message, action, project and destiny). What a difference, though, between the acritical confidence of the past and the critically proven and laboriously acquired confidence of the present. The negations and suspicions of criticism have constrained Catholics and

Protestants to scrutinize the history of these booklets in appearance so ingenuous, so transparent, as are the Gospels. After decades of research, the history of their formation has become more familiar to us. No matter how complex it be, the knowledge of this history, far from frightening us, reassures and confirms us.

Footnotes for Chapter V

1. W. Pannenberg, R. Rendtorff, T. Rendtorff, U. Wilckens, *Offenbarung als Geschichte* (Gottengen, 1965).
2. W. Pannenberg, *Grundzuge der Christologie* (Gutersloh, 1964). *Esquisse d'une christologie* (Paris, 1971), used in quotation.
3. *Ibid.*, p. 16.
4. *Ibid.*, p. 18.
5. *Ibid.*, p. 19.
6. *Ibid.*, p.19.
7. *Ibid.*, p. 20.
8. *Ibid.*, p. 23.
9. *Ibid.*, p. 24.
10. *Ibid.*, p. 26.
11. J. Moltmann, *Der gekreuzigte Gott* (Munich, 1972). *Le Dieu crucifie,* (Paris, 1974). Used for quotes.
12. *Ibid.*, p. 96.
13. *Ibid.*, p. 133.
14. *Ibid.*, p. 97.
15. *Ibid.*, p. 98.
16. *Ibid.*, p. 98.
17. *Ibid.*, p. 98.
18. *Ibid.*, p. 99.
19. Kasper, *Jesus der Christus* (Mainz, 1974).
20. H. Kung, *Christ sein* (Munich, 1974).
21. Ch. Duquoc, *Christologie* (2 vols., Paris, 1968, 1972).
22. *Ibid.*, pp. 97-109.
23. *Ibid.*, pp. 106-107.
24. Ch. Duquoc, *Christologie* (Paris, 1972), 2:10.
25. *Ibid.*, 2:11.
26. *Ibid.* 2:12.
27. *Ibid.* 2:13.
28. *Ibid.* 2:14.
29. *Ibid.* 2:15.
30. *Ibid.* 2:16.
31. *Ibid.* 2:17.
32. S. Schillebeeckx, *Jezus, het verhaal van een levende* (Bloomendaal, 1974).
33. Later we discuss the problems of criteriology relative to the Gospels.
34. Save in the case of recent theologians, such as Pannenberg and Moltmann.

Chapter VI

CATHOLIC EXEGETICS

Faced with Bultmannian and post-Bultmannian criticism, the attitude of Catholics had a moment of hesitation. Some, before the new methods of exegesis, elaborated and practiced by Protestants, had the impression that all that was certain up to then, was crumbling. Others, on the contrary, (the majority) recognized, in the new critique along with some dubious ingredients, or even unacceptable ones, that there were some perfectly assimilable elements. Rather than complete rejection, their attitude was to distinguish between philosophical principles and literary methodology. Such, among others, was the attitude of R. Schnackenburg, F. Mussner, W. Trilling, A. Wilkenhauser, H. Schurmann, K.H. Schelkle, A. Vogtle, A. Descamps, L. Cerfaux, P. Grelot, B. Rigaux, J. Dupont, I. de la Potterie, A. George, X. Leon-Dufour, R. Brown, etc.

We shall first point out a certain number of points on which, at the time of Vatican II, agreement seemed unanimous. We shall show next how the finding of criticism on the nature of the Gospels modified the course of research. The notion of author, in particular, has been made considerably more flexible. From now on there is less interest about external criticism than about internal, attention being given to distinguish the levels of tradition and to verify the organic continuity which goes from Jesus to the Gospels. Finally, we shall point out in what sense, after Vatican II, Catholic research is oriented, and what are the main themes of this research.

I. Points of Convergence

Among the points on which there is agreement, let us mention the following:

1) Our Gospels have been the object, in the period of oral tradition which preceded the first writings, of a process of formation at once lengthy and complex. They are the culmination of a lively history which extended over many decades.

2) It is not possible to write a complete biography of Jesus in the modern sense of the word, or in the spirit of the *Leben-Jesus-Forschung* (Quest for the Historical Jesus) of the 19th century.

3) The Gospels intend to show that Jesus of Nazareth is identically the Messiah, the risen Christ, the Son of God and, correlatively, that the risen and glorified Jesus is today identical with the crucified Jesus of yesterday. In the positive meaning of the term, their objective is apologetic.

4) We find, in the Gospels, some diverse literary forms and genres. Thus, the historicity which qualifies the account of the passion, does not univocally apply to the accounts of the infancy.

5) We can distinguish, in tradition, three levels: that of the evangelists, that of the primitive community, that of Jesus. Each of these levels represents a specific theological approach.

6) Catholic exegetics does not, however, admit that the primitive community exercised over the event Jesus (life and message) a creative and deforming action, to the extent of constituting a sort of opaque screen preventing all access to the reality of Jesus. It thinks, on the contrary, that we have at our disposal worthwhile criteria, critically proven, enabling us to understand, if not the *"ipsissima verba Jesus"* (an obsession of the past century), at least the authentic message of Jesus, and to

arrive at "truly happened" facts which pertain to the Jesus of Nazareth.

7) The most important point concerns the attitude of the historian in regard to the Gospels. He is quite aware that he is not, as the Liberal School believed, faced with "historically pure" facts, but with a kerygmatized history. While tradition does hearken back to the past, it also interprets it and represents it with relevance to the present needs of its hearers. The present text represents the sedimentation of multiple layers, some more recent, others more ancient. As a result, the task of the historian becomes more delicate and more arduous, but he does not despair of knowing who Jesus was. Since he finds himself faced with a unique situation, his method requires adaptation and initiation. For appreciating the historicity of the Gospels, the professional historian, formed in the methods of classical literary criticism, must go beyond its bounds and make flexible its procedures of research. For correctly handling the Gospels he must familiarize himself with a whole ensemble of specific problems: genesis of the texts (their compositional history and their literary forms); the life of the communities where they were composed; the function carried out by the texts (ensembles of texts or units which compose them) in the first Christian communities. Historical Criticism must be accompanied by a sound apprenticeship in the methods of biblical exegesis.[1]

These positions, essentially, have been confirmed by the Instruction of the Biblical Commission, in 1964; by the Dogmatic Constitution *Dei Verbum* of Vatican II, in 1965; by the discourse of Paul VI to the members of the Biblical Commission, in 1974.[2]

II. Critique of the "classical" position on the relation Jesus-Gospels.

The advances made during the last fifty years have had as an effect the revealing of the weakness of the traditional position on the relation Jesus-Gospels, as also the reason for this weakness.

This position was based on the testimony of the Churches of the 2nd century, notably that of Irenaeus, and on the Prologue of Luke (Lk 1:1-4). The Prologue presents the following elements: a) events happening during the life of Jesus, which knew their "accomplishment" with the birth of the Church; b) there exist eye witnesses of these facts; c) these eye witnesses, after the Pasch became servants of the Word; d) this apostolic preaching gave birth to various accounts, some oral, some written; e) after others, Luke also took up writing. He learned from living witnesses, he made use of written sources (especially of Mark) and, finally, he composed his Gospel.[3] The testimony of Irenaeus, on the other hand, constitutes, if not a reduction, at least an extreme stylization of what really happened: Matthew, he says, wrote his Gospel in Aramaic. Mark put in writing Peter's preaching; the Gospel of Luke contains Paul's preaching; finally, John composed his Gospel when he was at Ephesus.[4]

Under this perspective, there is no distance between the text and the Jesus event. The problem of the historical authenticity of the Gospels coincides practically with that of research on the authenticity of the author. The "classical" argumentation, basing itself on the apostolic origin of the Gospels, reasons thus: our Gospels have full historical value, for they have as authors sincere and-well informed men, that is, the apostles (Matthew and John) and disciples of the apostles, Mark, disciple of Peter and of Paul, and Luke, disciple of Paul. This concept of author is of grave consequence for exegesis. In fact, if the Gospels emanate, directly or indirectly, from eye witnesses, invested with an apostolic authority, it follows that everything they relate puts us into the presence of Jesus Himself. The text adheres to the event, and the weight of proof falls on one who doubts its historicity.

This concept of author is still found among recent authors, such as Lagrange and De Grandmaison. In his *Jesus-Christ*, De Grandmaison studies at length the sources of the history of Jesus, but makes but little use of internal criteria.[5] M.J. Lagrange, in his introduction to the commentary on

Mark, insists on the person of Mark and on the testimony of tradition on him as his subject. "The author of the second Gospel, he says, is John surnamed Mark, who reproduced Peter's catechesis: he was therefore well informed. Moreover, he seems worthy of belief. His testimony should then be received. This argument is sound."[6] Mark's intention was to relate the most serious of histories, that of God's intervention in the person of His Son. The historical value of the Gospel of Mark rests first on the quality of its author.

These two examples illustrate the approach to the problem of the historicity of the Gospels, which prevailed until very recently. Internal criteria are not neglected, but placed on a secondary level. The proof rests above all on external criticism, that is, that of establishing the authenticity of the author. Now this perspective was the object, in the last decades, of a radical change, attributable to the three following factors:

1) A more critical examination into the testimonies of the 2nd Century and of the texture itself of the Gospels, revealed that the modern concept of *author* could not be applied univocally to the authors of our Gospels. This concept brings out a very complex reality. The composers of the Gospels belonged to the primitive Church and to Jesus through an oral and written tradition of which they were the spokesmen, the interpreters and the theologians. Between Jesus and the present text, there are many levels and many mediations, the respective contribution of which must be appreciated.

2) Secondly, the "classical" position or the traditional one conceived the concept of testimony in too elementary a manner. It identified the testimonies of the Gospels with secular ocular testimony, in which the witness tells what he saw and heard with maximum objectivity. Now this concept of testimony, applied to the Gospels, is incomplete. In fact, the apostles are witnesses (of what they saw and heard) of the whole life of Christ, from the baptism to the resurrection (Ac 10:39), but they also testify to and, above all, about the profound meaning of His earthly existence, that is, of the salvation brought about by His death and resurrection (Ac 10:42-43). They testify to "facts" which signify the religious

meaning of things seen and heard. Moreover, factual testimony and testimony of faith are inseparable. John saw blood and water flow, but he testifies to the salvific value of the death of Jesus on the cross (Jn 19:35). The "classical" position had practically confused the biblical testimony with the secular.[7]

3) Thirdly, the "classical" position was practically unaware of the role of oral tradition in the formation of the Gospels. It did not know that between Jesus and the Gospels there is inserted a tradition which has its own history. During three or four decades, the Good Tidings was preached, commented on, made current, according to the milieux of life and according to the problems of these milieux. If it is true that the matter of the Gospels was preached thus in the primitive Church and that it served for catechesis, worship, polemic, mission, it follows that this matter was colored by the life of the Church and bears the imprint of the theological interpretation of this community. The activity of the Church, which actualizes and interprets the life and message of Jesus, constitutes one of the constituent characteristics of the profile of author proper to the Gospels. The study of this moment of tradition is to be credited to the School of Form Criticism. However, upon evaluating the role of oral tradition in the Gospels against the excesses of Source Criticism (Quellenkritik), Form Criticism underestimated the role of the evangelists and made them mere compilers of an extant tradition under the form of literary units of small dimension. The school of Redaction Criticism reacted against this new excess showing that each evangelist, not only had his project, his theological perspective, but also his language and compositional procedures which exegesis can discern and systematize.

This double mediation, which was discovered through researches by *Formgeschichte* and *Redaktionsgeschichte*, is from this time on certain. The concept of author of the Gospels, all at once, is found to be deeply modified. If, in fact, in the concept of author there are, as components, the successive interpretations of the apostles, of the primitive ecclesial preaching in the various milieux of life and, finally, of the evangelists, it no longer suffices to invoke the authority of Mark or of Luke to establish the historical authenticity of the content of the actual Gospel. There must be distinguished the respective contribution of Jesus, of the primitive community, of the evangelist, and shown the organic continuity which links the present text to the event of Jesus.

III. Three levels of "Traditionsgeschichte"

Gospel criticism, in order to be faithful to the very reality of the Gospels and to the true process of their formation, is led to distinguish a triple level of depth, which corresponds to three moments of tradition and to three different contexts of its history. These three phases of *Traditionsgeschichte* (Tradition Criticism) have furthermore, been acknowledged by the Instruction of the Biblical Commission and by the Constitution *Dei Verbum*.[8]

1) The first level is that of the event itself: teaching, actions and attitudes of Jesus; community living with His disciples; encounter with the environment; position taken in regard to this milieu and the reaction of the milieu to Jesus. By level of event, we do not mean only the level of the chronicle, but the level of the event and of the *meaning* it has for Jesus, in His life. This first level corresponds to the *Sitz im Leben,* (life situation) of Jesus.

2) The second level is that of the primitive community, after the Pasch *(UrKirche)*. The milieu of the apostolic and ecclesial preaching was quickly diversified. In it there is distinguished a Jewish milieu, a Greek milieu and a Roman milieu. The regionalism of communities signifies a diversity of mentalities, of cultures, of concerns, of problems, which the preaching must take into account. Besides, this preaching in no way is reporting or chronicling. It invokes the actions and teaching of Jesus, but in the light of the Pasch and of the whole history of salvation, with that fulness and depth of perception which comes to it from the Spirit. The Church has the

conviction that this liberty belongs to her, for the event of the resurrection has made the identity of Jesus stand out and projected a new light on His earthly career. The more tradition progresses in time, the more it deepens the meaning of the past. Thus, John represents a deepening of the synoptic tradition. The primitive preaching had, the first theological knowledge of the life of Jesus. It also was the first to make relevant His message. It showed how this message can clarify new situations, problems unheard of in the times of Jesus. The Gospels are thus the mirror of the preaching and life of the Church. The research of *Formgeschichte* is situated at this second level.

3) The third level is that of the composition of the Gospels, that of recounted history, of historiography: it is the level of *Redaktionsgeschichte.* The Constitution *Dei Verbum* has formulated the aspects of this compositional task. The evangelists submitted the gospel material to an operation of selection, of synthesis (seen especially in the Gospel of Matthew) and of adaptation to the needs and conditions of their readers. The literary genre adopted is that of a "Gospel," that is the proclamation of good tidings, and not that of a chronicle. The Gospels are kerygmatic and catechetical works. Their avowed objective is to arouse faith in Jesus Messiah and Son of God, yet still remaining faithful to the truth about Jesus.

Thus, after centuries of criticism, it seems that exegesis, in order to be faithful to the whole process of the formation of the Gospels or of the *Traditionsgeschichte,* should take the following path. After the preliminary stage of textual criticism (variants of the text in order to arrive at establishing with the greatest fidelity possible the original text), it studies the text in its present form (structure, unity, theology). This is the level of *Redaktionsgeschichte.* Next, it studies the stage in the course which were formed the traditions which gave birth to the first accounts: the milieu of life of these traditions, as well as their concerns. This is the level of *Formgeschichte.* Finally, it seeks, this time on the level of historicity properly so called, through usage of proven criteria, to determine, not only what the text says, but what happened. This is research on the Jesus level and on the meaning of the event itself (and not only of the interpretation which the author of the *related* event presents). In reality, the event is first; but, in exegesis, the inverse trajectory is to be followed evidently, since the text is the first known.

Moreover, in order to be faithful to the movement of tradition exegesis should verify, not only the respective contribution of each one of the three stages (Jesus, the primitive community, the evangelist), but it should also show the *organic continuity* which goes from Jesus to the actual text. In the concrete, this means first that there should be considered the original event, in the context of the life of Jesus, and with the meaning it takes on in this context: christological, messianic, eschatological. Then it is seen that, on this level, the event possesses a depth of meaning which is far beyond that of the explanation it has known subsequently. Thus, the miracle of the multiplication of the loaves, in the time of Jesus, is first presented as a manifestation of the *Agape* of God. Besides, there is a messianic and eschatological value: Jesus appears there as the new Moses who performs anew the prodigy of the manna in the desert, as the awaited prophet in whom the messianic hope is realized.

Then it must be pointed out how the event was read and understood by the primitive Churrch. Thus, in the multiplication of loaves, the Church saw an anticipatory sign of the eucharistic repast. A meaning made evident by the fact that it utilized the very terms of the Last Supper for describing the action of Jesus on the bread. The event is recounted, but made really present.

Finally, the compositional activity of the evangelist must be acknowledged and appreciated: interpretations and literary retouches. In the miracle of the loaves, Mark stressed the messianic aspect of the miracle, as well as its Christological import, by proposing Jesus as the Shepherd of His people.

If exegesis thus comes to retrace the whole history of tradition and to verify that it is not a divide between the earthly Jesus and the Christ of the Gospels, but an organic and living continuity, a deepening of conformity to the original message or event, it satisfies the essential demand of evangelical criticism. Let us add that it also responds to the requirements of Catholic theology, for which revelation is not only in the message of Jesus (Jeremias' position), nor solely in the kerygma of the Church (Bultmann's position), but at the same time, all of a piece, in the words and deeds of Jesus, with the apostolic interpretation recorded in Scripture. Concretely, for us, the object of faith, the deposit of faith, is Jesus interpreted by the apostles. There is ever question of the same reality, but identified and better understood. There is continuity and study in depth.

IV. The main lines of the development of research

Vatican II has been, for Catholics exegesis, a privileged moment, for it has not only permitted taking bearings for a new departure, but, fortunately, given occasion for so doing. Thus, far from declining, interest in the question of the historical Jesus, has considerably increased in the last decade. Present day research is aware that the problem is not confined to exegetics but is at the heart of all theological disciplines: obviously of fundamental theology, but also of dogmatic theology, especially in christology and ecclesiology. We have already emphasized that most of the recent christologies open up with a chapter on finding Jesus through the Gospels: Thus was brought about a phenomemon of enlarging the problem. Let us point out some of the major problems which hold the attention of present day research.

1) There is a much clearer awareness than before of the difficulties which all research on the pre-paschal Jesus inevitably runs into. Difficulties which affect the content, the form and the interpretation of tradition. On the level of *content* we know that oral tradition, then written tradition, brought about a selection of materials concerning Jesus. Whence the fragmentary character of our information and, consequently, fragile and complex for all reconstitution of the life and

message of Jesus. On the level of the *formation* of tradition, there must be distinguished, on the one hand, the case of the properly so-called logia of Jesus, subject to the multiple influence of milieu, procedures of transmission and of schematization, as well as to the risks of a translation (passage from Aramaic to Greek); and, on the other hand, the case of acts and deeds, attributable to Jesus, but which have received voice and form from the primitive preaching (for instance, miracles). On the level of interpretation, the process of kerygmatic transformation affects as well the phase of composition as that of oral transmission.[9]

2) More and more attention is being paid to questions of method. Criticism itself is subject to criticism. Consideration is given not only to the ways of finding Jesus, but to the validity and relative worth of these ways.[10] It is not enough only to classify the criteria of historicity: their value and their limits are discussed also. There is recognized the necessity of literary criticism and of historical criticism, but their competence and their respective fields of action are discussed. Some show themselves more sensitive to a demonstration enabling the establishing of the historical solidity of the *ensemble* of the evangelical tradition and, consequently, attach more impor-tance to the stages necessary for this verification, as well as for the quality, the linkage, the convergence of the arguments invoked.[11] Others, exegetes for the most part, carry out these verifications to the level of particular pericopes,[12] the two methods complementing each other showing how, in each case, the general criteria of historical authenticity apply. The authenticity of the ensemble clarifies the obscure zones of detail, while the particular verifications come to reinforce global certitude. Each worker has his terrain of specialized research, since no one can take all of it over.

3) Present day research is uniformly sensitive to the hermeneutic aspect of the problem Jesus. After having been, on this point, out-distanced by Protestant exegesis, Catholic reflection is presently very active.[13] Once there is admitted the complex process of transmission going from Jesus to the evangelists, through the interpretative mediations of the

apostles, of the first preachers of the faith, of the first Christian communities, of the first traditions (written and oral), of the first theologies, the *kerygma-history* problem seems more and more the problem of the relation text—Jesus. Since the Gospels cover a triple situation (Jesus, Tradition, Composition), which itself involves the historical: milieu of life and its problems; linguistic: the whole level of expression, there is no longer merely the question of confronting history and faith, Jesus and the Christ, but rather the text, speech, and the reality reached at the term of the analysis, that is, Jesus. There must conjointly be spoken of a problem of history and of hermeneutics, corresponding to a parallel process of history (of Jesus to the evangelists) and of speech (of the first logia to the evangelical texts) and consequently, of the understanding of the relation which links text and event.[14] Through this relationship of text to the event Jesus only becomes more precise, progressively, using the combined effort of literary and historical criticism.[15]

4) At the same time that Literary Criticism extends its field of action, Historical Criticism appears more and more indispensable. In fact, once having reached the term of its research, that is, the most ancient forms it can reconstruct, literary criticism must still ask itself in what measure do these forms carry contents faithful to reality. Research about Jesus cannot afford to bypass a study of the criteria which enable us to determine what authentically appertains to Jesus.[16] Before this contribution still quite recent, there is not a matter of falling into a fetishism, as if the criteria were magical keys enabling the solution of every difficulty; but there is the matter of no longer closing our eyes and minds to the perspectives it opens up. Criteriological research of the present day endeavors to define, to classify, to characterize the different criteria proposed, and to make precise the conditions for their valid use. It insists on the necessity of a supple and convergent usage, as well as on relationships of complementation and of support which unite literary criteria and historical criteria. Characterized by discretion, this research is promising.

5) Recent reflections on history have modified how we

regarded the Gospels. The positivist concept of history is passé. Pure objectivity is a myth. Whether he wishes or not, the historian projects himself into the past which he depicts. Historic fact, apparently so simple, so ingenuous, represents an ensemble of most complex noetic processes, which involve at the least two interpreters: the witness of the events and the historian. The evangelists, on seeking to express the ultimate meaning of the life of Jesus, that is, giving of His life for the salvation of all, place themselves at the heart of the concerns of history, such as it is conceived today. Despite their freedom in regard to coordinates of time and place, they are more faithful to Jesus than the most complete of chronicles. The Gospels, undoubtedly, refer to history, pertain to history, but in a mannner which must be defined right away. Present day research endeavors to define this unique literary genre which is called a "Gospel."

6) Finally, exegetics shows itself concerned about the mutual relationships between two types of research, that is historical research on Jesus and christology properly so called. Christology, in fact, could not utter whatsoever discourse it wishes on the Christ. What Jesus *truly was*, at the time of His earthly passage among us, is normative for all ulterior reflection: that of the New Testament, that of the councils, that of the theologians. So it is important to know Jesus, precisely in so far as He is the source and foundation of christology.[17] Jesus at the origins of christology, the christology of Jesus such are the themes which flourish in recent monographs and collective works.[18]

On other points, research is active, without coming however to that degree of consistency and extension which permits speaking of *lines* of research. Let us point out three of these points: a) the endeavor to reconstruct not only the great stages of tradition, but minutely to make precise the details of that whole process, as well for the actions as for the logia; b) the study of the basic vocabulary of the Primitive Church, raised by the question of the ministries in the Church, or by the question of tradition, helps us better to know the profound attitudes of the primitive ecclesial milieu in regard to Jesus; c)

the abundance of the material collected which is about the pre-
paschal period, poses anew the problem of a biography of
Jesus.

Footnotes for Chapter VI

1. P. Grelot, "L'historien devant la resurrection du Christ." *Revue d'histoire et de spiritualite,* XLVIII (1972) 222-227; F. McCool, "The Preacher and the Historical Witness of the Gospels," *Theological Studies,* XXI (1960), 528-529, 540-541.
2. Constitution dogmatique *Dei Verbum,* no. 19; approved November 18, 1965; "Instructio de historica Evangeliorum veritate," April 21, 1964, *AAS* LVI (1964) 712-718; "Discours de Paul VI aux membres de la Commission biblique," March 14, 1974 *AAS* LXVI (1974) 235-241.
3. W. Michaels, "Einleitung in das Neue Testament" (Bern, 1954); L. Vaganay, *La question synoptique. Une hypothese de travail* (Paris, 1954).
4. Test of Irenaeus: "Ita Matthaeus in Hebraeis ipsorum lingua scripturam edidit Evangelii, cum Petrus et Paulus Romae evangelizarent et fundarent Ecclesiam. Post vero horum excessum, Marcus, discipulus et interpres Petri, et ipse quae a Petro annuntiata erant, per scripta nobis tradidit. Et Lucas autem, sector Pauli, quod ab illo praedicabatur Evangelium in libro condidit. Postea et Joannes, discipulus Domini, qui et supra pectus ejus recumbebat, et ipse edidit Evangelium, Ephesi Asiae commorans." (Adversus Haereses, III, 1; PG 7: 844-845).
5. L. De Grandmaison, *Jesus-Christ,* (2 vols., Paris, 1928), vol. 1, pp. 118-124.
6. M.-J. Lagrange, *Evangile selon saint Marc* (Paris 1929), p. cxxvi.
7. R. Latourelle, "Evangelisation et temoignage," *Evangelisation* Documenta Missionalia IX (Rome, 1975) pp. 86-91).
8. In the description of these three levels, we follow, in its essential lines, the text of the Instruction of the Biblical Commission: Instructio de historica Evangeliorum veritate, *AAS* LVI (1964) 714-716.
9. F. Hahn, "Methodologische Uberlequngen zur Ruckfrage nach Jesus," in K. Kertelge, *Ruckfrage nach Jesus* (Quaestiones disputatae, 63, Freiburg i. Br, 1974), pp. 13-31; A. Descamps, "Progres et continuite dans la critique des Evangiles et des Actes," *Revue theologique de Louvain,* I (1970) 5-44.
10. F. Hahn, *op. cit.* pp. 11-17; F. Mussner, "Methodologie der Frage nach dem historischen Jesus," *ibid.,* pp. 118-147; A Descamps, "Portee christologique de la recherche historique sur Jesus," in J. Dupont, ed. *Jesus aux origines de la christologie* (Gembloux, 1975), pp. 23-45; P. Fruchon, *Existence humaine et Revelation. Essais d'hermeneutique* (Paris, 1976).
11. X. Leon-Dufour, *Les Evangiles et l'histoire de Jesus* (Paris, 1963); J. Caba, *De los Evangelios al Jesus historico,* (Madrid, 1970); I. de la Potterie, "Come impostare oggi il problema del Gesu storico?" *La Civilta Cattolica,* CIX (1969) qu. 2855, pp. 447-463; E Schillebeeckx, *L'approccio a Gesu di Nazaret,* (Brescia, 1972); H. Zahrnt, *Es begann mit Jesus von Nazareth* (Stuttgart-Berlin, 1960); F. Lambiasi, *L'autenticita storica dei Vangeli* (Bologna, 1976); A. Descamps, "Portee christologique de la recherchesur Jesus," in J. Dupont, ed. *Jesus aux origines de la christologie,* pp. 23-45. Our demonstration intends first to establish the historical

solicity of the ensemble of the gospel tradition.

12. For instance: I. de Potterie on the multiplication of the bread; X. Leon-Dufour and R. Pesch, on the passion; K. Kertelge, F. Mussner, A. George, on the miracles; J. Dupont, A. George, on the parables; X. Leon-Dufour, P. Benoit, H. Schurmann, on the meaning Jesus gave to His death.

13. We mention, among so many others, the works of: R. Lapointe, E. Coreth, F. Mussner, R. Marle, P. Fruchon, P. Grelot, H. Cazelles, P. Grech, Alonso-Schockel, R. Pesch.

14. P. Mussner, *op. cit.* pp. 120-121.

15. P. Fruchon, *op. cit.* pp. 114-118.

16. Among the more recent publications, we cite those of F. Lambiasi, F. Lentzen-Deis, R. Pesch, I. de La Potterie, E. Schillebeeckx, Lehmann, D. Luhrmann, N.J. McEleney, S. Zedda, R. Latourelle.

17. H. Jellouschek, "Zur christologischen Bedeutung der Frage nach dem historischen Jesus," *Theologische Quartalschrift* CLII (1972) 112-123; A. Descamps, *op. cit.* Dupont ed., pp. 23-45.

18. S. Zedda, Gesu storico alle origini della Cristologia del Nuovo Testamento, *Sacra Doctrina* XVI (1971) 433-448; J. Dupont, *op. cit.* note 11; I. de la Potterie, ed., *De Jesus aux Evangiles* (Paris, 1967); K. Kertelge, *Ruckfrage nach Jesus* (Freiburg, 1974); J. Gnilka, "Die Christologie Jesu von Nazareth," in *Jesus Christus nach den fruhen Zeugnissen des Glaubens* (Munich, 1970), pp. 159-174.

Part II
METHODOLOGICAL PRECISION

Chapter VII

SPECIFICITY OF THE LITERARY GENRE "GOSPEL"

The Gospels constitute, with the Acts of the apostles, the Epistles and the Apocalypse (Revelation), one of the four literary genres of the New Testament. The last two already existed in ancient literature. The other two, the first especially, that is the literary genre "Gospel," are a specific creation of Christianity. Nothing equivalent is found in other literatures, not even in the New Testament. The Gospels are unique, just as the Event to which they refer is unique.

I. From the oral Gospel to the Gospel of Mark

The term "Gospel" represents a usage which is very ancient in the Church. In the time of the first preaching of Paul, it is already a technical term, since he employs it without even feeling the need to explain it (1 Th 1:5; 2:4; Gal 2:5; 14; 1 Cor 4:5; 9:14; 2 Cor 8:18; Rm 10:16; 11:28).

1) This usage, it seems, has its source in the Old Testament. It is agreed that there is seen in Deutero-Isaiah the special context in which, the expression developed. There is not question, in this section, of the announcement of the particular triumphs of Yahweh, as in certain psalms, but of His

decisive victory and recognition of it by all the peoples of a Kingdom which inaugurates a new era. In this context, the figure of messenger takes on a special relief. It is he who as herald proclaims the sovereignty of Yahweh and, by his efficacious word, inaugurates the messianic, eschatological era.

In the key text of Is 52:7, the one "bearing good news," the messenger of joy announces, that, with the deliverance by Cyrus of the captives of Babylon, the era of salvation is opened up: "How beautiful upon the mountains are the feet of him who brinrs glad tidings, announcing peace, bearing good news, announcing salvation, and saying to Zion, 'Your God is King!' (Is 52:7). Psalm 96 echoes this Good Tidings. "Announce his salvation, day after day. Tell his glory among the nations.... Say among the nations: 'The Lord is King!'" (Ps 96, 2:10). In Is 61:1-11, he whom Yahweh has "anointed," is sent to announce to the lowly, to the poor, to the unfortunate, to prisoners, what they can expect from the new Kingdom which is proclaimed. The entering of all nations into the history of salvation, as well as the gift of justice, of peace, of joy, all typically messianic realities, introduce us already into the context and climate of the New Testament.

2) In the New Testament, it is Jesus who appears as the "messenger" of the messianic Good Tidings. In Him is fulfilled the prophecy of Isaiah: through His works and through the Good Tidings announced to the poor (Mt 11:5; Is 35:5-6; 61:1), the time of salvation becomes reality, as do the signs which accompany it. The essential content of this Good Tidings, is the imminent coming about of the Kingdom, of which Jesus proclaims the demands: "Reform your lives! The kingdom of heaven is at hand!" (Mt 4:17). Even if this Kingdom is not yet a brilliant and final manifestation, it is even now a presence full of grace in Jesus. The Kingdom effectively begins with Him: there where Jesus is, the enemy forces retreat, the power of life and of salvation announced by the prophets is working. Healing and exorcisms show that the kingdom of Satan is torn in pieces and that the Kingdom of God has arrived (Lk 7:22; Mt 12:28).

There is, then, explained the change of meaning which is observed in the language of New Testament. Jesus appears not only as the messenger of the Good Tidings, but also as the one of whom the message speaks. Jesus announces without doubt the kingdom, but definitively, this announcement concerns Jesus Himself, constituted messianic King by His resurrection and His exaltation to the right hand of the Father: it is He who saves. In the language of Christians, who consider the death and resurrection of the Christ as the heart of the Gospel, this perspective is even clearer. It is entire salvific activity of God, displayed by and manifested in Jesus Christ, for establishing the Kingdom of God, which is the content of the Gospel. This perspective is that of St. Paul.[1]

3) *Gospel* is one of the most used words of St. Paul: it is repeated sixty times in his epistles. The term designates as well the very action of proclaiming the Good Tidings of salvation (1Cor 9:14) as the content of this proclamation (Rm 1:1). This content is essentially linked to Christ and to His work of salvation (1 Cor 15:3-5). To proclaim the Gospel, for St. Paul, is the equivalent of proclaiming Christ, especially in His death and resurrection, which constitute the coming of eschatological salvation. In this perspective, there can be but one single Gospel. There can be attributed to Paul, if not the introducing of the term "Gospel" in the New Testament, at least its diffusion, for designating the active predication by the Church of the message of salvation.

4) Mark, on introducing the term into the synoptic tradition, does not disapprove of the Pauline usage, but comments on and amplifies it. Today, there could not be spoken of the literary genre "Gospel" without at once referring to Mark, for it is he who made it a reality, even if the term as used by him does not even designate the written Gospel. He, however, conceived his work in so intimate a relationship with the event and the proclamation of salvation that, it, wholly and entirely, justifies the title of *Gospel.*

It is remarkable that Mark employs the substantive *Gospel* seven times without any modifier (Mk 11:14, 15:8; 35; 10:29; 13:10; 14:9). He also uses as equivalents "for My sake" and "for Me," that is, Christ, and "for the sake of the Gospel" and "for the Gospel" (Mk 8:35; 10:29). Luke, on the contrary, never uses the noun, but the verb "evangelize." In Matthew the noun is found four times (Mt 4:23; 9:35; 24:14; 26:13), but always with a modifier ("the Gospel of the Kingdom" or "this Gospel"). This results in placing the accent on the content of the preaching of Jesus (the Good Tidings of the Kingdom) rather than on His person.

The first verse of the second Gospel represents a characteristic typical of Mark: "Here begins the gospel of Jesus Christ" (Mk 1:1). These words, at the head of Mark's book do not constitute a title, nor a definition of his work, but rather a sort of exergue, an inscription. On using the word *Arche,* Mark thinks of a *history*: the history of the manifestation of Christ revealing Himself on revealing what, through Him, God accomplishes in the world. *Arche* dispels right away the idea of a Kingdom established all at once in its totality and its perfection. On the contrary, the Kingdom knows a humble and disconcerting beginning, then a development, that is, the earthly existence of Jesus, and finally, a fulfillment, that is His resurrection and glorification. On the other hand, this beginning is something absolutely new, which evokes the "beginning" of Genesis: this time, there is question of the new creation, of the new times of salvation in Jesus Christ, and of a new status of man and of humanity.[2]

For Mark, the Gospel is even more an *event* than a message: it is the joyous proclamation of the event of salvation. This event embraces the whole existence of Christ, but, in relation to the culminating point of this existence (passion-resurrection), the rest represents a beginning: a "commencement." If Mark speaks first of John the Baptizer, it is because with his preaching the time of salvation was inaugurated. John's ministry is so intimately connected with that of Jesus it is part of the eschatological event. Even before Jesus appeared, it was already the Gospel of Jesus Christ. It is through John's ministry, through the baptism and preaching of Jesus, the salvation announced by the prophets began to be realized. The appointed time is at hand. It is the hour of the decisive intervention of God. Mark, starting out from the present time of the Church, wants then to go back to the beginnings of a history, that is, to the first manifestations in this world of the decisive action of God. His work presents a view of history in which the past and the present, though not confused, could not be disjoined. In his concept of the Gospel, Mark is distinguished from Paul, who thinks above all of the passion and resurrection of Christ. For Mark, the whole existence of Jesus, from the baptism to the resurrection, is a Gospel.

Many exegetes give to the genitive "Gospel of Jesus Christ" an objective meaning, that is, the Good Tidings concerning Jesus Christ. However, it seems to us legitimate to recognize with Marxsen and many others a meaning both subjective and objective: Christ proclaims and is proclaimed; He is at one and the same time Gospel and Evangelist, messenger and message. On revealing Himself, He reveals what God accomplishes through Him. Marxsen, though, follows Bultmann too faithfully when he identifies Christ with the kerygmatic Christ after the Pasch alone. In the Gospel, there is not only the Christ preached by the Church, but also the whole activity of Jesus. The whole earthly existence of Jesus is Gospel: from baptism to death.

Also, on closely linking his work to the event of the Good Tidings of salvation in Jesus Christ, Mark promoted the relationship between the oral Gospel and the written Gospel. He became, as it were, the catalyzer facilitating the change-over. Mark's work became the prototype of the Gospel. Consequently, Matthew, Luke and John adopted the literary design of Mark, even if they never described their work as a "Gospel."

5) It is only in the course of the 2nd Century that the word "Gospel" serves to designate our present canonical writings. The first certain examples of its use are found in Marcion around 140, Justin, around 150-155, and in the Canon of Muratori, in the second half of the 2nd century. Justin speaks of the "Memoirs of the apostles which are called Gospels."[3] The Canon of Muratori designates the Gospel of Luke as "tertius Evangelii liber," and the Gospel of John as "quartum Evangelium."[4] The present titles date only from the 3rd century. Even when the meaning of written Gospel became

dominant, the Church is ever aware the word designates above all the content of the work, that is, the proclamation of salvation in Jesus Christ, and that in reality there could be but one and only one Gospel. This is why Irenaeus speaks of the "tetra-morphic" Gospel.[5]

II. Why did the Gospels come after the Epistles?

It may seem astonishing that such important writings as the Gospels were written so late, more precisely, after the Epistles, and many decades after the events they relate. Even more, the Gospels and the Epistles present quite a different picture of the New Testament. In the Epistles, there are found very few allusions to the earthly activity of Jesus, to His teaching, to His words, to His discussions with the Pharisees, to His miracles. The preacher becomes the preached, and His death and resurrection seem the sole content and the sole preoccupation of apostolic testimony. In the Gospels, on the contrary, the earthly activity of Jesus is primary. He is the messenger of the Kingdom, and it is He who speaks and acts. What is the explanation?

Let us start by distinguishing two quite different questions: on the one hand, the *interest* shown about the earthly existence of Jesus in the primitive Church, and, on the other hand, the appearance in the Church of *successive accounts* on the earthly career of Jesus.

The interest in the person of Jesus of Nazareth, from then on professed as the Lord, is a certain and pristine fact, attested to by the studies of *Formgeschichte* on preexisting evangelical units and on the areas in which these units sprang up: ministerial, liturgical, and catechetical. Thus, the passion of the Savior, including the account of the Supper, is set in a continuous account and found a place in the liturgical milieu. Very soon also, for catechetical needs, the *logia* of Jesus were brought together, especially His parables. The discourse on mission, very archaic, brings together clearly the instruction of Jesus for missionaries. The accounts of miracles find a place in the preaching to the Jews, as signs of the messianic Kingdom, and to the Gentiles, as signs of God's might. The prologue of Luke attests to the existence of the tradition of these accounts of varying extent, under oral or written form.

Since the Gospel is not first of all a doctrine, but salvation accomplished in a concrete person, it is not possible to eliminate all interest in this historical person; it is not possible to avoid being in a certain sense a biography. In fact, that a man preached and healed many, then that he was arrested, judged, condemned, crucified, and that this man is the author of salvation, is something marvelous. It would be impossible to separate the event from the person in whom it took place. Salvation in Jesus of Nazareth commands interest in His existence among men.

But this historical interest in the historical person of Jesus still does not answer the second question: why the *successive accounts,* and why *so late*? On this point, we are reduced to probabilities, and at times to simple hypotheses.

Without doubt it is in order to respond to the new conditions of evangelization that the Church was brought to bring out the texts, more and more distinctly informative. Conditions were created by temporal and geographic remoteness and even more by cultural distance.

At the beginning, especially in Palestine, Jesus had no need to be presented. The inhabitants of Judea, of Galilee knew the characteristics, the works, the tragic destiny of Jesus. He had too strongly upset the religious life of the nation to be so soon forgotten. The coming of Jesus was a publicly known fact, belonging to the generation of witnesses. In 57, in the First Epistle to the Corinthians, Paul appeals to these witnesses still living (1 Cor 15:6). In this first phase of evangelization, there is question rather of fully identifying the one who was seen going about Palestine, of explaining that this man Jesus was actually the expected Messiah, even more the Lord, the Son of God among men.

But it was not the same for the pagans, strangers in Palestine and to the faith of Israel, such as the centurion Cornelius of Cesarea, the inhabitants of Antioch, the Greeks of

Athens or the Romans. For all of them, to announce the survival of an unknown would have been to lead them to think there was involved some new esoteric doctrine. Typical in this regard is the reaction of the Athenians to the preaching of Paul: "He sounds like a promoter of foreign gods" (Ac 17:18). Salvation, is too, linked with the historical person of Jesus: it was necessary to present Him. Clement of Alexandria states that Mark wrote his Gospel in response to the express desire of his audience in Rome.[6] The Canon or Muratori states that John wrote his Gospel at the request of the bishops of Asia.[7] It is difficult to verify the exactness of these traditions. One thing is certain, in contact with the pagans, and on being diffused, the Gospel, necessarily, and each day more so, must be related to the person of Jesus. This is why the teaching to the Gentiles has less scriptural arguments and more and more insists on details of a chronological and geographical nature which enables the placing of Jesus of Nazareth. The essential still remains the passion and the resurrection, but the historical framework is enlarged. In regard to this, the preaching of Peter in Cesarea (Ac 10:37-41) is as it were a canvas, a miniature of what the written Gospel will become. On the other hand, as the Gospel is addressed to various cultural milieu, at the same time it informs, it must also "make relevant." Thus it is that the same Gospel, presented to Judeo-Christians (Matthew), to Romans (Mark), to Greeks (Luke), to the inhabitants of Asia Minor (John), becomes our "tetra-morphic" Gospel.

There is still another question. Why this late return to a narrational description, after the universal announcement of salvation? Why the Gospels, in the second half and at the end of the first century? Why, after having preached Christ, the Lord, the Son of God, does the Church return to the Jesus, Rabbi of Nazareth, and to His earthly career? According to Kasemann, we have seen, the Gospels were written to oppose excessive spiritualizing tendencies, which manifested themselves in Corinth, or against the gnosis, that is, against the currents which abandon the earthly and historical figure of Jesus in order to reduce Christianity to a formless doctrine, or one which confines Christian revelation to individual or collective spiritual experiences, thus abandoning the Christ *extra nos* for thinking only of the Christ *in nobis*. There was concern to protect the Church against a mortal danger: that of thinking of the Christ who lives in us, in order to make little account of His personal, corporal, and historical existence. In the name of an ideal and mystically pure Christ, there would result the setting aside of Jesus Himself and of His humanity. There would come about forgetfulness of the fact that He lives in us, but after having existed as one of us and outside of us, and that the one now in glory was first humiliated and crucified.

The Church rejects a Christianity which does not pass through history. To react against these tendencies which are at least ambiguous, she renews her memory of the past. Returning to the history of what happened once for all, she, thus protects preaching. The present Lordship of Christ is inseparable from what is past. Salvation was worked before us and outside of us. Thus, the Gospel of the evangelists prevents the preached Gospel from becoming myth, gnosis, ideology.[8] C.H. Talbert, for his part,[9] thinks that the work of Luke, Gospel-Acts, is directed against gnosticism, and has as its objective to emphasize the character of Christ's authentic humanity. He thinks that this is why Luke, in his Gospel introduced the accounts of the infancy (chs. 1-2), the genealogy of Jesus (ch 3), and stressed the biographical in his account. It is for this same reason that the Acts manifest a clear preference for the name of Jesus. Finally, according to a tradition represented by St. Irenaeus and St. Jerome, the Gospel of John was written against Corinth which refused to recognize, in Christ, the Son of God truly become flesh, a man among men.

III. Characteristic traits of "Gospel" literary genre

We can now attempt to make precise in what the Gospels constitute a "specific" literary genre, even within the New Testament.

They cannot be likened to any of the ancient literary genres, neither to the type of great history, in the fashion of

Polybius, Thucidides, Titus-Livius, nor to the type of Greek biographies, nor to the genre of "Memoirs," in the manner of Xenophon writing about Socrates, nor to the literary portrait. In the New Testament, the Gospels represent a unique case. The other writings show they are not uninformed about the life of Christ; fundamentally, however, it is the event of the cross and of the resurrection which holds their attention. The rest of the activity of Christ is hardly mentioned. Only the Gospels are interested so visibly in the earthly activity of Christ as well. On the other hand, the composers of the Gospels are not writers working in a studio, with documents from archives, and preoccupied with writing a full life of Jesus, from birth to death. In fact, there is not found, in the Gospels, the unfolding of the origins of Jesus, of His formation, His character, of His personality. There is not found precise chronology, nor topography; which are nonetheless, fundamental coordinates in history. Indications of time and place remain vague, generic: "in the next place, at that time, after, in the house, on the lake, enroute, on the mountain." The very ensemble of tradition is structured by an elementary web with stereotypical joinings. In these conditions, how to characterize a genre which manifestly evolved within history and which, nonetheless, differs so widely and to a degree often so disconcerting? We can but describe each of its traits to allow the physiognomy which emerges from this description to be composed.

1) The Gospels are the proclamation of the Good Tidings absolutely unique and original *(Ur-Kunde)*, since they have as object the depiction of the prime Event of human history, that is the decisive intervention of God in Jesus Christ. The manifestation of Christ among men is the historically unique "beginning," the *Arche,* for in Him and through Him the salvation promised and awaited for centuries, is fulfilled. The "fulness of times" is "now," "today." Consequently, the Gospel cannot be an indifferent proclamation. It presents itself as an appeal for an ultimate decision. Nothing more important can henceforth be produced in human history, on the personal as well as on the collective level. All men are called to conversion. Whoever wishes to correctly read the Gospels, must let this

prodigious summons resound in him, this summons which, in Jesus, makes salvation known. The hearers of Peter, on the day of Pentecost, experienced this tremendous feeling and they "accepted the message" (Ac 2:36-41).

2) The Gospels *belong to a tradition already formed,* which itself was a rereading, in the Spirit, of the Event Jesus in the light of the Pasch, of the Old Testament and of the experience of the nascent Church. This dependence is expressed in the fact that they insert, in the framework of their account, units of sequences already constituted. The Gospels, before they are definitively composed works, are testimonies of a literature which they collect, organize and confirm. Let us, however, observe that this living tradition was taken up and fixed at various stages of its evolution before being finally inserted in the work of the last composer. The evangelists relate a tradition which underwent the influence of many theologies: theologies which were not completely obliterated by the final composition. On the other hand, the evangelists, in turn *rewrite*, each one following his own perspective, that which they received from prior traditions and theologies, for all have in mind to announce the Good Tidings of salvation to men of a certain area and to respond to their problems.

3) The *framework* of the Gospels, common to all, must be its structure and its themes essential to prior kerygma, such that it is possible to reconstruct it starting out from the Epistles of Paul (1Cor 15:3-5; 11:23-27; Rm 1:1-4); and speeches of the Acts (2:22-36; 3:12-26; 4:8-12; 5:29-32; 10:34-43; 13:16-41). The Gospels develop and amplify this traditional format, the great lines of which are the following. The time for the fulfillment of the promises arrived. Jesus is of the race of David. After the preaching of the Baptizer, He began His ministry in Galilee, healing the sick and freeing all those who had fallen into the power of Satan. Then he went up to Jerusalem, where He suffered and was crucified. He rose from the dead and appeared to numerous witnesses. He is now exalted. All men are invited to penitence and conversion. Mark retains this framework which is imposed on him, taking as base the passion and the resurrection. Proof that, for the Gospels, the death of

Jesus is the capital event, for in it was accomplished the salvation of mankind.

4) The announcement of salvation takes the form of a *historical narration*. Since first there is involved a "proclamation" of salvation, the Gospels cannot be conceived of as a life of Jesus: in proof of the failure of the liberal enterprise. On the other hand, this proclamation takes the form of an historical account (and this too characterizes the Gospels), for the salvation announced is an event which is connected with an earthly and historical existence. To describe the development of this existence, is at the same time to proclaim the event of salvation. Mark was the first to expound thus the Good Tidings in the systematized framework of the existence of Jesus. He did so, not out of simple love of the past, but out of respect for reality. In fact, it is not to any Christ at all that we adhere by faith, but to Him who has been glorified since He accepted the kenosis of His earthly, humble and suffering life. For Mark, this movement of the existence of Jesus, centered on the passion and resurrection, is a *profile* of the life of Jesus, with one single journey to Jerusalem, before the passion, and in a quadripartite framework which relates only the great utterances of His life. Mark, however, not only adopts the narrative form of events described in the past or in present, but clearly distinguishes the temporal levels. He describes, for the *present* Church, the history of salvation in its beginning, (preaching of the Baptizer, baptism and preaching of Jesus), its development in Galilee and in neighboring regions, and his tragic end (account of the passion following a most strict chronological sequence of events). Besides, the activity of Christ, as Son of man, covers the future, the present and the past. The Son of man, who was condemned before the Sanhedrin, is He who, from now on, has the power to pardon sins (Mk 2:10), and He who also will come one day on the clouds of heaven. Past, present, future flow together, but remain distinct.

In Luke, this historical perspective stands out even more, for the history of Jesus has a *prior extension*, with the accounts of the infancy, and a *posterior extension*, with the history of the apostles. The history of salvation is characterized by a historically authenticated continuity and by a process of development of which Christ occupies the center. Jesus as well as the Church passes through stages. Luke becomes thus the first historian of Christianity, striving to retrace and to fix the great periods of the history of salvation.

5) The Gospels are at the same time *narration* and *profession*: narration about Jesus and testimony of the community which believes in Him. Besides, narration and testimony are so intimately founded that the account is a profession, and the testimony of faith is a narration or a recital about Jesus, just as in the "credo" of the Old Testament, which are the succinct account of the salvific acts of God (Dt 26:5-9; 6:20-24; Jos 24:2-13). There is nothing like this found in profane literature. The basic reason for this is that, for the narrator-witness, the evangelist, the risen Lord, living and ever present, is identical with Jesus of Nazareth, Savior through His life and death. On relating this, there is professed: "Lord and Jesus." This is why the Gospels have also as their object the historical person of Jesus, Christ, and Lord, who is at one and the same time history and kerygma.

6) If the Gospels are the proclamation of salvation in Jesus Christ, made to human groups geographically and culturally distinct, they present a character of *relevance* and of *dialogue*. Each Gospel refers to a definite community and to a concrete situation: the community of Jerusalem, of Antioch, Greek communities, Asian and Roman communities. The Gospels record the dialogue of the Church with the men and the problems of these communities. Thus, the Gospel of Matthew, put out in Syria, in the years of the eighties, responds to the questions of a Judeo-Christian community in discussion with the synagogue which itself is being completely reorganized after the disaster of the seventies. The evangelist responds to these questions relying on a tradition which acquires its authority from Jesus Himself: from His message above all. Thus the dialogue of Jesus with the Jews of His times goes on, through the Church, with other associates and in other areas, the diverse Gospels being as it were the parts of this polyphonic

dialogue. The Gospels cannot be read abstracting from this relevant characteristic.

Let us conclude. If the Gospels deliberately adopt the narrative form proper to history for describing the earthly activity of Jesus of Nazareth, in His beginnings, in His public ministry and in His tragic destiny, it follows that the literary genre "Gospel" is not independent of the conditioning and of the questioning of history. On acknowledging historicity as a dimension of salvation in Jesus Christ, the Gospels submit themselves to the criteria of historical research.

Footnotes for Chapter VII

1. P. Lamarche, *Revelation de Dieu chez Marc,* "Le Point theologique," XX (Paris, 1976) pp. 33-34; P. Blaeser, "Evangile," in H. Fries, ed., *Encyclopedie de la foi* II, (Paris, 1965), pp.87-95.
2. P. Lamarche, *op. cit.,* pp. 31-32; J. Delorme, "Aspects doctrinaux du second Evangile," in I. de la Potterie, ed., *De Jesus aux Evangiles* (Gembloux-Paris, 1967), p. 84.
3. *I Apol.* 66, 3; RJ 129.
4. RJ 268.
5. *Adversus Haereses* III, 11, 7-8; PG 7: 884-885; RJ 215.
6. Eusebe, HE 6, 14; PG 20:552.
7. RJ 268.
8. E. Kasemann, "Blind Alleys in the Jesus of History Controversy," in *New Testament questions of Today* (London, 1969) pp. 32-41.
9. Ch. H. Talbert, *Luke and the Gnostics* (New York, 1966).

Chapter VIII

THE STATUS OF HISTORY AND THE HISTORIAN'S QUALIFICATIONS

When we come to the problem of finding Jesus through the Gospels, our procedure must be unprejudiced, but not without presuppositions. Particularly it presumes a certain concept of history and of many related realities (memory, historicity, historiography). These concepts, constantly invoked in the course of demonstration, demand preciseness, for they condition the very understanding of the problem being studied. Correlatively, there must also be defined the qualifications of the historian engaged in research on the event Jesus. These qualifications, indeed, by the very nature of the Gospels (narrations and professions of faith) require a procedure in which Literary Criticism and Historical Criticism work on a par. Before undertaking the properly systematic part of our demonstration, we must treat of a sort of basic semanticism and a justification of our premises.

I. Memory, history and historicity

Memory of the past, in our existence, is not simply an appendix of our personal life, a sort of filing cabinet for keeping the memoirs of our past. A. Bridoux writes that memory is what gives me the irrefutable certainty of the identity of my person and of the radical originality of my nature. Of all our certitudes, it is without doubt the strongest and most solidly anchored in the heart of man. All changes which may come about are as nothing compared with this fundamental identity. Further, they only cause it to be brought out more clearly.[1]

In the memory, facts are not simply collected and recalled: each event is set in a definite perspective and constitutes, with other facts thus conserved, a continuous, organic and significant series. Each event possesses a *before* and an *after*. But time and motion, as such, still do not constitute historicity. That comes into consciousness only when the past comes to life again and finds itself perceived as real. This is why it must be said that consciousness is essentially *memory*. Consciousness goes in research of real time, but at the same time it perceives it as an anticipation of the future. Consciousness is at once memory of the past and anticipation of the future, memory and prophecy, retrospective and prospective. This dialectic is possible, since Man's being is the will to be ever more and ever to be of more value. Faced with the future, consciousness becomes desire, hope, project. The past is transformed into future energy: man *pro-jects,* that is jets himself forward and thus builds himself up. The future is man in a state of project. A propos of this, E. Dardel[2] rightly observes that the future precedes the present. Indeed, it is on starting out from the future that man builds himself, for the future is the fanning out of his possibilities: it stands out, not to remain a *to come,* a future, but to become present. Nor, is passage of the future to the present brought about by means of an option, a decision and, finally an execution. In the option, man assumes one of the possibilities of his future, while, by action, he realizes himself: he makes himself present to one of the future promises offered to him. Intention and action are a joint pursuit.

This having been stated, what is to be understood by history? History is man's being, inasmuch as it is built following a rhythm of intention-realization, of project-execution, by way of decision. Historicity, in turn, is this very rhythm, viewed as a fundamental law of human being.[3] By way of the series of possibilities which are offered him, man builds himself his own history, ever following this dialectic of project-option-realization. Let us add that at the same time he builds his personal history, man becomes a moment of human history, for he cannot realize his personal history without becoming himself an integral piece of universal history. History is thus developed between two terms: the unity of the cellular project and the much wider unity of the history of humanity.[4]

The theology of history, widening even more the horizon makes clear that beyond each individual project and beyond the projects of humanity, there exists a superior project which includes and transcends the history of humanity, that is, the project of God Himself. History, in fact, can take on a meaning which man himself determines (as did Hegel and Marx), or a transcendant meaning, which escapes the mind of man. The Christian esteems that the ultimate meaning of history belongs to God. "What constitutes the profound reality of history," observes Marrou, "what is built up in the course of time, that which grows, the City of God, the Mystical Body of Christ, is by nature something which is not of the order of sensed experience and which necessarily escapes a most extensive area of our vision."[5]

II. Historical knowledge

1) The term "history" is ambiguous. It may designate the past of man (real history) or recounted, written history which is knowledge of the past. To avoid this ambiguity, authors distinguish between history and historiography, between (minuscule) history and (majuscule) history, between *History* and *Geschichte*. For the moment, we understand by history the real past of the Jesus of history, Jesus of Nazareth, in His earthly existence. When there will be question of historical work, we shall speak of historical research or of historical knowledge, or of historiography. The term real history itself

remains fluid. It may designate in fact the history of a man, the history of a people, the history of a way, the history of a cultural movement, the history of humanity. It serves to express the realization of one or of many projects, whether individual or collective.[6]

2) The concept of history which dominated the 19th century and which, for a long time, inspired the judgments bearing on this historical value of the Gospels, is that of the positivism represented by Ludwig von Ranke (1795-1886) and Theodor Mommsen (1817-1903). Now, following the canons of positivism, which aspire to give an exact and complete picture of the past, starting out from "historically pure" sources, this judgment of value can only be unfavorable to the Gospels, they evidently appearing as sources "contaminated" by the object of faith and by theological interpretation. So it is well to examine the postulates of positivism.

At the base of positivism, there is an ingenuous, acritical epistomology. This, in fact, considers the object of historical knowledge as a datum, already formed, and historical knowledge as the registering or the photographing of this object. The objectivity of historical knowledge consists in perceiving the datum as it is (*wie es eigentlich gewesen*), in registering bare facts, in their original truth, apart from all interpretation. The ideal of historical positivism is to arrive at the cold, neuter, impersonal exactitude of the natural sciences. It strictly keeps itself at the level of facts, in their pure materiality.

We must admit it, such an ideal is not only inaccessible, but contrary to reality. Facts are always accompanied by an individualist or collective interpretation, without which, furthermore, they would be unintelligible. Thus, to say that Kennedy was "assassinated" at Dallas, is more than a fact. To speak of a fact only, it would have to be said: "Kennedy, while visiting Dallas, was found bathed in blood, with two bullets in his body." But to say "assassinated" is already an interpretation of the fact and implies an intentional cause on the part of one or many persons. Every human fact, in practice, shows itself at the same time as a fact and as an interpretation, which is interpreted by a judgment. Outside of the human mind, which apprehends and judges, there is naught but a chaos of data. Objectivity, a propos of a historical fact, consists then in entering onto the horizon of a consciousness which perceives it and judges it. This principle is verified even at the level of scientific knowledge. Indeed, the pretension of penetrating the nature of things such as it is, is after a long time abandoned by men of science. They recognize they are the interpreters of reality, to a certain level of intelligibility. Their models or drafts are essays of interpretation of reality. So physical science itself is not in agreement with the principles of positivism.

Let us add that each human fact is rich in an indefinite number of interpretations, which await being known or rediscovered. Now this activity of discernment will always be imperfect, partial and unilateral. Besides, the materiality of the fact only constitutes one element among many others, of the becoming of a man realizing himself in a project. A man gave his life to a project; another man, the historian, endeavors to bring back this fact, by interpreting the intention which inspired it, by means of an explicative hypothesis. This is why, in each human fact, objectivity can only be defined by integrating the contribution of the subject which brought about the fact as an expression of his project, and the contribution of this other subject which brings it back in seeking to interpret it.

3) In historical research, as in all human sciences, always there intervene elements of subjectivity, individual or collective, which cannot be eliminated. Let us point out at least two of these elements:

a) The *choice of a perspective.*—If for instance, I am writing the history of the Counter-Reformation, this period appears as a moment of vigorous religious renewal; on the other hand, if I am writing a history of art, it appears as a period of decline. The choice of a perspective now takes over the interpretation of reality. Doubtless this choice is necessary, but it imposes limits on objectivity, for it reduces reality to only one of its dimensions.

b) *The emotional option.*—Emotional factors often play a

decisive role in judgments on persons or events., Thus, a judgment on the political role played by men such as Napoleon, Churchill, De Gaulle or Lenin, will depend to a large extent on initial emotional stands. The war of 1939-1945, viewed by French, the Germans, the English, the Americans, the Russians, will be seen under a different light, according to the nations concerned. Who will write the "objective" history of the Crusades, of the French revolution, of the Russian revolution? The existential option of the historian, believing or disbelieving, with his philosophical assumptions, conditions his whole work. Consciously or not, it inspires the choice of documents, the organization and the interpretation of materials, the synthesis at which he arrives. The Gospels, for example, narrate the walking of Jesus on the waters. Right away there come about personal options: miracle, pure symbols, hallucination, natural explanation, intent to deceive on the part of the narrator, etc. However, there is no intent to drown in total scepticism the possibility of a worthwhile historical research, but to evaluate it correctly. A first step toward objectivity consists, for the historian, in openly declaring the perspective he adopts and stating his assumptions. Then he can open himself up to another perspective, different from his own and even, if there is room and in the face of facts soundly attested to, simply renounce it.[7] Objectivity is first of all research of objectivity.

4) The relationship between real history and historical knowledge cannot be correctly defined except by starting out from an exact view of existence as historicity. Real history is human action inasmuch as a realized intention. And intention is the consciousness of man who *pro*-jects himself as a future possibility. It is the human subject in a prospective stage.

Historical research does not find itself before a purely material fact, deprived of all signification, but before a fleshed out intention, before a realized project. Thenceforth, what does historical. research propose? It is the *re-creative* interpretation of the creative intention of real history. It travels the road of life in reverse. While real history proceeds from project to realization, historical research proceeds from action to intention. It endeavors to find out the intention of the subject in the act by which it is carried out. Real history and historical research condition each other mutually. But, let us repeat, historical knowledge is only possible because real history is now "significant," and intelligible. It follows that historical research is only possible on condition it adopt, before real history, an attitude at the same time of affinity, in order to communicate with it, and of distance, in order to judge it correctly. "Comprehension" always implies these two steps.

a) *Affinity or co-nascence.*—A book, or a film, can be understood, without sharing the intention of the author himself, by a sort of divination. We must make ourselves contemporaries of the author and of his work. According to Claudel, to know, there must be *co-nascence.* We must abandon temporarily our position in order to enter into that of another, render ourselves disposable and ready to listen. To understand a text, is to understand a person. This supposes sympathy and the same wave length.

When there is question of exegesis, there must be abolished the cultural distance which separated us from the text in order to become contemporaries of the author. Indeed, exegesis cannot avoid the necessity of a return to the times and manner of speech in which the sacred word appeared, in order to find out the reality signified, with the intention of the author, in the milieu in which it came to birth. To read the sacred text is the fruit of a second spontaneity, which results from a rigorous hermeneutic exercise.

b) *Distance and judgment.*—On the other hand, for judging well an object, it is necessary to be able to detach oneself from it, step back, and set it on a much wider horizon. After a period of affinity, there must be a period of withdrawal, for understanding the object in its changed appearance. The historian is like a judge. He becomes suspicious. He does not stop understanding, but he seeks to integrate the first time (of connaturality, of sympathy, of life-with-another) in a second, lumping it together and summing it up, which permits him the better to appreciate and to judge, or go beyond his own horizon. Thus, the poetry of Baudelaire acquires a much richer meaning in the light of the literary outburst of symbolism, to which it gave birth. Likewise, romanticism may be judged starting out from German and French romanticism and concluding that romanticism is "mystery." But the study of Italian romanticism will quickly oblige revision of this somewhat simplistic judgment.

By distance, we do not understand simply a psychological distance, but as well a *temporal* distance. In fact, rightly to appreciate an event or a historical movement of a certain dimension, it is necessary that the ferment of contradictory opinions be first appeased. It is also necessary that, for evaluating the importance and the intensity of a curve, it be possible to compare it with other curves.[8] Thus, there was needed many decades, and even centuries, for measuring the force of the impact of nascent Christianity.

c) *Distance and continuity*—For judging well, there must be not only distance, but continuity in distance; if not, there is a hiatus. Gadamer emphasizes, "It is important there be seen in temporal distance a positive and producitve possibility given to the understanding. It is not a yawning abyss, but thanks to the continuity of provenance and of transmission, it is opened up to the light by which all tradition is offered to our attention."[9]

It comes about that the situation of affinity, whether then and there a datum, or due to a chronological contemporaneity with the event and its milieu of origin, or also because it maintains the tradition, brings about the horizon in which a document came about and thus makes the reading of this text chronologically distant from me. The exegetical task consists then simply in clarifying the meaning of the text, if it is obscure or ambiguous. But it also happens that tradition represents a series of re-readings or interpretations made in the course of centuries, in cultural horizons each time diverse. In this case, hermeneutic work is necessary. There is involved reconstructing the original cultural situation and discovering the initial meaning. This situation is that of our Gospels, which represent a series of successive re-reading of the real existence of Jesus.

d) *Distance and study in depth.*—The temporal distance is not simply an obstacle to overcome. It is also a source of study in depth, for it permits multiplicity of observations and perspectives. Inserted in a new framework, a fact, a text acquires more intelligibility. It discloses latent riches. Each work, and even each word, each action anticipates an indefinite series of readings. The understanding of a text, of a work, of an event, is an unlimited, indefinite process.[10]

It follows that real history remains open to an ever richer knowledge of the past. The art of the historian is to capture these harmonies which are diffused throughout the centuries. This is why, too, it is possible, by reason of the change of horizon, to re-write ceaselessly history. Israel, for instance, never stopped meditating on its past in order to perceive the latent riches therein. The Old Testament represents a constant re-reading of these fundamental events which gave birth to Israel as a people: Exodus, the Covenant, the Chosen. Each generation took up on its own meditation on these events, endeavoring to discover the inexhaustible meaning of them. On renewing the knowledge of the past, history opens up new possibilities for the future.

III. Application to the problem of the Gospels

The observations we have just made on history and historical knowledge, enable us now to state that our Gospels are much closer, than the holders of positivism thought, to the concepts of history and to historical fidelity. In fact, what the Gospels relate to us is the earthly history of Jesus, but with the profound meaning which it has through Jesus Himself. Jesus, likens the will of the Father even to that abyss of charity which brings Him to the cross. Here is the fundamental project of Jesus. That the intention of the evangelists was truly to bring home this meaning of the salvific oblation of the life of Jesus, can be verified from the importance they give to the account of the passion (for instance, in the Gospel of Mark). The truth is that two aspects are constantly stressed by the Gospels.

1) On the one hand, the event itself, in its reality of an event "truly happened." The Gospels, however, also point out

the meaning of the event, that is, that meaning which belongs to the event itself, which is "interior" to it. The meaning is, then, not an element superadded by—tradition. It is joined with the event. The meaning fructifies, but it is not created. Thus, the death of Jesus is not a simple demise. The oblational character of this death belongs to its reality. The function of the historian is to find out, beyond the diversity of recensions, the reality of the event and its significance. Such is the element of truth which positivism contains: historical research should find again the pre-paschal Jesus, in His totality of meaningful-event.

2) On the other hand, if the event has a meaning it is not for satisfying curiosity, as a pure object of information: it is presented as a summons, as an appeal to conversion and to an authentic life. The reality of Jesus is not neuter. It puts into play the existence of the one who encounters it. Such is the valuable element of the New Hermeneutic. The historian, as such, does not have to decide for others. He can, however, show that the call for the decision of faith belongs to the message of Jesus. He can also show that the Christian interpretation of Jesus is coherent with the aim, historically present in His existence.

Already, indeed, in the times of Jesus, His earthly existence had a meaning. His words and deeds were not pure enigmas. His life was presented as scanned by options. The community of Jesus and His disciples participated in this project and performed acts which involved it: for example, the mission of the Twelve. The pre-paschal consciousness of the event, does not transmit it under the form of raw, insignificant material. It already contains, without separating them, the event and its first understanding. Doubtless an imperfect understanding, but born out of reality.

Thus, from the beginning, the event appeared as meaningful, but this meaning was not immediately and fully perceived. The tradition of the faithful understood the past to the measure it applied it to the present. The Gospels are the expression of this plenitude of meaning implicitly contained in the pre-paschal event, but imperfectly grasped by the apostles.

They represent the fructification of the past and of its original meaning. They collect the past as an event that "happened," to which they never stop referring (fact and meaning), but, at the same time, the various recensions and diverse theologies bring back the whole meaning, plenary of the event. They also manifest the indefinite possibilities of the revelance and application, which the real existence of Jesus represents. The historian, however, can and must ask whether the diverse expressions of a same plenitude, are legitimate explanations of it. Beyond relevance, he seeks for that which was made relevant.

IV. Qualification of the historian

In our hypothesis, the historian who explores the Gospels, is a believer. Far from being unfavorable, this qualification is advantageous for him, for it sets him right away in the perspective in which the Gospels were written: of the faith. Otherwise, it would have to be concluded that the ideal position, for appreciating the doctrine of a philosopher, is that of scepticism; for understanding a religion of salvation, that of an atheist; for grasping the meaning of a committed life, that of a man without an ideal. The believing historian is required to state his assumptions, but not required to abandon them, under pretext of an impossible neutrality. The believer can carry on, in the interior of his belief, activities of a philosopher, a historian, a philologist, on condition, however, that he respects he techniques and methods of the disciplines he practices.

The believing historian accepts the Gospels, such as they are presented in reality, that is, as works in which narration and profession, event and interpretation are blended in one and the same text. The historian, therefore, does not give up the successive interpretations incorporated and recorded in the actual text: he even starts out from there. These interpretations are needed by him for linking the present to the past and for having access to the past.

The very nature of the documents he is examining, obliges him to acknowledge the priority of Literary Criticism over Historical Criticism. The event is first, but there is a literary priority of testimony over event. Before asking himself whether the event truly "happened," the historian must therefore pose the questions: What was the predominant intention for preserving the account? In what context was it transmitted? To what extent was it made relevant? What is the import of the compositional activity of the evangelist? To procede thus is not to renounce the critique of historicity, but to assure rather the validity of the procedure. For, in order to appreciate the relationship of a document to the past, first it should be read according to its perspective. The historian then has the right to ask whether the meaning read in the texts which make relevant and interpret the past, is faithful to the original event and to the meaning contained in it. After all, it is the event which is speaking. Of this he must be assured.[11]

This time too, historical verification cannot do without hermeneutics. The point of departure of research is always the present text. Basing himself on literary and historical information, the historian follows in reverse the evolution of the tradition, from the written stage to oral stage. He examines each stage as to its context, its proper perspective, its relation to the anterior stage and to the following stage. He seeks to determine in what measure each stage could stress, limit or twist the meaning of the events he wants to know in their totality. Each stage of the tradition supplies thus the illumination which directs toward an anterior stage, which in turn leads toward that which preceded it, till the events sought, that is, the life of Jesus and the pre-paschal community, appear at the end of this long trail.

In this process of discernment of structures and superstructures of the Gospels, priority comes back to Literary Criticism (the level of *Redacktionsgeschichte*). In a second time, which corresponds to that of *Formgeschichte*, Literary Criticism and Historical Criticism go together. In a last stage, Literary Criticism must give way to Historical Criticism. In fact, once the successive forms of tradition are known, and once the oldest literary form accessible to us is known, there remains to establish that the message borne or the event recounted are authentically of Jesus. Now it is by recourse to the criteria of historicity properly so called that this last operation is accomplished.

At the end of exploration, the historian finds himself ever in the face of events and of a meaning. Never does he reach "meaningless" events. His ambition, furthermore, is not to get hold of a dead, neuter past, in order then to contemplate it as a cold and disinterested spectator, but to take hold of a pre-paschal Jesus already meaningful and a source of meaning. This is why he can next, in a complementary procedure, survey the path of tradition for reading in it the development of the meaning implied, but not explicit, in the original events. Having left the text read in the present, the historian goes back to it, but never separating the event from its meaning. The present text appears as the "precipitate" of a temporal and significant evolution of which he strives to reconstitute the stages and verify the fidelity. In this research, an indissoluble and reciprocal link unites the interpretation and the historical reconstruction, for a stage of tradition only finds as its perspective one reset in its "mileu of life" and, inversely, the knowledge of this perspective enables the knowing of how tradition has treated the material received. The relation of the text and of tradition to the event Jesus, is not made precise save little by little, by point effort of *history* and of *hermeneutics*.[12]

Thus, when there is question of the Gospels, the historian cannot underplay the present, nor the successive interpretations of tradition incorporated in the text. He only reunites the past as "past" inasmuch as understanding of events permits. The past only works for him as past if he accepts seeing how it unfolds, as a blooming flower, for constituting the present of the Gospels. It is a rough road, but there is no other.

V. Results

1) Recent considerations on the nature of history, on its aspiration and its limits, have in good part rehabilitated the Gospels as a way of finding Jesus. Indeed, historical research conceived as the recreative interpretation of the project of real history, shows that the evangelists on introducing the reader to the ultimate meaning of the life of Jesus, that is, His oblation to the Father for the salvation of man, place themselves at the very heart of history and its concerns. In their freedom in regard to the coordinates of time and place, they remain more faithful to Jesus than the strictest of chroniclers. The object of the Gospels, as that of the kerygma, is the real history of Jesus, as a project carried out as an offering to the Father.

2) The historian, on the other hand, accepts the Gospels such as they are. It is by way of these testimonials of faith that he endeavors to reach Jesus in His human historicity. It is on stripping away one by one the superimposed layers of tradition that a way is opened up to the event Jesus, to this eternal objective which justifies the interior pretension of faith itself. If the Gospels intend to evoke events of which they prolong and unfold the meaning, the historian must be assured that the proposed meaning is truly that of the past event. His undertaking, no matter how historical it may be, cannot by-pass assiduous collaboration with Literary Criticism, nor can his task as a historian abstract from hermeneutical concern.

3) We shall make precise, in the third part, the historical procedure which we have just outlined. We shall define in particular the respective contribution of Literary Criticism and a Historical Criticism in their concrete exercise.

Footnotes for Chapter VIII

1. A. Bridoux, *Le souvenir* (Paris, 1953), p. 6.
2. E. Dardel, *L'histoire, science du concret* (Paris, 1946) pp. 58-59.
3. A. Rizzi, *Cristo verita dell'uomo* (Rome, 1972), p. 48
4. Ibid., pp. 35-50.
5. H. I. Marrou, *Theologie de l'histoire*, (Paris, 1968), p. 61.
6. A. Rizzo, *op. cit.* pp. 79-80.
7. Ibid., pp. 84-88.
8. H. G. Gadamer, *Wahrheit und Methode*, (Tubingen, 1960). Quoted: *Verite et methode*, (Paris, 1976), p. 138.
9. *Ibid.*, p. 137.
10. *Ibid.*, p. 139.
11. P. Fruchon, *Existence humaine et Revelation. Essais d'hermeneutique* (Paris, 1976) pp. 114-118.
12. *Ibid.*, pp. 145-149.

PART III

OUTLINE OF A DEMONSTRATION

The third part of our expose is a time of properly so called demonstration. To tell the truth, the first time likewise belongs to demonstration. Indeed, two centuries of research ending with a firm conclusion on the possibility of a historic finding or Jesus of Nazareth, constitute a sufficient argument for establishing confidence, even on the level of science. This concurrent testimony of exegetes is an argument of external criticism itself based on usage of internal critique. It remains for us, however, to collect and, above, all, construct in an organic way the considerations which have emerged in the course of these two centuries. Besides, the history of criticism reveals that some important arguments have been omitted, and some others hardly sketched, which we must now present or elaborate.

This demonstration appeals to external criticism and to internal criticism. Discussion on the former, has been predominant for a long time, not to say exclusive and has become quite brief. Not because it is depreciated, but in the face of the evidence gathered on the process of formation of the Gospels, there is no longer any reason to delay by handling questions on the authenticity of author. The real problem is on the level of the mediations which separate us from Jesus, and of the fidelity which qualifies each one of these interpolations.

In the demonstration aimed at establishing the historical authenticity of the Gospels, we can in fact distinguish two major points of articulation or, if it be preferred, two on which the whole structure hangs: the mediations of the primitive Church and the mediations of the evangelists. Internal criticism, on which rests the weight of demonstration, endeavors to determine to what extent this twofold mediation maintains or interrupts the continuity which goes from Jesus to us.

Logically, on the level of exegesis, it is the mediation of the Gospels which is first accessible, since the text is incontestably first. On the other hand, chronically, on the level of the historical formation of the Gospels, as on the level of historical research on the Gospels, it is the mediation of the Church which is primary. In fact, Redaktionsgeschichte could not be set nor understood without first studying Formgeschichte. It is the School of Forms which is at the origin of all modern research on the Gospels. It is responsible for the most serious problems which must confront the criticism of today. It is, finally, what, by reaction, brought, about Redaktionsgeschichte.

The radical positions of the School of Forms obliged historical criticism to make a certain number of verifications. Reduced to the essential, of a linear design, if it be wished, these verifications, which constitute the body of the demonstration, come to four:

1) Between the group of Jesus and His disciples, before the Pasch, and the nascent Church after the Pasch, is it possible, even highly probable, that there was a faithful and active transmission of the sayings and deeds of Jesus?

2) Second, can we establish there had been, on the part of the primitive Church, concern for the faithful transmission of the sayings and deeds of Jesus? Can there be discerned, in the nascent Church, a will for "continued" fidelity to Jesus?

3) Third, this concern for fidelity—is it maintained at the level of the composition of the Gospels? The astounding freedom we observe in the treatment of the material received, is it compatible with a true and controllable fidelity?

4) Finally, is it possible to establish the reality, the very fact of this fidelity to Jesus? It is the problem of historical authenticity.

There is question of verifying that there was the possibility of faithful transmission, a concern and a will for faithful transmission, an actuality of faithful transmission. If theses verifications are carried out, our confidence in the Gospels is historically founded. The demonstration follows a linear procedure, but each argument comes back to one and the same center: Jesus. There is at the same time concatenation and convergence.

Chapter IX

THE CONTRIBUTION OF EXTERNAL CRITICISM

For appreciating the historical value of the Gospels, internal criticism first relies on the text itself (analysis of the literary texture, study of the content); external criticism, on the other hand, looks on the text from "without," to respond to questions concerning the author, the date and place of composition, the sources, the integrity of the text.[1] In the case of the Gospels, external criticism calls on extra-evangelical writings (Epistles of Paul, Acts of the Apostles) and above all on the testimonies of the post-apostolic Churches (2nd and 3rd centuries), which speak explicitly of the Gospels.

For a long time, external criticism enjoyed an almost exclusive and uncontested authority, while internal criticism was held suspect and accused of subjectivism. Today, the positions are reversed: internal criteria are in the forefront of criteriology, while external criticism has fallen into almost total discredit. Many exegetes treat it like a poor relative. Others esteem it superfluous and simply leave it out. Here, as elsewhere, the truth is probably in the middle. If contemporaneous research has shown that external criticism, due to the very character of the Gospels and of the history of their formation, has no longer all the importance once attributed to it, it is not however dispensed from interrogating it. Even if its contribution is minimal, used over sparingly or neglected, in our judgment, on three precise points, it still has something to teach us: on the authors of the Gospels, on the authority of those in the Church of the first centuries, on the attitude of the Church in the face of deformative tendencies of the apocryphal and the gnostic writings.

I. The concept of author

The historian ever pursues, substantially, one single objective: to bring together events, persons and their project, by way of documents. In the case of the Gospels, as we have seen, the problem, up to the 19th century, is posed in very simple terms. The Gospel is attributed to the author designated by a tradition which as a rule does not go back beyond the 2nd century. This author, apostle or disciple of an apostle, is a first-hand witness, graced besides with the charism of inspiration. Ancient exegetics places thus the Gospels in a privileged condition: the access to reality is direct. The reader, thenceforth has little need of internal criticism.

1) *Perspective of testimonies of the 2nd and 3rd centuries*

In general, it can be said that tradition has a tendency to "individualize" the authors and to put them in intimate relation with an apostolic authority.

The most ancient texts which we possess (Papias, the Canon of Muratori, the anti-Marcionist prologues, Ireneaus of Lyons) consider Mark and Luke as authors in the formal sense. Contemporaneous criticism, in general, accepts this testimony and reasons thus: if the tradition of the 2nd century had falsely designated Mark and Luke as evangelists, it would have had to propose rather (gratuitousness for gratuitousness, falsity for falsity) the name of two eye witnesses, that is, two apostles, for these would have been in a better position for guaranteeing the content of both Gospels. If the Churches of the 2nd century kept the names of Mark and Luke as authors, they doubtless did so under the pressure of facts.[2]

However, it is to be noted that tradition has a tendency to

bring Mark and Luke closer to apostles in order to give their Gospels all the prestige of apostolic authority. This is so with Papias who presents Mark, not only as a companion of Paul, which we know from elsewhere, but also as the interpreter, the spokesman of Peter.[3] Further, Clement of Alexandria asserts that Mark wrote his Gospel while Peter was still living. Now prior testimonies of Irenaeus of Lyons, of Papias and of the anti-Marcionist prologues hold the contrary. We have no doubt that here is the beginning of a legend and an example of this tendency to strengthen the links between apostles and evangelists.[4] One thing is sure, on proposing Mark as a companion of Paul and spokesman of Peter, there is made of him a privileged witness of the life of Jesus. As for Luke, tradition is satisfied to recognize in him a companion of Paul. Tradition has reason to propose Mark and Luke as authors, so much the more so that internal criticism confirms its testimony. However, it "over values" their quality as witnesses. Mark is much more a faithful "reporter" of original preaching than a spokesman of Peter.

Tradition attributes the first Gospel to Matthew and the fourth Gospel to John. Now, we know today that the first Gospel is a substantial recasting of the Aramaic work attributed to Matthew, along with elements coming from other sources, notably from Mark (indirectly and directly). On the other hand, we know that the fourth Gospel, if it has its source in the testimony of John, does no less represent the influence of a community of specific characteristics, in which the Joannine tradition was long preached and matured.

It is certain, the ancient Church has a tendency to "personalize" the authors of the Gospels and to place them under the aegis of an apostle. This concept of author, which prevailed up to the 19th century, is of great consequence. If our Gospels, in fact, have for authors eye witnesses or disciples of eye witnesses, they put us in the presence of events and of Jesus Himself. The distance is abolished between Jesus and the Gospels, and internal criticism is superfluous.

2) *The concept of author submitted to criticism*

Unfortunately, this concept of author does not stand up against the data of contemporaneous criticism. If the first and fourth Gospels were directly attributable to Matthew and John, the character of "eye witness testimony" would not fail to become apparent visibly and irrefutably in the composition. The same holds for Mark and Luke. Exegesis even doubts they are second hand witnesses, in the sense that they would have collected depositions from eye witnesses (from Peter, for instance) to put them into writing afterwards. Their texts do not bear the mark of "things taken down directly."[5]

Let us not conclude, however, that modern criticism ends up only with negative results. A certain number of ancient data are found confirmed, while some others, subjected to a new light, are better understood.

A propos of the first Gospel, criticism acknowledges that its author, an unknown person, is a Judeo-Christian, who spoke Greek, quite fully conversant with the Jewish and Rabbinic milieu, who preserved and utilized in substance the Aramaic work attributed to Matthew. Criticism equally acknowledges that Luke is a doctor, a companion of Paul (Ac 13-28), and that he is a Christian sprung out of paganism. It is acknowledged that Mark was a companion of Paul and that his Gospel influenced the canonical works of Luke and Matthew. Peter's influence, confirmed by tradition and admitted by such critics as V. Taylor,[6] is contested by many an exegete. Mark depends much more on the original preaching, of which he is the faithful "reporter" and "transmitter," than of Peter. On the contrary, Paul's influence on Mark is more and more acknowledged. The christology of Mark, notably, could have been inspired by Paul and would thus constitute a key for the interpretation of the christology of the Synoptics. John's personality lost much of its preciseness as direct author of the fourth Gospel. On the other hand, we know better the history of the composition of the fourth Gospel, as well as the qualities as writer and as theologian of its author.[7]

3) *A new profile of author*
    Briefly, internal criticism revealed to us that the modern

concept of author could not be applied univocally to the authors of our Gospels. The composers of the Gospels are connected with the events of the ministry of Jesus by an oral and written tradition spread throughout many decades. So there must be eliminated the idea of a composition of the Gospels on the basis of direct testimonies, coming from men who participated in the events, and right away recorded by our authors. Between Jesus and our texts, there are many mediations the respective contribution of which must be appreciated. From this fact, Matthew and John have acquired a profile of author which is defined by the ensemble of characteristic tendencies and traits which only internal criticism has enabled us to find. As much is to be said, in due proportion, of Mark and of Luke. The study of oral and written sources used by the composers, has opened up the way to *Quellenkritik* and *Formgeschichte*. The composers themselves are not simple reporters of tradition. They are also interpreters and theologians. They have their perspective and their literary procedures. The study of this compositional activity has given birth to *Redaktionsgeschichte*.

Thus, what the evangelists lost as individuals, as personal authors, they have regained as servants of tradition and as theologians. This discovery of the new profile of author has been imposed by a more attentive examination of the ancient testimonies and, above all, by the examination of the very texture of the Gospels. Internal criticism has observed, in our present texts, some divergencies and even some incoherencies which could not be attributed to an eye witness, even written down second hand. In order to explain them, exegetics has been constrained to change field. It must pass from external criticism to internal, from critique of author to the problem of the sources and to the problem of their formation.

II. The authority of the Gospels

External criticism provides us with a second important datum. By way of all the texts, a conviction arises and is forcibly expressed, that is, the incontestable authority which the Gospels enjoyed in the ancient Church. This authority is manifested in various ways:

1) In the most faithful conservation of the very text of the Gospels. Thus, the discovery of the papyruses by Bodmer (published in 1956-1958) attests that the text of the Gospel of John, in its present form, was already in circulation at the end of the second century.

2) In the fact that, as early as the 2nd century, there is a reading, during liturgical ceremonies of the text of the Gospels, and this reading has the same importance as that of the prophets. Justin writes a propos of this: "The day of the sun (Sunday), there is an assemblage of all the inhabitants of town and country, and there is read the Memoirs of the apostles or the writings of the prophets."[8] In another passage, Justin, who addresses himself to the pagans, makes clear that these "Memoirs" are called Gospels.[9]

3) In the fact that the Church, when she engages in discussion with heretics, appeals to the Gospels, as a decisive argument. This is so with Irenaeus of Lyons when he addresses himself to the Ebionites, to the Marcionites, to the Docetes, and to the Valentinians. Furthermore, Irenaeus observes, each of the sects, when they break with the Church, always keep a link with one of the four Gospels, at least for justifying their doctrinal position. Thus, the Ebionites, fanatical Jews, relied on Matthew; Marcion and the Marcionites, hostile to the Jews, rejected the Old Testament, but attached themselves to Luke; Cerinthus and his disciples invoked the Gospel of Mark, while Valentinus and his followers based their speculations on the Gospel of John. In their way, the heretics confirm thereby the authority of the Gospels.

4) Finally, all the testimonies are unanimous in acknowledging that the authority of the Gospels derives from the fact that, by them, we have access to Christ. Through the Gospels, in fact, we know the preaching of the apostles about Christ. It is for this reason that the local Churches, although diverse in language, mentality and culture, recognize our four Gospels as norms of faith and of life. It is for this reason equally

that the apocrypha are rejected. Let us present the texts of some of these testimonials.

Papias:

Here is what the Elder said: "Mark, who was the interpreter of Peter, has written with exactitude, but still in an orderly manner, all that he remembered of what had been said or done by the Lord. For he had not heard nor accompanied the Lord; but, later, as I have said, he accompanied Peter. The latter gave his teachings as needed, but without making a synthesis of the Lord's words. In this way, Mark did not make any mistake in writing as he recalled it. He had but one purpose, that of putting aside nothing of what he had heard and of being deceived by nothing he related."[10]

Irenaeus of Lyons:

The Lord of all things has in fact given His apostles the power to announce the Gospel, and it is through them that we have known the truth, that is, the teaching of the Son of God... For it is not through others we have known the economy of our salvation, but rather through those through whom the Gospel has come to us. This Gospel, they first preached; then, by God's will, they have passed it on in the Scriptures, that it may be the foundation and the pillar of our faith.[11]

Tertullian:

First we establish that the evangelical argument has as authors the apostles, to whom the Lord Himself gave the charge of promulgating the Gospel; the disciples of the apostles also, not alone, but in union with the apostles, for the preaching of the disciples might have been suspected of ambition for glory, without the support of their masters, as well as of Christ Himself, who established the apostles as teachers.[12]

Origen:

In the time of the New Testament, many "have attempted" to write Gospels, but all have not been accepted ... Matthew,

Mark, John and Luke did not "attempt" to write, but, filled with the Holy Spirit, they wrote the Gospels. The Church possesses four Gospels; the heretics, a very great number. Thus "many have attempted" to write, but only four Gospels are approved; and it is from these that there must be drawn, in order to set it in light, what is necessary to believe about the person of our Lord and Savior. I know that there exists a Gospel which is called "according to Thomas" and another "according to Matthias"; and we read even some others so as not to seem ignorant on account of those who imagine they know something, when they know these texts. But, in all this, we approve of nothing save what the Church approves: there are, it is to be admitted only four Gospels.[13]

Eusebius of Cesarea:

Having come to this point, it seems reasonable to us to recapitulate the list of writings of the New Testament, of which we have spoken. And, without any doubt, there must be placed first of all the holy tetrad of the Gospels, which follows the book of the Acts of the Apostles. After this book, there must be cited the Epistles of Paul, after which there must be sanctioned the first attributed to John and likewise the first Epistle of Peter. Such are the books universally received.[14]

These testimonies are evidently not expressed in scientific terms and do not know of critical demands. They have the same tendency, as we have seen, to exaggerate the bond which joins the Gospels to the apostles. One fact, however, remains incontestable: the very firm, unanimous, spontaneous conviction that, through the Gospels, we truly know Jesus and His message, for the Gospels contain the preaching of the apostles about Jesus.

It can be difficult to reject the import of such testimony, even if it is acritical and ingenuous in its expression, for it comes down from all generations close to the event (let us think of Irenaeus and Papias), who faced martyrdom to defend their faith in the message of Christ, transmitted by the living tradition of the Church and recorded in the Gospels. Without doubt, it belongs to internal criticism to determine the precise relation which exists between the message of Jesus and the actual text of our Gospels; to discern, in the very texture of the Gospels, the traces of making relevant and interpreting due to the re-reading and deepening of the events. Literary Criticism, however, will never be able to nullify this massive, incoercible persuasion of the first Christian generation. By way of the Gospels and by way of the living tradition of the Church, we truly meet Jesus of Nazareth: His life and His message.

III. Attitude of the Church

This persuasion is such that it enables the Church to take a position in regard to currents which, from the beginning, tend to deform the message of Christ. These currents are represented by the attempt of the apocrypha and by that of the gnostic writings.

1) *The attempt of the apocrypha*

The apocrypha, satisfying the popular taste for the marvellous, yield to the temptation of "completing" the Gospels, either to fill out the lacunae of an information, which they regard as insufficient, on certain periods of the life of Jesus (especially that which preceded the public ministry), or in order to enrich the account of the resurrection with details suited to establish its reality in an irrefutable way, in the face of incredulity.[15] This attempt is already the "temptation" to write a life of Christ which may be a complete reconstruction of the past, in order to answer the demands of popular curiosity or the requirements of a certain apologetic seeking to explain the discord or the silence of our accounts, or to found further the reality of the major events of the life of Jesus.

Tatian's enterprise, in his *Diatessaron*, responds more or less to this purpose. In fact, Tatian was struck by the incoherence, the discontinuity, the inexactness of many evangelical accounts so he undertook to write a consecutive account of the life of Jesus. Matthew served as a basic text, completed by John for the beginning and the end, by Luke and

Mark for the rest.

This attempt by the apocrypha betrays the Gospels in two ways. On the one hand, it plays up to popular curiosity, by seeking before all in the Gospels a source of teachings; on the other hand, it tends to separate the event from its meaning, to give it a "plus-value," treating it for itself, as something of value in itself.[16]

Since the middle of the 2nd century, our four Gospels have been considered as a compact ensemble, as a *numerus clausus*: they are four, no more, no less. All other texts which claim the title of Gospels, are rejected as apocrypha. These four Gospels are considered as the four forms of the sole Good Tidings of salvation. This conviction is inscribed in the expressions of Irenaeus, who speaks of "the quadriform Gospel; of Tertullian," who speaks of "the evangelical proof" (the four Gospels constituting a single juridical proof that can be brought against the heretics); of Eusebius, who speaks of "sacra quadriga" of the Gospels. These formulas, which view the Gospels as a single four square block, are the expression of a peaceful and long time acquired possession.

2) *The attempts of the gnostic writings*

This second current, which long ago anticipated Bultmann's undertaking, contrary to the apocrypha, sacrifices the event to the meaning, and interprets the Gospels starting out from doctrinal assumptions, alien to tradition. Thus the dualism of Marcion, who opposes the good God of the New Testament to the just God of the Old Testament, represents a personal doctrinal position, his own principle of interpretation. On proceding thus, Marcion subordinates the Gospels to his system and substitutes his personal view for that of the Gospels. This time, the moderation of the Gospels is offset, no longer for the sake of piety, but for the sake of understanding. The result is worse.[17]

The primitive Church knows the apocrypha and the gnostic writings. She is perfectly aware of the dangers they represent: danger of sacrificing meaning to event (apocrypha), which becomes an object of curiosity, rapidly transformed by popular imagination; danger of sacrificing the event to the meaning (gnostic writings) under the dominant pressure of the human mind.

In order to avert both dangers, the Church had only recourse to one sole criterion of discernment. It is only in the four Gospels according to Matthew, Mark, Luke and John, that the authentic message of Christ can be understood, the message acknowledged and taught by the living tradition of the Church. The decisive criterion, is the agreement between the Gospels and the apostolic tradition, which itself refers to the living Christ.

These data of external criticism do not say all about the relationship Jesus-Gospels. However, they have their weight. They suffice even now to create a favorable presumption in regard to the Church and her fidelity to Jesus of Nazareth.

Footnotes for Chapter IX

1. G.J. Garraghan, *A Guide to Historical Method* (New York, 1946).
2. A. Descamps, "Progres et continuite dans la critique des Evangiles et des Actes," *Revue theologique de Louvain* I (1970) 7-8.
3. Eusebius, *Hist. eccl.* III, 39; PG 20:298-300.
4. *Ibid.*, VI, 14; PG 20:552.
5. A. Descamps, *art. cit.*, 11-13.
6. V. Taylor, *The Gospel according to St. Mark* (London, 1957), p. 82.
7. A. Descamps, *art. cit.*, 14-15.
8. "Solis dicta die, omnium sive urbes sive agros incolentium in eumdem locum fit conventus, et memorias apostolorum aut scripta prophetarum leguntur, quoad licet per tempus" (Justinus, *Apologia* I, 67).
9. "Nam apostoli, in memoriis suis, quae vocantur Evangelia" (Justinus, *Apologia* I, 66).
10. Eusebius, *Hist. eccl.* III, 39.
11. Irenaeus, *Adversus Haereses*, III, 1.
12. Tertullianus, *Adversus Marcionem* IV, 2; PL 2:363.
13. Origenes, *In Lucam homilia* I.
14. Eusebius, *Hist. eccl.* III, 25.
15. R.McL. Wilson, ed. *New Testament Apocrypha*, vol. I, *Gospels and Related Writings* (London, 1963), pp. 366-369.
16. X. Leon-Dufour, *Les Evangiles et l'histoire de Jesus* (Paris, 1963) pp. 50-53.
17. *Ibid.*, pp. 54-56.

Chapter X

THE MEDIATION OF THE PRIMITIVE CHURCH AND THE PROJECT OF THE SCHOOL OF FORMS

The study of written and oral sources utilized by the evangelists opened the way to *Quellenkritik* and to *Formgeschichte*. We shall briefly treat the first, for its contribution was soon exhausted.

No explanation has as yet succeeded in supplanting decisively the theory of Two Sources. This theory, as is known, makes Matthew and Luke depend on Mark for the narrative portion, and on the *Quelle* (source) for words (a source reconstructed from the *logia* common to Matthew and Luke). This theory evidently does not explain all the material of the Synoptics. Likewise the *Quellenkritik* next interested itself in the composition by Mark and in the portions by Matthew (more than a fifth) and by Luke (more than a third), which is not explained by the theory of Two Sources. None of the numerous theories proposed for solving this problem have been convincing. P. Vielhauser could write, whether rightly or wrongly, that with the theory of Two Sources, *Queelenkritik* had finished its task.[1] It should hand it over to *Formgeschichte*, otherwise, it finds itself at an impasse.

I. The School of Forms: its project

The School of Forms, with its leaders (K.L. Schmidt, M. Dibelius, R. Bultmann, G. Bertram, M. Albertz), represents the major effort of modern criticism to break the "steel ring" which holds prisoner written sources, and to go back over the course of tradition to its origin, that is the preached Gospel.

In fact, before having been put in writing, the Gospel was preached, made relevant, applied to the diverse situations of the Church. It knew a whole life, a whole tradition of interpretation. The merit of the School of Forms has precisely been to study this first stage of the history of the evangelical tradition.

Starting between 1919 and 1922 the School dominated criticism up to the recent works of *Redaktionsgeschichte*, with Conzelmann (in 1954) and Marxsen (in 1956). So it is to render justice to FG,[2] and at the same time a principle of sound method, to study the mediation of the primitive community (between the event and the text) starting out from the very works of those who made of this stage of tradition the main object of their researches.

At first sight, FG presents itself as a *literary* enterprise. Indeed, it identifies, describes and classifies the literary forms in which our evangelical accounts flowed. But then it sets up a bridge between literary form and the milieu which engendered it. It asks what are, in the ecclesial community, the precise situations in which such an account could come about, be developed and be transmitted into the stream of tradition. It is interested in the genesis, the formation and the evolution of the oral traditions, prior to the written texts. It asks what laws presided over this evolution. In more general terms, we shall say that FG, after having considered the horizontal dimension of the Gospels—the breaking up into literary units—views then next in their vertical dimension. It descends down to the deepmost layers, the most ancient layers of tradition, for tracing back the path which goes from the evangelist to the Church, then from that to Jesus. Definitively, its project is of a *historical* nature. Its ambition is to retrace the whole history of the evangelical tradition: from the oral Gospel to the written Gospel. In a first period, its method is literary, but its final aim rests on history. The underlying principle of the school, is that the primitive community is responsible for this whole process of formation of the evangelical tradition.

In a word, FG wants to write the pre-history of the Gospels, an ambition expressed in the title of the work of R. Bultmann: *Die Geschichte der Synoptischen Tradition*, or in that of Vincent Taylor, *The Formation of the Gospel Tradition*. The undertaking of FH has rightly been compared to that of geology which studies the successive forms of the earth's crust, or to that of morphological linguistics which retraces the forms of a word in the course of centuries; or also to the modern procedures of analysis which enable to be discovered, in a tableau, the successive forms that the artist gave to his work, starting out from all the first sketches. Analogously, FG aspires to rediscover the most ancient forms of tradition and the successive states it has known, in the course of the years which preceded putting the Gospels in writing.

If the undertaking ended in a certain historical scepticism, even in a radical and negative judgment, with Bultmann, about the possibility of finding Jesus through the Gospels, it is due less to the method itself than to the principles which inspired its representatives: the sociological principle of creative community; the principle of rationalism with mind closed to the hypothesis of an intervention of God in history under the form of Incarnation, miracle, resurrection; the theological principle of a faith which, for assuring its vertical relation to God, divorces itself from history.

A viewing of fifty years (from 1926 to 1975) however, enables us to make a right discernment as to the contribution of FG for retaining the assimilable elements, which above all are found at the literary level.

II. Originality and merits of FG

The Instruction of the Biblical Commission (April 1964)

invites exegetes to utilize the positive elements of FG, without specifying, however, what these elements are.

1) Paradoxically, FG has restored the value of the whole importance of oral Tradition. Dibelius never stops repeating: "In the beginning was the kerygma." The Gospel was predication before being Scripture. Tradition precedes Scripture. In fact, during a period from 25 to 30 years, the matter of the Gospels was preached in the primitive Church. It served as ministry, catechesis, worship and polemics. It follows that this matter was colored by the whole life of the Church and that it bears the mark of relevance and of the theological interpretation of this community. The Gospels are the "privileged witnesses" of this Tradition, since they are inspired. But that Tradition continues on, no less inspired, after the Gospels. Protestant theology, up to then, had given absolute primacy to Scripture. The reflux of Tradition, at the heart of the Gospels, such as FG conceives it, in reaction against *Quellenkritik*, constitutes then a point of novelty in the horizon of Protestant thinking.

2) FG (especially Dibelius) has correctly underlined, a propos of the Gospels, the inconsistent character of the coordinates of time and place, their value being more often compositional than historical. Certain pericopes, it is true, are well set (for example Bethany, Naim, Jericho); but, most of the time, there is in the evangelical account such fissures that a full sequence of events of the life of Jesus is impossible. The Gospels are not of the *biographical* literary genre. Thereby the project of the Liberal School crumbles. Mark, to be sure, intends to describe the concrete and historical existence of the man Jesus, who lived in a very definite region, and whose ministry, in its origins, its development, its difficulties and its tragic end he depicts. Jordan, Galilee, Jerusalem are the privileged places of His presence. But apart from these grand lines, the historian has little to help him reconstitute the film of the life of Jesus. It is on the contrary better served when there is question of describing the *economy* of His life.

3) In all times, and in all literatures, there has been had the more or less confused perception of the diversity of literary

genres: a speech, a drama, a lyric, a text of a law, a chapter of Titus-Livius call for different commentaries. The originality of FG has been its applying the principle of literary genre, not only to the Gospels, in their globality, but even in "minor units" which compose them. The ambition of FG has been to draw up in some way some sort of complete inventory of the literary genres and sub-genres of our Gospels. Thus, in the *narrational* material, the School distinguishes paradigms (Dibelius) or apothegms (Bultmann), summaries, accounts of miracles, legends, myths, the account of the passion; and, in *doctrinal* matter—allegories, parables, sentences of a sapiential, polemical (controversies), prophetic, apocalyptic type, disciplinary norms, precepts of life, words in which Jesus speaks of Himself ("Ich-Worte"). These very same units have their sub-divisions. Thus, the wisdom genre can take on the manner of an exhortation, an explanation, a proverb, an apologia.

In this flood of literary genres, species and sub-species, what holds the attention of FG, are not so much the purely stylistic elements (for instance, the play of antitheses, of parallelisms, of hiatuses), which rise from literary virtuosity, rather than from the "revelatory" elements of a *context of life*. In other words, the school considers not so much the literary impression of the author (compositional aspect of his work) as the impression made on the author by the social and religious milieu. What is of interest is not so much the personal contribution of the author as the socio-religious influence of the community which constrains the author to have recourse to such a literary form rather than to another.

We are therefore in the presence of a new type of literary analysis. FG observed that our Gospels have a manifestly molecular structure: they resemble a mosaic of pericopes, which in turn flowed in characteristic literary forms. Thus, in the hypothesis that Mark was the "personal" author of the whole second Gospel, FG would be sensitive above all to the diversity of the forms of his Gospel. When the school discerns in it a paradigm or an account of a miracle, what interests it, is not so much the existence or the absence of sources in Mark, as the "typical" literary structure observed, as well as the socio-religious milieu in which such a structure could arise: a liturgical, catechetical or ministerial milieu, a milieu of pagans or of converts.[3]

4) In fact, and this is another positive characteristic of FG, it endeavors by the analysis of the forms to know the life of the primitive Church, which it represents thus as a living organism.

It is the conviction of FG that for each style, or for each *typical* literary form, there corresponds a milieu, a socio-religious context, a particular *Sitz im Leben*. Indeed, if, in reality, it is the milieu which imposes the adequate literary form, it follows that the knowledge of the forms leads indubitably to the knowledge of the corresponding milieu. There is inter-action, a constant play of the text and of the milieu.[4]

This principle of the School, which consists in going from the literary forms to the milieu and, inversely, from the knowledge of the primitive Christian milieu to the multiple literary forms of tradition, is of itself legitimate. We know, indeed, that life and literary form condition each other mutually. A business letter, written in an administrative bureau, has an imprint which betrays its origin. A sermon and a chronicle of political events are wholly different. No one is deceived. Life imposes the form, just as the form reveals the milieu. In the case of the Gospels, however, it is not always possible to determine with certitude the original *Sitz im Leben*. Indeed it happens that in the course of tradition the primitive *Sitz im Leben* may have been modified, or that the present text represents the sedimentation of many successive contexts.[5] Therefore it must be determined, not only what is the actual text of an account or of a logion, at times different from one Gospel to another, but also the original context which goes back to the time of Jesus Himself.

The literary types revealed by FG send us back to the milieux which we may briefly check.

For those who are "outsiders," that is pagans and Jews of the Diaspora, the Church adopts the style of ministerial or kerygmatic predication: the global announcement of the Good Tidings of salvation, centered on the event of the death and resurrection of Jesus. In this milieu, normally there is found place for the accounts of miracles and exorcisms, as attested to in the discourses of Peter in the Acts (Ac 2:22; 10:38). To the Jews, familiar with the Old Testament, the Church shows in Jesus the fulfillment of the messianic promises.

Directed to the converts, there is place for repeating the essential of the kerygmatic predication and for giving it a stereotype form. Thus the first symbols, creeds of the Church are born. Adhesion to the kerygma is inseparable from the perfection of moral life: whence the instructions, the exhortations to vigilance, perseverance, etc. The liturgical milieu, characterized by the breaking of the bread (Ac 2:42), commemorates the symbolic deed of Christ through the account of His death and resurrection and through the hymns to Christ the Savior. The Acts tell us that the first Christians showed themselves "devoted to the Apostle's instruction." (Ac 2:42). In this milieu of converts, catechesis evoked the teachings (parables, rules of life) and the major mysteries of the life of Jesus (baptism, temptation in the desert, transfiguration); it also studied in depth the messianic proof.[6]

Thus, at the level of method, FG, by analysis of literary forms, opened up knowledge of the milieux and functions, of the activities of the primitive Church. An undertaking of itself justifiable, although not without risk, for, on making analysis of forms an instrument of historical knowledge, the school brings about a delicate passage from literary criticism to historical criticism.

Nonetheless on the literary level the school of forms represents the most important contribution of modern exegesis. It set in focus an extremely precise and sharp instrument of analysis. By way of internal criticism, it has come to clarify the multiform activity of the Church as a living community, with its life of prayer, its difficulties in the face of the surrounding world, its ministerial and catechetical effort.

III. Negative aspects of FG

A judgment on FG, even if it wants to be respectful and

sympathetic, cannot however, ignore or be silent about a certain number of deficiencies or of very serious excesses.

1) The school pays attention above all to the primitive community. For Bultmann, the sole problem of primitive Christianity is the reconstitution of the life of this community, illumined by faith in Christ, and of this community there is concern to know the milieu, the problems, the activities. The knowledge of Jesus as a real and historical source of this community has lost interest. Bultmann sees even a real, radical discontinuity between the pre-Paschal community of Jesus and His disciples, and the post-Paschal community of the primitive Church. Faith has no need of the historian.

2) On thus concentrating all its attention on the primitive community, FG has a tendency to exaggerate the *creative power* of this community, likening it to anonymous collectivites, spontaneous forces ferments of culture whence come myths, legends, folklore. A theory dear to the Germans of the 18th and 19th centuries for explaining the formation of canticles, then of the homeric poems and songs of heroic deeds. This theory, evidently, comes at the right moment for explaining the presence in our Gospels of a material which the school generally considers bereft of historical value. This simplistic application of the theories of Herder and of Gunkel to the case of the Gospels, constitutes the feeble point of FG, its "original sin." The School keeps silent unjustifiably about the presence, in the primitive Church, of the apostles and *witnesses* of Jesus (a term not found in Bultmann's work) and especially about all we know of this community through extra-evangelical sources: in particular through the Acts, the Epistles of Paul and John.

In fact, the primitive community is not an amorphic society, without structure. It is not in the line of mollusks, but of vertebrates. In this community, in fact, those having authority to direct it, are precisely those who were close friends of and ate at the same table with Jesus: His witnesses.

The Acts of the apostles, indeed, describe to us a community gathered round its chiefs, the apostles, Peter at the head. His was the initiative of the election of Matthias (1:15-

26). The day of Pentecost, he spoke first (2:14). When Peter and John are arrested, it is Peter who addresses the Sanhedrin (4, 8). Peter puts Ananias and Saphira to death (5:5-9). The twelve call the disciples together and choose the seven deacons (6:5-6). The apostles send Peter and John to Samaria "to confirm" the baptized (8:14-17). Peter addresses Cornelius and the pagans (10:34-43). The apostles protest against some who without any instructions from them have upset others with discussions (15:24). The apostles promulgate and dispatch the decree of Jerusalem: "It is the decision of the Holy Spirit and ours" (15:27-28). Of Peter it is said "he was making numerous journeys." (9:32) He preaches in Lydda, Joppa, Cesarea. Of the Christians, on the other hand, it is said they "devoted themselves to instructions of the apostles" (2:42). And when these had to choose between two ministries, they concentrated on the ministry of the word (6:4).

On the subject of this primitive community, Vincent Taylor justly observes, and not without humor:

On this question of witnesses FG appears very vulnerable. If it is correct, it must be said that the disciples rose up to heaven immediately after the resurrection. In Bultmann's perspective, the primitive community lives in a "vacuum," isolated from its founders by walls of an inexplicable ignorance. Like Robinson Crusoe, it must do the best it can. Incapable of being informed, it must invent the "situations" for the sayings of Jesus, it must put on His lips sentences over which its memory has no control. All this is absurd... Even if it disconcerts the peace and security of the theories (of FG), the influence of the witnesses on the formation of the Tradition cannot be ignored. . . For having neglected this factor, FG gains in internal coherence, but loses in credibility for carrying out its task, which is that of describing the *Sitz im Leben* of Tradition.[7]

Up to a certain point, the facts are more correct than the theories. The collectivity, to be sure, excercises a real influence on the author, but, properly speaking, it does not create it. In the case especially of so original a religion, so dymanic as that of Christianity, how to conceive this, without admitting as point of departure the immense personality of Jesus is a problem. History attests to it. At the origin of every great ideological movement, there is ever a powerful personality: Plato, Aristotle, Mohammed, St. Thomas, Karl Marx, etc.

Let us add that the primitive community is in no way an *anonymous* society. On the contrary, it is perfectly identified with a good number of its personages of first rank. Besides the apostles, known by all, it counts the relatives of Jesus (James), the disciples, such as Matthias, Barnabas, Barsabas, Silas, Mark, Cleophas, Nicodemus, Joseph of Arimatias, Manson, the deacons (one of whom was Stephen), the 120 brothers of whom Peter speaks at the moment of the election of Matthias (Act 1:15). the 500 brothers witnesses of the resurrection, of whom Paul speaks, (1 Cor 16:6), the mother of Jesus and her immediate entourage.

The image of primitive Church, such as it is shown by way of the first writings of the New Testament, is then not one of an amorphous and anonymous community, but rather that of a structured community which has its religious guides, perfectly identified, who are first and above all the witnesses of the life and ministry of Jesus, that is, the apostles. Such is the nutritive environment of the evangelical tradition.

3) In the genesis of the evangelical tradition, FG has set its whole attention on the role of the primitive community. At the same time, it has undervalued the role of the evangelists, considered as simple compilers of preexistent units. The Gospels thus present the image of a conglomerate of artificially grouped fragments, an archipelago spread out over the ocean of Tradition. *Radaktionsgeschichte* has had to correct this unilateral view of things and set in light the personal, literary and theological import of the evangelists.

4) In so far as FG endeavors to describe and classify literary forms, then to trace the history of their development, it remains in its domain. But when it employs, for designating the forms, a terminology which, from the beginning, implies a judgment of historicity, it "extrapolates." Thus, when it qualifies as myths or as legends a portion of the evangelical matter, it now takes on the content. Even if Dibelius uses the

term "legend" in a literary sense, he insensibly glides onto the historical plane.

There is a further feeble point the school has. It overestimates literary criteria to the detriment of historical criteria. Thus Bultmann, on account of the likenesses of structures he perceives between the accounts of miracles, in the Gospels, and the prodigies attested to by Greek literature, concludes that both are without historical value. From the moment that the accounts of feats accomplished by Epidaurus are legendary, so too are the evangelical accounts. This is an illegitimate deduction. Nothing, in fact, on the literary plane, is more like to a veridical account of an extraordinary cure than an imagined account. What is most important of all, in the case of the Gospels, is not only the attestation to the fact, but the moderateness of the account, the immediate religious context, and even more the multisecular context of Christianity. The analogy of the literary forms therefore is not an absolute guide for arriving at a judgment of historicity.

5) As often happens, the explanation of certain positions of FG is to be sought, not so much in its explicit statements but in its presumptions, its *Vorverstandnis*. The Instruction of the Biblical Commission observes justly a propos of this that the philosophical and theological options which inspire the School, often come to vitiate it, either the method itself, or its literary conclusions. To be sure, if it stated, as does Bultmann, that the Incarnation, the resurrection and the miracles are unacceptable, because they have no meaning for modern man formed by science, it must be concluded that the evangelical accounts which propose such things as realities of history, belong to the literary genre of legend and of myth.

IV. Three Major Problems

The great merit of the School of Forms has been to provide us with a strict method of literary analysis of the Gospels and means of coming, through the study of the texts, to the mileux which saw them born. This progress, however, has not come about without bringing forth some grave problems.

1) In regard to the past, FG exaggerated the hiatus between Jesus and Christ, between the pre-paschal community and the post-paschal community. Criticism should ask whether such a position is founded on history. It should make precise the nature and degree of continuity which join these two communities.

2) FG exaggerating the creative power of the primitive community, has deformed the image of the Church. The school studied especially the *sociological* milieu of the primitive community and its *external* activity. But it neglected the most important study of its interior comportment, its profound convictions which inspire its attitudes and its conduct. In fact, instead of imagining a creative community, semi-conscious and but little scrupulous, there ought, following a sound historical method, have been researched in the texts what knowledge this contemporaneous community of the Gospels could have of its historical relation to Jesus. The primitive Church, does it live under the sign of fidelity to Jesus or of creative imagination? By having neglected extra-evangelical literature, FG deprived itself, on this point, of a priceless support.

3) In regard to the evangelists, the school of forms has quite simply misunderstood their role. Absorbed by the study of primary units, it was not sufficiently concerned about the final composition of the Gospels.

The study of these three major problems corresponds to the first three critical *verifications* of our demonstration.

Footnotes for Chapter X

1. Cf. W.G. Kummel, *Einleitung in das Neue Testament* (Heidelberg, 1967), p. 15.
2. To simplify, we will use from now on FG for *Formgeschichte* and RG for *Redaktionsgeschihte*
3. A. Descamps, "Progres et continuite dans la critique des Evangiles et des Actes," *Revue theologique de Louvain* 1 (1970) 27-29.
4. *Ibid.,* 29-30.
5. Thus, in the Gospel of Mark, the account of the Eucharist, which had first a liturgical context, makes part of the course of events which lead to the tragic end of Jesus (Mk. 14:22-25). Cf. X. Leon-Dufour, *Passion, DBS* (1960) 1456-1458.
6. X. Leon-Dufour, *Les Evangiles et l'histoire de Jesus* (Paris, 1963), pp. 266-279.
7. V. Taylor, *The Formation of the Gospel Tradition* (London 1933), pp. 41-43.

Chapter XI

JESUS AND HIS DISCIPLES OR THE PRE—PASCHAL COMMUNITY

The primitive Church constitutes the meeting-point between Jesus and the evangelists. They, in their turn, assure continuity between the primitive Church and us. But if there is a hiatus, from the beginning, between Jesus the preacher and the Christ preached, between Jesus and the primitive Church, who can assure us that the kerygma is still the Gospel of Jesus? The *first critical verification* consists in defining the relationship really existing between the pre-paschal community, on the one hand, and the post-paschal community, on the other. Between these two groups and these two moments, it is possible there is a veritable continuity, not only of time, but also of "tradition?"

It is known that FG is interested before all else in the community after the Pasch. Bultmann holds even that the sole real problem of primitive Christianity is the reconstruction of the life of this community. The problem of "the real history" of Jesus is of no interest. He says, further, the most ancient stage that can be reached by way of criticism, is that of the Palestinian community.

The researchers of FG have as their point of departure the community of faith born on The Pasch, the life and attitudes of which it studies. But the question arises immediately: Is it admissible that the history of Christianity began thus with paschal faith, and that this faith is responsible for the whole Christian tradition? Kasemann, as has been seen, energetically, combatted this idea of a real discontinuity of tradition, and showed the inconsistency of such a position. However, he did not establish, by a genuine proof that a continuity of tradition is something not only possible, but highly probable. H. Schurmann[1] posed this question and endeavored to anwer it. Counter to Bultmann, he holds that there exists between the group of the disciples of Jesus and the post-paschal community, not only a continuity of "remembrance" (a rather fragile ethereal bridge), but a real continuity of *tradition*, including the transmission of a message and of an activity. Besides he holds that the fact of this continuity can be scientifically established by the very method and techniques of FG. If the School of Forms, continues Schurmann, has not pushed its research up to the study of the pre-paschal milieu, it is not on account of the limitations of its method, but out of motives of a dogmatic order. Indeed, according to Bultmann, it is not possible to have tradition if there is no faith, for it is faith which marks the beginning of a community and determines the laws of transmission of this tradition. Now Christian faith did not begin until after the Pasch. The School of Forms in this way places a screen before its eyes which makes it short-sighted. It is like a camera set to take pictures of nearby objects, but at a distance. Why not, rather, try to see what is distant, without being blinded by the light of the Pasch? Perhaps we will in this way see a certain number of objects stand out on the more distant horizon of the historical Jesus before the Pasch.

I. Starting point and method

The starting point of Schurmann's reflection is a minimal but irrefutable fact, even for a radical supporter of FG, that is, that Jesus during His public life, had disciples, and that this group of Jesus and His own constituted a "community." Of itself, this phenomenon implies already an effective continuity between the periods before and after the Pasch, and authorizes important conclusions.

It is undeniable equally that this first community constitutes a definite milieu *(Sitz im Leben)*, with its own activities. Thenceforth, there is question of knowing whether this pre-pascha milieu is truly typical and is distinguished from the post-paschal *Sitz im Leben.* The accent, as is seen, is less on Jesus than on the community gathered around Him, and on the activities and attitudes which characterize it. In particular, there is question of knowing whether the attitudes of this community are of a nature which favors the faithful conservation of the words of Jesus.

At this moment there reappears Bultmann's well known objection: Between the community before and the community after Pasch, there is certainly a temporal and sociological continuity, but there is a real discontinuity, for faith intervenes as a new decisive, element, creative of a new community. To this objection, Schurmann replies (as does Kasemann also) that it could not be reasonable to speak of a purely sociological community, for the sole fact that a group of persons set out to follow Jesus, and that this group constitutes a "community" of disciples, obliges us to think that, before the Pasch, there existed an adherence of belief in the word and the person of Jesus. That there is a discontinuity between the two moments, is something too evident. But it is undeniable, on the other hand, that sociological continuity implies already a continuity of adherence to Jesus.

The experience of the Pasch, then of Pentecost, gave to the belief of the disciples, as also to their predication, a new clarity, depth and support. But this discontinuity is not a hiatus. Evidently, for anyone who declares impossible the existence, before the Pasch, of every form of belief, it is useless to speak of continuity of tradition. But in virtue of such a psychological, sociological or historical principle, can it be asserted that such an attitude of faith is impossible? Is it not, on the contrary, more coherent to think that belief in Christ after the Pasch was only possible because, precisely before the Pasch, there already existed in the hearts of the disciples a belief at the very least embryonic, imperfect, but quite real? To acknowledge the

Pasch as a messianic "accomplishment," there had to be at the very least the suspicion of a messianic "coming."

If an adherence to Jesus (which most assuredly has not the absoluteness of post-paschal belief, but is not always real and profound in it) unites the group of disciples of before and of after the Pasch, it is quite legitimate to conceive of a continuity of tradition. Consequently, FG, on restricting its researches to the postpaschal period, makes an unjustifiable renunciation and reduction. FG has no other motive than its dogmatic veto.

So Schurmann proposes, starting out from the method and techniques of FG, to explore the pre-paschal period. He says, that it is an essential project for, to prove the existence of a continuity of tradition is the only means of going back from the post-paschal community to the group of the disciples of Jesus and to Jesus Himself.[2]

A first characteristic of originality, in Schurmann's project, is therefore to study the pre-paschal community starting out from the very method of the School of Forms. A second characteristic consists in distinguishing, in this community, a double *Sitz im Leben*: the one, *external*, constituted by the visible situations and activities of this community, such as the liturgical, ministerial and catechetical life; the other, *internal*, constituted by the interpersonal relationships which unite the members of this community, in the profession of one and the same faith and respect for the same values. FG studied the external *Sitz im Leben*, but neglected to study the spirit which animated the community. Yet, it is these internal bonds and this spirit which are formally the motivating factors suited to arouse, maintain and assure the faithful transmission of a tradition. In his study, Schurmann gives equal attention to this double *Sitz im Leben*: external and internal.

II. The Community of Jesus and His Disciples:

Internal *Sitz im Leben*

In a first period, Schurmann studies the milieu constituted by the intimate life of Jesus and His disciples: in other terms, the internal *Sitz im Leben* of the pre-paschal community.

Even in a reductive perspective, no one could deny that Jesus preached and had disciples, chosen and formed by Him. Jesus welcomed the crowds, but He chose His disciples. The tradition on this point is firm. On many an occasion, Jesus makes an appeal to the men whom He has picked out and recruited to be His companions. Of these good men, He demands they leave all to attach themselves to Him and share His labor.

This group made up of Jesus and His own forms a community "apart," distinct from the surrounding environs, precisely because the disciples follow the Master closely and have faith in Him. This community is not of an occasional nature, fostered by passing encounters, but one that presents a characteristic of stability. The whole tradition presents us with the image of Jesus who is never separated from His disciples. To be attached to Jesus is concretely to follow an itinerant preacher. Jesus does not teach as a rabbi, in the setting of a synagogue. He preaches along the highways, He passes from village to village, He traverses Galilee, then Judea. When the Kingdom is about to come, it is not the time to sit down, to settle down, but to warn all the people. The disciples share the precarious life of Jesus. They are always with Him and, consequently, become the witnesses of His life and of His teaching.[3]

This stable presence of "disciples" about Jesus is not a spontaneous fact. It postulates a cause. This cause, beyond the call of Jesus, is their belief in His word. Let us make clear that the decisive element of this belief was not, at the beginning at least, the perception in Jesus of some christological attribute, but the esteem and admiration felt for His word, proposed by Him as the final word of God before the end of time. Jesus appears as the bearer of the definitive revelation of God. On the level of teaching, His authority strikes His hearers. No one has spoken as this man. On the level of action, His prestige is unprecedented: Never have we seen anything like it. The attestations about the impact produced by the appearance of Jesus are of incontestable historicity.

Such is the milieu in which the teaching of Jesus resounded. The men, called by Him, are grouped about Him and live in closest intimacy with Him. They are won over by Him, fascinated by His word. How to think, afterwards, they would have let this word evaporate or sink into oblivion? The familiarity with such a Master authorizes us rather to think that they preserved the treasure of His word with a sovereign respect and that they did everything possible to guard it unchanged.

If we admit the belief (in the sense of a profound attachment) of the disciples in the word of Jesus, we are in the possession of an important methodological principle, that is, that the word of Jesus, as such, was deemed worthy of being preserved and transmitted, and, as a matter of fact, *could* be, by reason of the intimacy of life of Jesus and His own. Such a *Sitz im Leben* suffices to explain the interest for the words of Jesus, as well as the interest to preserve them. Further, the very fact that the *logia* of Jesus have been transmitted to us, is already a sign of this esteem and interest. Attachment to Jesus explains in particular the preservation of *logia* which could with difficulty be understood while Jesus was living, since they were deliberately obscure and prophetic, quite oriented toward the future. Let us think especially of the *logia* concerning the tragic destiny of Jesus. Invented after the Pasch, they would not have been able to preserve the enigmatic character of such discourses.

The belief of the disciples in the word of Jesus explains not only the "possibility of a tradition," but even the very physiognomy of this tradition. In fact, the attitude of a community in regard to the word of a rabbi, or of a sage, differs necessarily from that which is adopted toward a prophet, a fortiori toward a messianic and eschatological prophet. That disciples gather around a teacher, or a sage, or a chief, or a prophet, or a messianic figure, is not at all an identical phenomenon. The figure which becomes the center of attraction of this community, determines right away the kind of adherence to the person and the firmness of the tradition he engenders.

Now it is clear that Jesus was, for His disciples, more than a rabbi or a sage, and that the circle of His disciples could not liken itself to that of teachers of Israel. The pre-paschal community belongs rather to one made up of prophets and their disciples. The analogy is to be found in this direction. The word of Jesus, in fact, resounds as the decisive word, as the ultimate revelation of God at the supreme hour of the imminent coming of the Kingdom. And, on the other hand, the personality of Jesus imposes itself as that of a prophet, much more than as that of the greatest among them. Jesus conducts Himself as a gatherer of men, as the shepherd who leads His flock.

There is conceived the importance from then on for the disciples to preserve, even more than the literary form, the message itself of Jesus in its original content. The characteristic of urgency and of unicity of this message constitutes a guarantee of a fidelity much superior to that of all rabbinical techniques, without denying thereby that Jesus had recourse to the mnemotechnical means in use in that epoch.

Briefly, a) the intimate community of Jesus and the disciples called by Him, in its stable and permanent form; b) the attachment of the disciples to the prestigious personality of Jesus, soul of this community, center of attraction and of the cohesiveness of the group; c) the authority of His unique and decisive word. These convergent traits constitute a *Sitz im Leben* which is internal, sufficing to explain the possibility and effective continuity of a tradition of the words and deeds of Jesus.

III. The pre-paschal activity of the disciples: External Sitz im Leben

The study of the internal *Sitz im Leben* does not make superfluous the study of the external *Sitz im Leben*. On the contrary, both mutually clarify each other. Understanding of the intimate life of the community opens up to us the meaning of its external activity. This, in turn, reveals to us factors which assure the process of tradition a fresh consistency. Two of these factors are the ministerial activity of the disciples and the exigencies of the pre-paschal community life.

1) Schurmann's thesis is that Jesus preached and presented His message with the precise intention of providing His disciples with a suitable instrument, in view of a ministerial activity to perform, not only after the Pasch, but while He was still living, as ambassadors and preachers of the Kingdom. If, indeed, Jesus addressed a particular appeal to the men whom he selected to be His companion, this appeal signifies without any doubt at all that they will have a part in His religious mission. A good portion of the logia which have been handed down to us, proceeds, it seems, from this intention of furnishing the disciples with an instrument of evangelization. In regard to this, the *mission* of the apostles before the Pasch constitutes a *Sitz im Leben* particularly important for understanding the origin and the process of transmission of the evangelical tradition.

It seems, indeed, probable that Jesus gave to His words a special "force," with the precise intent precisely to impress them in the memories of His disciples. The very fact of one or likely more "missions" of disciples before the Pasch, authorizes us to think that Jesus truly had this in mind. Thus, the parables, with their incisive character, seem destined to be developed and interpreted according to the diversity of situations. They are presented in a "typical" original situation, in order that they may later be taken up again, explained and made relevant indefinitely.

If Jesus proposes to entrust to His disciples a "mission" without Him and as early as before the Pasch, He must prepare them, the more so since there are involved men lacking in culture and education, or rather men belonging to a milieu of oral culture, in which there are memorized the psalms, the law, the prophets. In this context, the sole means for Jesus to avoid His message of salvation and His moral demands being degraded and "banalized," was to present them in a more or less stereotype form.

Matthew, Mark and Luke relate that Jesus, after an important period of ministry carried out among His disciples, sends them out on a mission (Mt 6:7). On this point, some authors, such as Dibelius and Bornkamm are in agreement with Catholic exegetes acknowledging that the disciples shared the activity of Jesus, before the Pasch. The intention of Jesus to send His own on a mission is attested to in Mark (3:14-15; 6:7), as also in the instructions He gave about their mission, (Mt 10:5-6; Lk 10:8-12) of which the main point represents a very ancient core. The context, the wordage, the train of thought in this discourse, reflect in fact a pre-paschal situation. The collaboration of the disciples in the activity of Jesus is expressed through the power given them, on the one hand, to preach, on the other, to expel demons and to heal: two powers and two activities equally part of the ministry of Jesus.[4] On returning from their mission, the apostles, reunited around Jesus, tell Him all they have done and everything they have taught (Mk 6:30).

This first preaching by the disciples has as its essential themes the announcement of the Kingdom (Mk 1:15; Mt 10:7) and the exhortation to penitence (Mk 6:12).

The subject of the Kingdom was surely developed and explained. To it may be affixed the triple blessing on the poor (Lk 6:20-21), the parables of the Kingdom, the logia on the imminent coming of the Kingdom (Lk 13:18-21; Mk 4:2-9; 26-29), on the end which is coming (Lk 17:34 ff). Let us add that the announcing of the Kingdom is unthinkable without the accompaniment of the *sign* of its coming. How indeed, could Jesus send His disciples to preach so unheard of *Tidings* without providing them with arguments capable of opening the eyes and ears of those who heard them? These signs were, in the perspective of the messianic promises, the liberation of the possessed and the healing of the sick, in strict liaison with the announcement of salvation (Lk 11:20; Mk 3:27). Finally, it was impossible to preach the Kingdom without referring to Jesus Himself in whom the Kingdom is at the same time announced and made present. The theme of penitence, seemingly, was still more strongly stressed than that of the Kingdom, with all related themes: necessity of vigilance, threats of judgment against the unbelief and impenitence of Israel. All these logia and so many others, in the unpublished content, have been the matter of the mission or the missions of the disciples, and the elements of a tradition constituted before the Pasch.

2) A second factor suitable for explaining the formation and transmission of a tradition is the undeniable fact of a *life in common*. Without doubt, the group of the first disciples had no definite rule, such as had the sect of Quamran, but it had its norms of life meant for strengthening the bonds between the members. The disciples must leave family, goods, profession to attach themselves to an itinerant preacher and follow Him everywhere. This radicalism of Jesus is explained by the fact that His call is addressed to the men who must devote themselves entirely to the Kingdom. To this demand of communitarian life is connected a whole ensemble of logia which we can arrange in three groups:

a) Words directed to justify the risk of following Jesus and to strengthen the courage of the wavering. Certain logia (for instance: Lk 9:60, 62; 14:28-32) expressing the demands of Jesus directed to those who wish to follow Him have so radical, so sharp a tone that they are explained only in the pre-paschal context of a material following of Jesus.

b) A group of precepts directly concerning the disciples, although they still retain their full meaning after the Pasch, are much better explained in a pre-paschal context (Lk 12:22-31, 33; 10:4-7).

c) A last group of logia can be considered the "rules of the community" of those who have faith in Jesus. For instance, the invitation to conduct oneself as the servant and the last one of all the brethren (Mk 9:35; Lk 22:27).

IV. Estimate of a research

1) The origin and the transmission of the logia of Jesus began before the Pasch, in the very circle of the disciples of Jesus. FG is mistaken in confining itself to the study of the post-paschal community. Without a doubt it is interested in the early logia, but it is disinterested in the community whence they came to light. Schurmann has shown that it is now possible by the very techniques of the method of FG to establish that the *transmission* of the logia of Jesus has its origins in the group of disciples of Jesus. The initiator of the transmission is Jesus Himself, as is attested in 1Jn 1:1 ff; Lk 1:2; Acts 1:21-22. Through the pre-paschal community there is access to Jesus. If the transmission rested exclusively on Pasch and Pentecost, without being able to go back to the Jesus of history and to the circle of His disciples, it would not rest on an historical datum. It would be hardly distinct from a gnosis.

2) The principal merit of Schurmann is having applied the method of the School of Forms to the study of the pre-paschal milieu, having distinguished in it a *Sitz im Leben* at the same time external and internal, and having shown that the undeniable discontinuity presented by the Pasch, does not prevent an undeniable continuity of adherence to the word and person of Jesus, as well as a continuity of ministerial activity. After the Pasch, Jesus is better known, better understood. His word reveals itself more clearly as being the word of the Lord. There follows that His authority, far from diminishing, even increases. Adherence to His word gains in depth. The preaching of the Kingdom goes on, but becomes more precise. The Kingdom announced by the prophets, after centuries, has now arrived. There is no hiatus, but continuity and depth. The momentary discontinuity does not wipe out memories nor break the continuity of the process of tradition and fidelity to Jesus. Pasch is not an atom bomb which annihilated everything, but a flame which illumined all.

3) Another merit of Schurmann is that of having opened the way to a similar undertaking, this time concerning the post-paschal community. FG, in fact, in its researches on the

primitive community, neglected to study the *interior* attitudes which inspire and direct that community's external activity. Now, it is the knowledge of these attitudes and profound convictions which enables us to qualify the ecclesial milieu as faithful or unfaithful to Jesus. Schurmann himself did not study the internal *Sitz im Leben* of the post-paschal community, but his works have made such an undertaking possible.

4) Without doubt Schurmann, in the analysis of the external *Sitz im Leben, would have been able to complete and strengthen his exposition by studying, not only the discourse of mission, but also the accounts of calling and the numerous logia of the tradition of the sequela Jesu.* His basic argumentation no less keeps its validity and succeeds in establishing that a veritable continuity, not only temporal and sociological, but also of *tradition*, that is, of adherence, activity and message, is possible and highly probably between the pre-paschal and the post-paschal community. It brings about at one stroke the first of the critical verifications which our exposition presents.

Footnotes for Chapter XI

1. H. Schurmann, "Die vorosterlichen Anfange der Logientradition, in H. Ristow und K. Matthiae, ed. *Der historische Jesus und der kerygmatische Christus* (Berlin, 1962), pp. 342-370. In this chapter we follow, in essentials, Schurmann's exposition. On a certain number of points, however, we complement his exposition by A. Descamps' excellent article "Aux origines du ministere. La pensée de Jesus," *Revue théologique de Louvain* II (1971) 3-45. For other interesting material cf. M. Hengel, *Nachfolge und Charisma. Eine exegetisch-religionsgeschichtliche Studie zur Mtt. 8, 21f und Jesu Ruf in die Nachfolge* (Berlin, 1968).
2. Without excluding however the medium of properly called historical criteriology.
3. A. Descamps, *art. cit.* 29-32.
4. V. Taylor, "The Mission of the Twelve" in *The Life and Ministry of Jesus*, pp. 113-119.

Chapter XII

SPEECH AND ATTITUDES OF THE PRIMITIVE ECCLESIAL MILIEU (I)

Even if it is established, with Schurmann, that there is real continuity of tradition between the pre-paschal and the post-paschal community, it has not however been verified that, undergoing changes and the event having happened so long ago, the ecclesial milieu evolved and maintained itself under the sign of fidelity to Jesus. On the other hand, even if it is established that the evangelists, in spite of an evident compositional freedom, but one which was controllable, were substantially faithful to their sources, it must well be acknowledged that, behind the written sources used by them, there is ever found the same one and only source, that is, the ecclesial milieu in which the evangelical tradition was formed and developed. No matter with what kind of bias the problem of the Gospels is addressed, it is always brought back to this fundamental question: What is the nature of the ecclesial milieu, matrix and nurturer of the tradition? This question, since it involves the very intervention of the Church, in her twofold relation to Jesus and to the evangelists, is even more pointed than that of the relationship between the pre- and post-paschal communities. The *critical verification* of the primitive Church to Jesus is the second major point of our exposition.

It is here, we think, that Schurmann's distinction between

Sitz im Leben—external and *internal*—finds a new application and a new fruitfulness. The School of Forms studied especially the sociological environment (external *Sitz im Leben*) of the primitive Church, in its liturgical, missionary, cathechetical activity. This analysis has its importance, but it only reveals a portion of the reality. The same happens for the post-paschal community as for the pre-paschal community. What is most important is to know its interior attitudes and the spirit and mentality which inspires its external behavior. In this regard, observes Gerhardsson,[1] it may be astonishing that not one of the pioneers of the School of Forms, Dibelius and Bultmann, paid any attention to the concept of "tradition," even though so fundamental for understanding the Christianity of the years 30-50.

Therefore there is question, by a kind of psychoanalysis, of perceiving what are the spontaneous reflexes, and we might also say, visceral reflexes, of the primitive community in regard to Jesus and His word and, consequently, the psychological and mental structure of this community. We think it is possible to undertake such a research, by means of semantics, starting out from the *words* the frequency of which is such, in the nascent Church, that they fill in some way the whole horizon of Christian consciousness and express its profound orientation. We appeal to the texts which directly describe the primitive Christian environment, that is the Epistles of Paul and the Acts of the Apostles. The reference to Jesus, in this literature, though less direct than that in the Gospels, is not less significative. We know indeed that a community, just as an individual, betrays or better reveals itself through its *speech*, in the choice of terms it uses[2]. Let us make clear that, to be really informative, these words must reach not only a high degree of recurrence, but must appear in important contexts. In the present case, it is to be known whether the mentality shown by the basic vocabulary of the Epistles of Paul and the Acts, goes on in the sense of fidelity to Jesus, or of creative fiction, or fable.

If we, through the study of favored words, arrive at a determination of the *internal Sitz im Leben* of the primitive community (tendencies, attitudes, convictions, mentality), we are in possession of an important norm for appreciating the quality of the ecclesial environment in which the evangelical tradition was formed and developed. The fidelity of the evangelists to the Church is vouched for by the very fidelity of the Church to Jesus. We shall therefore have demonstrated not only that there is a continuity of Jesus to the Church, but also a continuity of the Church to Jesus, for the attitude of the young Church, in the years in which the tradition is formed, remained radically that of fidelity.

Among the words which thus show the attitude of the primitive Church in regard to Jesus, we can distinguish three groups which form about Jesus, three concentric zones. The first, general, but very early, is related to the idea of tradition: *receive* (paralambanein) and transmits (paradidonai); the second concerns the immediate collaborators of Jesus: *witness* (martus), *apostle* (apostolos) and *service* (Diakonia) of the word; the third concerns the most extensive and universal activity of all preachers of the Gospel: *teach* (didaskein), *proclaim* (kerussein), *evangelize (euangelizasthai), Gospel* (euangelion). In the examination into these words, there is less involved an exhaustive semantic investigation than to grasp how these key words and this basic vocabulary of the primitive Church give us access to the Christian consciousness and subconsciousness before Jesus.

I. Paradosis or tradition

1) *Receiving and transmitting in the Epistles of Paul*
The Epistles of Paul, which go back to the years 50-60, that is before the composition of the Gospels, attest to the whole importance of this category in Christian consciousness. The substantive *tradition* (paradosis) is found 12 times in the New Testament and designates the content of transmission. The verb transmit (paradidonai) is found 120 times, in various senses. In relation to paradosis or tradition, it designates the act of transmitting. This transmission is found in reference to

institutions passed on orally (Mk 7:3, 4, 5, 9), or a teaching communicated by other persons (1Cor 15:3).

Paul, as is known, was first a Pharisee and, as such, a faithful observer of the Tradition written or oral of the Torah: "You have heard, I know . . . of my progress in Jewish observance far beyond most of my contemporaries, in my excess of zeal to live out all the traditions of my ancestors." (Gal 1:13-14). Paul abandoned these traditions to take on that of Jesus. However, when he designed this new tradition, he preserved the terminology he received from Judaism: *receive* (paralambanein) and *transmit* (paradidonai). The apostle has nothing of his own. He received all he must transmit, even the authority which confers on him the power to transmit. In the Epistle to the Galatians, he, the most independent of the apostles, states that he submitted his Gospel to the Church of Jerusalem to confirm its authenticity and "to make sure the course I was pursuing, or had pursued, was not useless" (Gal 2:1-6).

Paul established a strict correspondence between *receive* and *transmit*, notably in two important passages which concern the resurrection (1Cor 15:3) and the Last Supper (1Cor 11:23). The identity of the received and the transmitted emphasizes Paul's fidelity in carrying out his mission. The content of the tradition in the texts mentioned, is the essential mysteries of salvation and their profound meaning: Supper, passion, death, resurrection. The authority of the paradosis derives from the fact that the Apostle faithfully transmits what he received—the mission of transmitting: "It makes us ambassadors for Christ, God, as it were appealing through us." (2Cor 5:20).

In many another passage, there is found, if not the same terms, at least the same attitude. Thus, the Thessalonians should act according to what they "received" from Paul: "You know the instructions we *gave* you in the Lord Jesus" *(didonai)* (1Th 4:2). They are urged to be faithful: "Hold fast to the *traditions* you received from us, either by word or by letter" (2Th 2:15; 3:6). To the Philippians, he writes: "Live according to what you have learned and accepted, what you have heard and seen me do" (Ph 4:9). He compliments the Corinthians who keep the "traditions" he "transmitted" (1Cor 11:2). He praises the Colossians for their fidelity: "Continue, therefore, to live in Christ Jesus the Lord, in the spirit in which you received him. Be rooted in him and built up in him, growing ever stronger in faith as you were taught" (Col 2:6-7). On the contrary, he accuses those who have abandoned the Gospel he preached: "If anyone preaches a gospel to you other than the one you received, let a curse be upon him!" (Gal 1:9). To abandon the tradition of the Gospel of Paul, is equivalent to abandoning the Gospel of Christ.

It is not by chance that Paul uses the terminology of the Jewish paradosis: He indicates thereby that the action of *receiving* and of *transmitting*, in a Christian milieu, resembles the manner of transmission used in Judaism. The second Epistle to Timothy contains another example of the Jewish and rabbinical influence on the Pauline concept of the paradosis. Every tradition which claims to be authentic, must produce the uninterrupted list of those who transmitted it. The Epistle to Timothy enumerates five of the links of the tradition: Christ (2Tm:10), Paul, apostle and teacher (2Tm 1, 2), Timothy, disciple of Paul (2Tm 1:6), then the faithful (2Tm 2:2) and other man (2Tm 2:2). On thus listing the witnesses of the tradition, without interruption, Paul manifests its fidelity and, consequently, its authenticity and authority.

In the pastoral epistles, we find, instead of paradosis, which betrays a rabbinic origin, the term *paratheke*, borrowed from the Greek juridical vocabulary. The exhortation to fidelity becomes: "Take as a model of sound teaching what you have heard me say, in faith and love in Christ Jesus. Guard the rich deposit" (2Tm 1:14).

If we analyze the data thus collected in the epistles of Paul on the paradosis, we ascertain that the term at times designates those condensed formulas of Christian faith which are the first "credo" (1Cor 15:3 ff.). These formulas Paul received as the nucleus of his Gospel. He hands them down just as he received them, showing he is not the master but the servant of the word. In the Jewish and rabbinical concept to which it belongs, the category of *paralembenein-paradosis* implies an attitude of fidelity to what is received and transmitted. It is not one of believing, of innovating, of transforming, but of transmitting. The word reveals a mentality and a milieu dominated to concern to preserve the word received, like a deposit, a heritage. The authenticity of the tradition is assured by the qualified chain of "transmitter," which goes from Christ to the apostles, from the apostles to their disciples and from them to the faithful. It must be emphasized that Paul's tradition, as that of Jesus (Ac 1:1) is made up of deeds and examples, as well as of instructions (Ph 4:9). A community which lives thus under the sign of the paradosis, lives under the sign of fidelity and of risk-taking innovation.[3]

2) *Tradition in rabbinic Judaism*

In his epistles St. Paul has preserved and applied to the Christian tradition the vocabulary of the rabbinical tradition. So two representatives of the school of Upsala, H. Riesenfeld and especially B. Gerhardsson, his pupils, largely basing themselves on this, have studied methodically the nature and means of the transmission of the Jewish tradition. This tradition is found in the written Torah and in the oral Torah which comments on, interprets and amplifies the written Torah, notably in matter of penal law.

The written Torah, or Pentateuch, is the object of extreme veneration. Three types of institutions assure its faithful transmission. First, there are the professional copyists, thoroughly trained. Then, there are the elementary schools where there is taught the reading and memorizing of the sacred text with no altercation. Finally, there is the public reading, in the Temple or in the synagogue, of the written Law.

Gerhardsson then studies with particular attention the transmission of the oral Torah, that is, the commentaries and interpretations of the Law made by the great rabbis. Higher institutions assure the fidelity of this transmission. The origin of these schools remains obscure, but they appear as the prolongation and development of many centuries old institutions in Israel (for instance the Recabites, in times of

Jeremiah, the Nazarenes, the disciples of the prophets.

The methodical and controlled transmission of the Torah is entrusted to the *Tannaim*. These specialists in memorizing—a veritable living library are at the disposition of the students. The ideal of these *Tannaim* is to be, as it were, a tank which does not lose a single drop of water it contains.

At the base of rabbinical pedagogy for transmitting the Torah, there are two principles. Above all, is *memorization*. Under the direction of his teacher, the pupil memorizes the text, section by section, and repeats it indefinitely. Our civilization of "printed paper" can hardly conceive the efficaciousness of such a pedagogy. And, yet, not very far back is the period when the press dethroned memory and oral tradition. For a long time, mankind progressed through the spoken word. Even today, a good part of mankind entrusts its cultural patrimony to the memory. Indians, Greeks, Romans, Jews, all the great civilizations were first memorizers. The laws, the sacred books and the great classics were memorized. They were first memorized and then commented on.

The second principle of this pedagogy is to preserve *unaltered* the text thus memorized. Gerhardsson studies the techniques employed for assuring this faithful transmission of the *ipsissima verba* of the Law. These are the usage of resumes or summaries, rhymed sequences, parallelisms, anti-theses, key words, recourse at the beginning to a proverb which brings to mind the doctrine explained by what follows. Most of these techniques are now found in the psalms or in the prophetical books. The essential technique is repetition. A rabbi never stops repeating the Law. It is ever on his lips.

The rabbinical tradition preserves not only the teaching of the great masters, but also their decisions, their manner of acting and their examples. The pupil learns in this way as much by sight as by the word. The teacher's life is the Law in action.

In the second part of his work, Gerhardsson applies these data of the Jewish tradition to the Christian tradition. The existence and the influence of an oral tradition is everywhere attested to in the history of primitive Christianity. It is expressed in the declarations of Papias, Justin, Irenaeus,

Clement of Alexandria, and in the extra-evangelicals of the New Testament, such as the Epistles of St. Paul and the Acts. The conviction is universal that at the origin of the Gospels there is an oral tradition, which is maintained, even after the setting down in writing of the oral Gospel.

Let us sum up the conclusions Gerhardsson reached at the end of his study.[4]

1) His basic thesis, which is equally that of Riesenfeld, is that Christianity did not begin with the preaching of the Church, but with Jesus and the holy Tradition of His words and deeds.[5] The Gospel of Jesus Christ is not only the Good Tidings concerning Jesus Christ, but also the Good Tidings brought by Jesus Christ.

2) But Jesus Himself could not be understood without reference to the Jewish tradition to which He belonged. Jesus was born and lived in a Jewish environment. He is rooted in it by His history and His whole earthly existence. He was nourished by the Law, He memorized and chanted the psalms. He came, not to abolish the Law, but to accomplish it.

3) From the beginning of His preaching, He is considered as a Teacher in Israel. And nothing warrants our thinking that His methods of teaching differed from those in usage at that time. As the rabbis, He teaches in the synogogues and in public places, by His examples as well as by His words. Familiar with the Torah, He comments on it and interprets it. Also like the rabbis, He had to train His pupils to memorize His teaching. Everything invites us to believe that the veneration of the pupils for the Teacher contributed to assure the faithful transmission of His words and deeds.

4) Gerhardsson rightly makes us observe that the Twelve remained in Jerusalem for fifteen or twenty years, that is, throughout the whole period of the formation of the evangelical tradition. They teach in the name of Jesus and testify to what they saw and heard. The faithful, on their part, "devoted themselves to the apostles' instruction" (Acts 2:42). It is this environment, dominated by the presence and influence of the College of the Twelve, which makes us think of the rabbinical schools, that fixed the tradition about Jesus.

5) This tradition was developed according to two preferred forms. a) One was the form of the *midrash*, equally used in the apocalyptical circles and in the sect of Qumram, that is, the interpretation of Scripture in the light of the teaching of Jesus and of the new ecclesial experience; b) the other was under the form of response to doctrinal questions and to problems of life raised by the members of the community: a response drawn from Scripture and from the tradition of Jesus. In this task of interpretation and of relevance, the logia of Jesus are evoked, repeated, explained, following the practice of rabbinal circles. Also there is evoked the behavior of the Teacher in the diverse situations of His earthly existence (for instance His polemics with the leaders of the nation).

6) Jesus being considered as the Teacher par excellence, much more than as Messiah, the young Church accords His words an authority incomparably superior to that of the rabbis. It is remarkable, at any rate, that His logia were never confused with those of other rabbis. They constitute a unique case.

7) The logia of Jesus have been collected according to diverse principles of classification. Most often, the unit is based on the same theme (parables of the Kingdom, counsels to the ministers, accounts of miracles), or quite simply based on a mnemotechnical medium such as key word, antithesis, parallelism etc. The logia of Jesus circulate from mouth to mouth, following a pedagogy of which Christ Himself is the initiator.

8) After having so strongly emphasized the normative fidelity of the oral transmission, Gehardsson had to explain the actual variants of the logia and the diverse versions of one and the same event. On this point, he is brief. These variants, he says, can derive from the very teaching of Jesus, or from attempts later on to make the tradition relevant, or from the compositional activity of the evangelists. One thing is certain, when they undertake to compose their Gospel, they make use of a material already consistent, that is, the Tradition *of* Jesus *on* Jesus, written or oral, but clearly distinct from the teaching

of the rabbis.

3) *Judeo-Christian tradition and other milieux of oral culture*
    Before making a judgment of the worth of Gerhardsson's contribution to the understanding of the concept of *tradition* in primitive Christianity, it seems to us useful to compare this Judeo-Christian milieu with the civilization of oral culture, contemporaneous with Judaism, or at least governed by the same laws. This is the case of India, of Africa and of the countries of Europe where the great epic poems were born. These comparisons, no matter how brief they are, are illuminating.
    1) The *Vedas*, or sacred books of Hinduism, go back to the years 1,000 to 200 B.C. These books, as also most of the sacred books of India, which make up a veritable library, were handed down orally. The fidelity of this transmission is extreme, assured as it is by a severe training of teachers and students. These texts were handed down without notable alteration for centuries, thanks to a number of strict techniques: counting the meters and the words, repetition of the text on reversing the order of the words etc. These procedures show the profound concern to preserve in their full integrity the sacred traditions of the country. The attitude of Hinduism in regard to its traditions is rightly compared with that of Judaism in regard to the Law, so much the more since both religious currents are parallel in time.
    2) J. Vansina, in his study of the oral tradition in the African environment,[6] especially in the Congo, observes that the texts of a religious and ritual character were brought there with an exceptional fidelity. In the popular mentality, to alter the words would be to expose themselves to the worst supernatural sanctions. Also, the ritual formulas were memorized and recited most carefully, most of the time by specialists (priests and sorcerers). The motive and the guarantee of this fidelity is the religious nature of the source. Religious poetry, as well as the great myths in which the concept of the universe, share the same fidelity.[7]
    3) A. Lord,[8] after having studied the Slavic and Greek

poems (Odyssey and Iliad), as well as the medieval songs of heroic acts (of Roland, of Beowulf), concludes that the dynamism explaining the faithful preservation of the great poems is the profound conviction that the tradition which they carry, contains the secret of life and happiness. All the oral techniques are at the service of this conviction. The artist lets himself be seduced by the literary form. Right away the dynamism of the tradition is weakened and fidelity feels the effects. The singer of the epic poems, is not an artist but a seer. The models of thought he has inherited were conceived, not to serve art, but religion, in the most profound sense. The techniques of memorization are all at the service of this ultimate purpose.

By a variety of approaches we are led to one and the same conclusion. We see that in areas of oral culture, religious traditions are the object of an exceptional veneration and preservation. These environments are of a preservative type and the techniques of memorization are at the service of the religious message.

In this much wider perspective of the history of religions in an area of oral culture, what is to be thought of Gerhardsson's work?

Two main faults have been charged against it. The first[10] (by Morton Smith), is having presented a description of the rabbinical schools which corresponds to the situation of Judaism after 70 rather than to that of the Palestine of the time of Jesus. The objection is only partly justified. As a matter of fact, these rabbinical school after 70 are not the result of spontaneous generation. They have an origin and a preparation which goes back to the Jewish milieux of the Old Testament. These schools, rather, represent a systematization and an apprenticeship of oral techniques which lasted a long time in Israel. Furthermore, these techniques are found in most areas of oral culture. Gerhardsson's excess is rather that of having pressed too far the parallelism between the College of the Twelve and the rabbinical schools. Even if the group of Jesus and His own, later the College of the Twelve, presents an analogy with the rabbinical milieux, it could not be claimed, on the basis of this similitude, that the tradition of Jesus has been handed down with the almost mechanical fidelity of the traditions concerning the Torah. Gerhardsson is over optimistic about the possibility of reaching the *ipsissima verba Jesu*.

This overestimation of the forces of preservation of the techniques of memorization does not take into account another real fact (the second objection, by W.D. Davies), that is, the liberty of the Church in regard to the words and deeds of Jesus. Gerhardsson, in his conclusions, acknowledges, it is true, the phenomena of making relevant and interpreting the Tradition, but he does not suspect the astonishing freedom the primitive Church assumes for probing ever more deeply the original word. He overestimates the dynamism of the oral tradition and underestimates the forces of relevance working in the Church. He confuses historical fidelity with absolute literality of the words of Jesus. Now, the originality of Christianity is not only in the personality and teaching of Jesus, who is more than a Rabbi, but also in the new type of transmission which His presence and the mission He confides to His own authorize.

The rabbinical analogy, however, if it is not pressed to extreme, but set on the much wider horizon of the forces of oral tradition, in a Jewish milieu, qumran, or in the religious milieux of oral tradition (India, Africa and Europe), gives support and consistency to the argument drawn from the Epistles of St. Paul and from the first writing of the Fathers on the effective and efficacious existence of a milieu of oral Tradition in primitive Christianity.

Yet this tradition is more than a phenomenon of memorization and of mechanical transmission (we add this objection to the preceding). It is above all, as the Epistle of St. Paul attests, the expression of a profound mentality. It is by fidelity to Him whom the Catholic Church proclaims as Messiah and Lord that the Church preserves and transmits the words and deeds of Jesus. The existence of such a mentality is not an invention of later Catholicism, but a fact of history. The category of the *paradosis*, as a mentality and a process of transmission is at the heart of the primitive Church. But it is first the interior will of fidelity which inspires and guarantees the fidelity of the process of transmission.

4) *Twofold dynamics of the tradition*

Evangelical tradition represents a unique case, just as Jesus did Himself. It is animated by a twofold dynamism. This is a dynamism of conservation and preservation, joined to an attitude of fidelity and, partly too, to the fact of the transmission of the logia of Jesus in a milieu of oral culture. It is also a dynamism of relevance and of study in depth, linked to the fact that the logia of Jesus must shed light on ever new problems of life.

On the one part, then, dynamism of *conservation*, is attested to by the Epistles of St. Paul. In this regard, it could not be denied that memorization played a capital role in the conservation of the evangelical tradition. In fact, the apostles without having studied in the rabbinical schools, belong to a milieu of oral culture. In such a milieu, the force of memory is in inverse ratio to the habitude one has for writing. Not only are the apostles sons of the synagogue, but they lived in close familiarity with the greatest of Teachers. Here memory is sustained and vivified by the authority of the word.

It cannot be concluded thereby that Jesus is responsible for all the present forms of our Gospels. The obsession of the *ipsissima verba* is vain and contradicted by the facts. The fidelity of the tradition is not of the *ne varietur* type. There is question of a fidelity which safeguards above all the foundation and the meaning of the message, but also respects the "imprint" in its most characteristic traits, often very close, of the original formulation.

The accounts (of miracles, for instance) are evidently not of Jesus, but they flowed in literary forms and structures very simple, often identical, even when the content varies from one account to another) (for example, an account of exorcism and the account of the stilled tempest). The fact means that these accounts were handed down from mouth to mouth, in a stereotype form which helps memorization and conservation.

This dynamism, however, is adjusted to another, which disproves the thesis of a mechanical transmission. The Church, indeed, has received the word of Jesus, not as an inert treasure, but as a living word, capable of illumining new situations. The action of this dynamism is visible and controllable, especially in the words in which the message is preserved, but at the same time made relevant according to the new conditions of the Church. Thus, the parable of those invited to the feast, in Luke, becomes in Matthew an allegory, that is an application of the initial and typical parable of Jesus to the whole history of the Jewish people. It is the same for the accounts of miracles (for instance, the account of the healing of the epileptic child).

A purely literal fidelity would rapidly lead to a fossilization of the message of Jesus, without true creativity. On the contrary, uncontrolled relevance, without concern for fidelity, would lead to the sacrifice of the essential points of the message. This twofold dynamism of the Tradition is already inscribed in the attitude and mentality of the primitive Church.

Footnotes on Chapter XII

1. B. Gerhardsson, *Memory and Manuscript. Oral Tradition and written Transmission in Rabbinic Judaism and Early Christianity* (Upssala, 1961).
2. Thus, a liberal, or a conservative has his own vocabulary. The former will speak of progress, the future, planning, evolution, liberation, revolution; the second, on the contrary, of protection, of guarding, of defending.
3. It can be astonishing to see the total absence, in the epistles and in the Gospel of St. John of certain characteristic terms of the predication and transmission of the Christian message, so often found in the rest of the New Testament. Thus, in this *Gospel* (76 times), *evangelize* (54) both terms absent from St. John. Likewise *paradidonai*, in the sense of communicating a doctrine, and *paradosis*, are wholly wanting. In reality, there is less a matter of an absence than of a substitution of terms. In fact, if the Joannine works be grouped in relation to preaching and its transmission, three themes and three actions are to be distinguished. a) The first is that of *communicating* the message, which is found in such verbs as: to give (83 times), to testify (43), to speak (63), to say (272), to teach (12). b) The theme of *receive* is found in hear (74), see (39), take (52). c) The theme of *preserve* is found in observe (25), remain (67), have (118), know (82). These words enable us to understand what is the Joannine concept of the transmission of the message. With St. John, the chains of tradition are reduced to two: *hear* and *announce*. There is wanting a link between announce and hear. The traditional chain is asserted but reduced to a binary structure. Thus, in Jn 17:8: "I *entrusted* to them the message you *entrusted* to me, and they *received* it." There is seen in John that the origin of the movement of tradition is in God Himself. Jesus is the first subject of this transmission. He is the one who sees and hears the Father, who receives from Him and renders Him testimony (Jn 3:31-32; 8:26). Paul, on the contrary, as Luke, places the beginning of the tradition in Jesus. John, on making it with the trinitarian life, must have recourse to more general terms, susceptible of a broad application, rather than the technical terms already in use, limited to human transmitters. Thus, to *transmit* (paradidonai) is less suited for designating the action of the Father with regard to the Son. *Give* (didonai), more general, is better suited. Likewise, instead of the Gospel which designates the specific announcing of the message of salvation, John uses the expression, the *words* (remata). On this subject see: C.M. Martini, "Osservazioni sulla terminologia della predicazione nell' opera giovannes," in *Atti della XVII Settimana Biblica* (Brescia, 1964), pp. 111-122.
4. B. Gerhardsson, *op. cit.*, pp. 324-335.
5. *Ibid.* p.324; R. Riesenfeld, *The Gospel Tradition* (Oxford, 1970), p. 28.
6. J. Vansina, *De la Tradition orale. Essai de methode historique* (Tervuren, Belgium, 1961).
7. *Ibid.*, pp. 122-126.
8. A. Lord, *The Singers of Tales*, (Cambridge, USA, 1964).
9. *Ibid.*, pp.220-221.
10. M. Smith, "A Comparison of Early Christian and Early Rabbinic Traditions," *Journal of Biblical Literature*, LXXXII (1963), pp. 169-176.
11. W.D. Davies, "Reflections on a Scandinavian Approach to the Gospel Tradition" in *Neotestamentica et Patristica*, Festschrift O. Cullmann (1963), pp. 14-34.

Chapter XIII

SPEECH AND ATTITUDES OF THE PRIMITIVE ECCLESIAL MILIEU (II)

II. Witness, Apostle, Ministry of the Word

These three categories are found in the Epistles of St. Paul or in the Acts. *In Luke as in Paul*, they express a well determined theological objective. That is why they are relevant to our purpose which is to discern the profound attitudes and motivations of the primitive Church in regard to Jesus. *Witness* and *apostle* qualify the Twelve, in their activity and in their very being, but through reference to the person of Jesus and to His mission in the world. Service of the word *(Diakonia tou logou)* defines the relation of the apostle and of the witness to the word of Jesus. They are in the service of this word. The three terms express an identical willed fidelity.

1) *Witness and testimony*

Recourse to the category of testimony, in the New Testament, is not occasional, but repeated and intentional. A simple statistic on the frequency of *martus* (witness) and of its derivatives (nouns and verbs) is highly significant. The term comes up 198 times.

"Testify" and "witness" belong above all to the terminology of the Acts and to the theology of Luke. "To testify"

characterizes the apostolic activity the day after the resurrection. The title "witnesses" designates in the highest degree the
apostles. Four characteristics define them as such. The first, as
prophets they have been chosen by God (Acts 1:26; 10:41). The
second, they have seen and heard Christ (Acts 4:20; 1Jn 1:1-3),
they have lived close to Him (Acts 1:21-22) and, consequently,
possess a living, direct experience of His person, of His
teaching and of His works. They ate and drank with Him,
before and after His resurrection (Acts 10:41). In a word, they
were the close friends and messmates of Christ. Others can
preach; in the strict sense, only the apostles can testify. The
third, they received a mission from Christ for testifying (Acts
10:41), and, to carry out this mandate, they were invested with
the power of the Spirit (Acts 1:8). The fourth, they were
committed. They had an attitude which is shown by an
absolute fidelity to Christ and to His teaching acknowledged as
truth and salvation of man. The Acts keep repeating that the
apostles announce the word of God with assurance (*parresia*),
that is, with a supernatural courage, fruit of the Spirit which
acts in them and triumphs over the all too human reactions in
the face of the difficulties of the apostolate: timidity, human
respect, fear, fear of persecutions and of death. Moved by this
interior courage the apostles declare: "Surely we cannot help
speaking of what we have heard and seen" (Acts 4:20). St. John
says the same: "What we have heard, what we have seen with
our eyes, what we have looked upon and our hands have
touched—we speak of the word of life . . . we bear witness to it"
(1Jn 1:1-3).

For taking the place of Judas and becoming a "witness of
the resurrection," Matthias had to fulfill these conditions. He
was a companion of the apostles "while the Lord Jesus moved
among us," that is, from the baptism which marked the
beginning of His ministry, to His glorification as Christ the
lord (Acts 1:22; 2:36). So there is no interruption of continuity
between the earthly Jesus and the glorified Christ. The apostles
are the juncture between the times of Jesus and the times of the
Church. Besides, it is significant that Luke, at the beginning of
the Acts (Acts 1:13), repeats the list of the apostles, thereby

showing that they are the ones who assure continuity between the pre-paschal and the post-paschal community. The name of Judas is not on the list. Thenceforth it was replaced by that of Matthias chosen by God (Acts 1:26). The authority of witness, in fact, does not come from him, but from God who sends or chooses him. Thus, called by God, having seen and heard Jesus, open to the understanding of the Scriptures, fortified by the Spirit, Matthias is qualified to transmit with fidelity what concerns Jesus and to become a witness of His resurrection (Acts 1:21-26).

Testimony, indeed, at the same time is based on the things seen and heard, and on the meaning of the events which happened. There is a twofold dimension, it is at the same time narration and confession.

On the one hand, since the apostles lived intimately with Christ, they are eye and ear witnesses to His whole career, from His baptism to the resurrection (Acts 4:20). "We are witnesses to all that he did in the land of the Jews (Galilee) and in Jerusalem." (Acts 10:39). But first of all, they are witnesses to the resurrection, for it is the essential fact which authorizes all that precedes and all that follows. This Jesus whom the Jews have crucified, has risen (Acts 5:31) and He appeared (Acts 10:40). "We testify to this: (Acts 5:32), the expression which again and again comes up like a *leitmotiv*.

But the testimony, in fact, is not only about the phenomenal, empirical reality of the words and deeds of Jesus. The apostles testify above all to the salvific bearing of these facts. They are witness to the profound meaning of His earthly existence, that is, to the salvation brought about by His death and His resurrection (Acts 5:31; 10:42).

Acts 10:37-43 brings together in one and the same text these two essential components of apostolic testimony. Peter first recalls the events of the life of Jesus: His ministry, His miracles, His crucifixion, His death, His resurrection, His apparitions. "I take it you know what has been reported all over Judea about Jesus of Nazareth, beginning in Galilee with the baptism John preached; of the way God anointed him with the Holy Spirit and power. He went about doing good works and healing all who were in the grip of the devil, and God was with him. We are witnesses to all he did in the land of the Jews and in Jerusalem. They killed him, finally, hanging him on a tree, only to have God raise him up on the third day and grant that he be seen, not by all, but only by such witnesses as had been chosen beforehand by God—by us who ate and drank with him after he rose from the dead" (Acts 10:37-41).

After this testimony on the earthly career of Jesus, the text links up with a testimony which this time is about the interior and supernatural dimension of this historical reality. "He commissioned us to preach to the people and to bear witness that he is the one set apart by God as judge of the living and the dead. To him all the prophets testify, saying that everyone who believes in him has forgiveness of sins through his name" (Ac 10:42-43). The terminology of this second part is ever that of testimony, but the reality attested to is beyond empirical observation. However it belongs to the same object, for it expresses the profound meaning, the innermost being of what the eyes and ears have perceived. This Jesus of Nazareth, whom the apostles and the Jewish people saw and heard, is from now on identified as the Judge of the living and dead. His death is not an ordinary one, as are others, for it saves us from sin, brings about our salvation.

In the apostolic testimony described by the Acts, there is an indissoluble union of the historical event (horizontal dimension) and of its religious and salvific import (vertical dimension). The same is true in the kerygma of Paul. For him, *Jesus* persecuted, crucified, dead, risen, glorified, is *Christ*. Far from denying or reducing the historical or phenomenal reality, this apostolic testimony reaffirms and confirms it, for finding out its interior dimension, which is beyond perception. It does not confer historicity on an event which did not occur, but discloses the transcendant import of what occurred. Without Jesus, (his works and words), the testimony has no longer support. It collapses.[1]

Not to leave anything out, there must be added to apostolic testimony a third element. When it states the meaning of the historical event, the testimony does not give an arbitrary interpretation, but supports on it true history: that of Jesus and that of the Jewish people. Thus, when Peter, on the day of Pentecost, declares: "Therefore let the whole house of Israel know beyond any doubt that God has made both Lord and Messiah this Jesus whom you crucified" (Acts 2:36), he bases his interpretation on the facts of the life of Jesus which authorize it, that is, His miracles, His resurrection and His apparitions. Peter states this precisely. This Jesus "was a man whom God sent to you with miracles, wonders, and signs as his credentials. These God worked through him in your midst, as you well know . . . God raised him up again" (Acts 2:22-24). The resurrection itself is founded on the apparitions (Acts 10:40-41), and these in turn are founded on experiences of an intense realism, such as eating and drinking (Acts 10:41; Lk 24:42) and touching (Jn 20:27). Peter's testimony on the identity of Jesus of Nazareth, as Messiah and Lord, is based on the historical reality of His life and His works. The same concern is found in the Gospel of John: "Jesus performed many other signs as well—signs not recorded here—in the presence of his disciples. But these have been recorded to help you believe that Jesus is the Messiah, the Son of God, so that through this faith you may have life in his name" (Jn 20:30-31). The apostolic testimony refers to history under two titles. It states the meaning of an event which it assumes and reaffirms on interpreting it; and the interpretation it gives it is itself based on the authenticity of the words and deeds of Jesus.

The category of testimony states not only a reference to Jesus but also that the reference to Jesus is willed. If Jesus did not perform the works He did, the apostolic testimony no longer has value and the Gospel no longer exists.

2) *The title of apostle*

According to the Semitic substratum, the term signifies a delegate, an ambassador, who carries out a plenipotenciary mission in the name of one who has authority and who makes himself in some way present through his delegate. The apostle represents the one who orders him: "I solemnly assure you, no slave is greater than his master; no messenger outranks the one who sent him" (Jn 13:16). Although the term does not have an absolutely univocal meaning, it is found in all the writings of the New Testament, with the exception of the Second Epistle to the Thessalonians, the Epistle of James and the Epistles of John. Used alone, or in conjunction with doctors and prophets, the term is characteristic of the apostolic age.

1) *Apostolos*, in the Epistles of Paul, is a favorite term. The testimony of the First Epistle to the Thessalonians, in this regard, is important, not only due to the antiquity of the document (in 51), but also because the term is still without malodor of controversy. Paul presents himself as "apostle of Christ" (1Th 2:7), charged with announcing the Gospel (1Th 4:4; 2:9). Through him it is God Himself who addresses the Corinthians: "This makes us ambassadors for Christ, God as it were appealing through us" (2Cor 5:20). The apostle is an ambassador of Christ, charged by Him. His mission of apostle, Paul received from the risen Christ, not from men (Gal 1:1).

This mission of evangelization. The traditional trilogy: "Apostles, doctors, prophets, which are found in the Epistles to the Corinthians and to the Ephesians (Eph 4:11-12), concerns equally the missionary ministry, and is like the one Paul received from Antioch.

2) In Luke, the concept of apostles is closely linked to that of *witness*. The apostles are men chosen by Jesus during His public life and who, before the ascension, had charge of a definitive mission. They thus became witnesses of His teaching, of His works, of His passion and of His resurrection. In Luke, delegation of power and function of witness are but one, as it appears in the account of the election of Matthias. For Luke, the apostles are not only ambassadors of Christ, but especially men who take on the functions reserved for the Twelve, notably that of qualified witness of the life and resurrection of Jesus.

Here there can be asked whether Jesus, during His public life, gave His disciples the title of apostles (Lk 6:13). The question is debatable. There is certainly no doubt that Jesus called a certain number of men to follow Him and become His disciples. There is no doubt furthermore that Jesus, during His public life, chose a certain number of His disciples "to be with Him," assigned to proclaim the Kingdom of God, to expel demons and heal the sick. The forming of a group of "Twelve" belongs to the oldest tradition (Mk 3:14; Lk 9:1). Nonetheless the same cannot be said for the term "apostle" and for the expression "Twelve Apostles." Present day criticism esteems that *apostolos* originated in Antioch and designates itinerant missionaries. It is this title which is applied to Peter and to Paul. The expression "the Twelve Apostles" seems to result from the fusion of both expressions: the "Twelve" and the "apostles," in use in the primitive Church.[2]

3) *Servant and ministry of the word*

1) In St. Paul, *diakonos* is not a technical term. It was first applied to all itinerant missionaries, and included the apostles (Rm 16:1; 1Cor 3:5; 2Cor 3:6; 6;4; 11;23; Eph 3:7; Col 1:23-25). Next, it designated the collaborators of the apostles, of Paul in particular, such as Crescens, Titus, Luke and Mark, who travelled with him as the needs of evangelization required (2Tm). The term is related to the missionary ministry. In the Epistle to the Collossians, St. Paul presents himself as diakonos of the Gospel, diakonos of the Church for sowing the word of God (Col 1:25). Inasmuch as he is servant of the Gospel, the apostle is diakonos of Christ (2Cor 11:23). Even more, *doulos*, slave of Christ (Tt 1:1; Rm 1:1), is a term which expresses with even greater force his belonging to Christ. He "taught about the Lord Jesus Christ" (Acts 28;31).

Diakonia has a parallel meaning. In the Second Epistle to the Corinthians and in the Epistle to the Romans, it first means the ministry of the word; then, in the second place, the material service of the local Churches (for instance, the collection for the poor). It is in the Epistles to Timothy that the diakonia is used in its full meaning. For Paul, the diakonia, is the office of announcing the Gospel, an office which he received at the moment of his apostolic calling (1Tm 1:12). Paul exhorts Timothy to be a good *diakonos* of Jesus Christ (1Tm 4:6): "perform your work as an evangelist, fulfil your ministry" (2Tm 4:5). Timothy must proclaim the word, refute, exhort, with a tireless patience and with solicitude to instruct. Paul, as the rabbis of his time, transmits his authority to the one of his disciples who will assure the transmission of the word of God and of the Gospel in its integrity. The diakonia essentially is a ministry of the word.

2) In the Acts of the apostles, the supreme Christian service, that is, the proclaiming of the Good Tidings of salvation in Jesus Christ, is designated by the ministry of the word" (Acts 6:4). This *diakonia tou logou* is identified with what Luke calls the *didache* of the apostles (Acts 2:42). In the Acts, the service of the word is in relation with the functions of apostle and of witness.

When there is question of choosing, between Barnabas and Matthias, to succeed Judas, the first faithful prayed thus: "O Lord ... make known to us which of these two you choose for this apostolic ministry (*diakonia—apostole*) replacing Judas, who deserted the cause" (Acts 1:24-25). One of the essential functions of the apostles is the service of the word. Likewise, when the apostles have to choose between waiting on table and serving the word, they choose the ministry of the word: "It is not right to neglect the word of God in order to wait on tables ... This will permit us to concentrate on prayer and the ministry of the word" (Acts 6:2-4). The apostles free themselves from other tasks in order to devote themselves wholly to the ministry of the word.

On the other hand, for the apostles, this ministry of the word, in the concrete, is identified with the testimony they must give of Jesus: His words and His deeds (Acts 1:1), to all He did from the baptism to the ascension (Acts 1:22). In the prologue of his Gospel, Mark states that "eyewitnesses" have become "ministers of the word" (Acts 1:2).

The word spoken of, is the "word of God" (Ac 4:31; 6:2; 11:1; 12:24; 13:5), the "word of the Lord" (Ac 6:7; 8:25; 13:49; 15:49), which is identically the word of Christ. Thus, when it is said, in Acts 11:1, a propos of the conversion of Cornelius and of his family, that the Gentiles have received the "word of God" this evidently means the message about Jesus and salvation in Jesus. In the Epistles of Paul, the word of God, the word of the

Lord, signifies equally the word about Jesus Christ. This usage was already established in the Epistles to the Thessalonians (1Th 1:6, 8; 2Th 3:1).

This word is acknowledged, not only as word about God, in which the apostles would express their own religious concepts, but as word of God under the same title as the word of the Old Testament. The same attitude of respect and of service due to the Torah, becomes, in the New Testament, respect and ministry of the word of Jesus. This is why Paul is said to be *diakonos* of the Gospel (Eph 3:7) as well as *diakonos* of Christ (2Cor 11:23). Such an attitude, evidently, is the expression of a fidelity.

III. Teacher, preacher, evangelist, Gospel.

These terms which belong to the vocabulary of evangelization, are not reserved only to the apostles. Their collaborators in the diffusion of the Good Tidings equally qualify. In the Acts verbs are most common; in St. Paul, the noun *Gospel* prevails.

1) In the *Acts* the testimony of the apostles is diffused by their predication or kerygma. If these terms overlap in the apostles' concrete activity, still to testify is a properly apostolic activity based on a privileged situation (that of those who have seen and heard), while to *announce , proclaim, preach* accent the dynamic, publicizing nature of this testimony and also is applied to other preachers than the apostles (Acts 15:35; 18:25) such as Paul, Barnabas, Silas, Philip, Timothy.

Testimony expresses fidelity to a unique experience and courage to make it known. Kerygma expresses loudness, power, expansion, notoriety (Acts 2:14; 8:5; 10:42; 19:20; 20:25). Thus, Peter and John "evangelize" numerous Samaritan villages (Acts 8:25). Paul and Barnabas "evangelize" the village of Derbe (Acts 14:21). In a vision, Paul understands he must "evangelize" Macedonia (Acts 16:10). *Evangelize* and *teach* are often used together. Paul and Barnabas at Antioch: "teaching and preaching the word of the Lord" (Acts 15:35; 5:42; 18:28, 31).

What the apostles announce, preach, proclaim, teach, and what their hearers are invited to hear and receive is "the good news of Jesus" (Acts 8:35), "the good news of the Lord Jesus" (Acts 11:20), "about Jesus" (Acts 18:25), "about the Lord Jesus Christ" (Acts 28:31). The common term in all these texts, and the unifying elements, is *Jesus*, identified as Christ and Lord.

More explicitly, it is said that Paul, in Damascus, "soon began to proclaim in the synagogues that Jesus was the Son of God" (Acts 9:20). In Thessalonica, Paul addressing the Jews of the synagogue, explains to them starting out from the scriptures that Christ had to suffer and rise from the dead: "This Jesus I am telling you about is the Messiah:" (Acts 17:1-3). To the Greeks of Athens, Paul spoke of "Jesus" and "the resurrection" (Acts 17, 18).

If, beyond these brief and synthetic formulas, we pass on to the examples of predication which are the great discourses of the Acts (2, 3, 5, 10, 13), evangelization seems to us like the proclamation of the work of salvation which God carried out in the world by the ministry, the passion the death, the resurection and the glorification of Jesus. Early evangelization announces the Event par excellence, with its transforming consequence for whoever believes in Jesus. The salvation of the world is brought about by faith in Christ and by the baptism which brings about the remission of the sins and confers the Spirit, the supreme gift. Evangelization, as testimony, establishes an indissoluble bond between the event and its salvific import. But the constant point of reference is the historical person of Jesus from now on identified and confessed as Christ Lord, Son of God in whom the promises of God the Savior are accomplished.

2) Evangelization is one of the fundamental themes of Pauline thought: The noun *Gospel* comes up 60 times; the verb *evangelize*, 21 times.

Paul defines himself through the Gospel. He was "set apart to proclaim the gospel of God" (Rm 1:1). If God tore him away from Judaism, it is for preserving the Gospel. God revealed to him His Son, "that I might spread (evangelize) among the Gentiles the good tidings concerning Him" (Gal

1:15-16; 2:7). Paul from then on, "is its (the Gospels') servant" (Col 1:23; Eph 3:7).

To preach the Gospel or to evangelize is his primordial task. "Yet preaching the gospel is not the subject of a boast; I am under compulsion and have no choice. I am ruined if I do not preach it:" (1 Cor 9:16). "for Christ did not send me to baptize, but to preach the gospel" (1 Cor 1:17). Not that the sacraments are useless, but the sacramental order depends on the announcing of the word. It is not enough that Jesus lived, died and rose that salvation might come. It is necessary that these salvific facts be made known. There must be men who preach the Gospel (Rm 10:14-15). This is why Timothy, following Paul's example, must "preach the word" courageously and resolutely (2 Tm 4:2).

In the language of Paul, the Gospel designates the Good Tidings revealed to the world. In half the cases, the term is used absolutely, without need of characterizing it by a noun or an adjective. Often, the accent is on apostolic activity. The Gospel then is equivalent to the act of announcing (1 Cor 9:14; Ph 4:15). Elsewhere, it refers to the content of this announcement (Rm 2:16; 2 Cor 11:4), to the message itself such as known in the primitive community.

In Rm 1:1-2, are found grouped both aspects, active and objective. Paul is the apostle for "to proclaim the gospel of God," that is what God "promised long ago through his prophets, as the holy Scriptures record."

The content of the Gospel, in the rare cases where Paul expresses it explicitly, is identified with the history of Jesus, notably His pass, His death and His resurrection. In Rm 1:3-4), the Gospel concerns the Son of God "descended from David according to the flesh" and constituted Lord by His resurrection. In 1 Cor 1-5, the essential content of the Gospel preached and confessed, is the death, burial, resurrection and apparitions of the risen Jesus. For Paul, there is the heart of the Gospel.

There is no hiatus between the Gospel and the Old Testament. The Gospel is nothing else but the revelation of salvation worked by God in Christ at the end of time. The concrete equivalence between *Gospel* and *mystery* shows it clearly (Rm 16:25; Col 1 25-26; Eph 1:9-13; 3:5-6). Paul says: "Now to him who is able to strengthen you in the gospel which I proclaim when I preach Jesus Christ, the gospel which reveals the mystery hidden for many ages but now manifested through the writings of the prophets, and, at the command of the eternal God, made known to all the Gentiles that they may believe and obey only him, the God who alone is wise, may glory be given through Jesus Christ unto endless ages. Amen." Rm 16:25-27). In both cases, there is question of the economy of salvation, but envisaged under different angles. On the one hand, there is involved a hidden secret, then unveiled, revealed, manifested and communicated; on the other, a Good Tidings, an announced proclaimed message. A hidden and revealed divine plan, a proclaimed divine plan: Gospel and mystery have the same object and the same content. The Gospel is the new economy of salvation, unveiled and accomplished in Jesus, by His life, His death and His resurrection, inasmuch as it is made known and is propagated by predication and by the divine force which is within it.

Paul speaks only the very same way about the Gospel (1 Th 2, 44), or of "the Gospel of God" (Rm 1:1; 15, 16), of "the Gospel of His Son" (Rm 1:3), of "the Gospel of Christ" (Rm 15:19-1;) 2 Cor 2:12; Gal 1:7; Ph 1:27), of "the Gospel of our Lord Jesus" (2 Th 1:8).

Instead of the Gospel, but in the same technical sense of Christian message, Paul also uses the term "word" (Col 1:25-26; 1Th 1:6), of "word of God" 1Th 2:13; Rm 9:6; 1Cor 14:36), of "word of the Lord" (1Th 1:8; 4:15; 2Th 3:1), of "word of Christ" (Rm 10:17). This word is "word of salvation" (Eph 1:13), "word of life" (Ph 2:16), "word of truth" (2Cor 6:7; Col 1:5; Ep 1:13:; 2Tm 2:15), "word of reconciliation" (2 Cor 5:19).

In certain texts, Paul sums up in one word the totality of this mission as apostle. "It is not ourselves we preach but Christ Jesus as Lord, and ourselves as your servants for Jesus' sake." (2Cor 4:5). Likewise the new life is in Christ "taught you in accord with the truth that is in Jesus, " (Eph 4:21). Correlatively, the faith which responds to this predication is to "believe in Jesus" (Rm 3:26), "confess Jesus is Lord" (Rm 10:9; 1 Cor 12:3).

The object of Paul's preaching, as of the testimony of the apostles, in the Acts, is always *Jesus* of Nazareth, in His life and in His death, fully identified, by His resurrection, as Christ, Lord and Son of God.

IV. Conclusion

Although it is not exhaustive, the semantic examination we have pursued, authorizes at least one conclusion. A community, the fundamental attitudes of which are those of mission, of testimony, of tradition, and of ministry, is quite a different thing from a community which shifts at every breeze, without axis, without point of reference, unconscious of its past and unconcerned about its future. A human group, whose explicit wish is to transmit integrally what it has recieved, to attest to what it has seen and heard, to act as delegate and representative of the one who sent it, and to regard this ministry as superior to all others, this group decidedly lives under the sign of a *fidelity*. This attitude of fidelity is expressed by the words which are found throughout and impregnate the Epistles of St. Paul and the Acts of the apostles, main extra-evangelical writings. The soul of the primitive Church was as it were fashioned and moulded by these basic words. St. Paul and the Acts, without the terms of apostles, witness, Gospel, ministry, tradition are inconceivable. To eliminate or reduce them would be as if to deprive a language of its basic vocabulary. To enumerate them is to describe the first reaction, the fundamental reflexes, the essential attitudes of the primitive Church, it is to define its speech and its mentality. Now what is important here, is that this basic vocabulary, in its original usage, aims at but one thing, has but one intent: Jesus and fidelity to Jesus. If this is so, we have the right to assert there is, in the primitive Christian milieu, not only continuity of tradition between Jesus and the Church (as Schurmann has established), but also concern for and will for "continued" fidelity of the Church to Jesus. The rejection of the apocrypha and of the gnostic writings, in the 2nd century, confirms that this attitude of the Church, consequently, has not been belied.[3] In order to achieve the demonstration thereof, there must however, be verified the *fact*, the *reality* of this fidelity by recourse to the criteria of historical authenticity.

Footnotes for Chapter XIII

1. R. Latourelle, "Evangelisation et temoignage," in *Evangelisation* ("Documenta Missionalia" IX, Rome, 1975), pp. 77-110; *Id., Théologie de la Révelation* (Bruges-Paris, 1969), pp. 51-60; *Id. Le témoignage chrétien* (Tournai-Montreal, 1971), pp. 18-22.
2. A. Lemaire, *Les ministeres aux origines de l'Eglise* (Paris, 1971), pp. 179-180; A. Descamps, "Aux origines du ministere. La pensée de Jesus," *Revue théologique de Louvain,* II, (1971), pp. 19-24.
3. Chapter IX, paragraph III: "Attitude of the Church."

Chapter XIV

THE MEDIATION OF THE EVANGELISTS AND THE CONTRIBUTION OF REDAKTIONSGESCHICHTE

The School of Forms did not exclude from its project the study of the role of the evangelists in the formation of the Gospels, for its ambition was to retrace the entire history of Tradition, in conformity with the fundamental principle of the school, that is, that our Gospels are the result of a long tradition. In fact, however, absorbed in the meticulous analysis of the primary units of the Gospels, Dibelius and Bultmann speak relatively little of the stage of the last composition. FG reduces to the minimum the part played by the composers. They are treated like compilers, further more rather ingenuous, which collected more or less adroitly diverse elements of tradition. Fortunately, the pendular movement which characterizes the history of criticism of the last two centuries, brought it back to consider more attentively the quality of authors of the evangelists. After around twenty years, research is conducted on the evangelists' contribution and on the role played by the communities and environments within which they drew up their Gospel. Labors ever more numerous enabled the making more precise the theological intents of each evangelist and at the same time understanding how they treated previous material. Consequently, the difference was toned down between the "theological" Gospel of John and the "historical" Gospels, that is, the Synoptics. Mark, Luke and Matthew were "promoted" theologians, under the same title as John. It even came about, due to emphasizing the theological preoccupations and the compositional activity of the evangelists, that there arose suspicion about their fidelity to Jesus. After the screen of the early Church, we would now have the screen of the evangelists.

Thus, FG denied all initiative to the evangelists. RG, on the contrary, pays attention only to their initiative and freedom. The exact evaluation of the role of the evangelists becomes a needed moment in the demonstration of this historicity of the Gospels. The astonishing freedom, not to say the kind of flippancy of the evangelists in regard to the material received, obliges us to *third critical verification*. To what extent is this freedom compatible with a certain and controllable fidelity to previous tradition? So we have two motives for studying RG: an external motive, that is, the problem brought out by FG, which has undervalued the contribution of the evangelists; an internal motive, that is, the exact evaluation of the mediation of the evangelists in the history of tradition.

I. At the origins of Redaktionsgeschichte

The expression "Redaktionsgechichte" is taken from the work by W. Marxsen on the Gospel of Mark.[1] It treats of a discipline which endeavors to discover the *form* and the *content* of the materials used by the evangelist for discerning the nature and the extent of his work in the arranging of the preexisting material, as well as in the compositional touches which are proper to him. So we might just as well call it "Kompositionsgeschichte" (Compositon Criticism).

In principle, the method of RG may be applied to the Gospel of John or to any other writings of the New Testament. If, in fact, it studied especially the Synoptics, it is first of all because we possess two of their sources.

RG is not absolutely new. Exegetes did not wait until our days to study the characteristics of our Gospels. It is still true, however, that ancient exegesis did not distinguish so clearly what is owing to the compositional work of the evangelist and what belongs to the previous tradition.

The origins of RG go back to the discussion, at the beginning of the century, on the Gospel of Mark. The Liberal School, indeed, persuaded that it was possible to know Jesus *as He was,* relied above all on Mark, the source of Luke and of Matthew, the nearest events and also the most trustworthy from the historical point of view. While Luke and Matthew showed some theological intentions, the Gospel of Mark appeared pure and uncontaminated.

It was Wrede, in his work on the messianic secret, in 1901, who tolled the knell for this confidence, upon establishing that the Gospel of Mark, just as that of Matthew and of Luke, reflects a "theological" concept. According to Wrede, the idea of a "secret" encompassing the messianic consciousness of Jesus, is a "creation" of Mark. It has no historical foundation in the life of Jesus. Wrede was correct on two points. It is true that the Gospel of Mark includes a theological view. Consequently, it is true that the exegete should endeavor to define the characteristics of this Markian theology. Wrede, before its time, was a practitioner of RG. However, he conceived over simply the work of the evangelists. In particular he did not grasp that, in order to appreciate correctly their compositional work, there must be known precisely the prior history of tradition.

In this perspective, it seems better that RG just took the place of FG in its research on the history of tradition. It is the second time of a process of which FG, historically, constituted but the second stage. The School of Forms did not scrutinize sufficiently the compositional activity of the evangelists. Dibelius considers then especially as "Sammler" (collectors), compilers. Bultmann, following close upon Wrede, considers Mark, it is true, as more theological than Matthew and Luke. However he thinks that Mark has not much room for manoeuvering, for his aim is limited or contradicted by his sources. On describing the compositional operations of Matthew and Luke, Bultmann makes precise that Matthew is not as consciously a guide as Mark by some dogmatic concerns and that he rather reflects his ecclessial milieu. As to Luke, if he arrives at a more continuous history, joined together by some special themes (the Spirit, pity for the poor, etc), his procedures are still rudimentary. Visibly, the attention of FG is on the history of the evangelical tradition more than on the history of the composition of the Gospels.

RG went into full swing beginning after the war of 1945. However, R.H. Lightfoot in *History and Interpretation*, 1934, may be considered a precursor. He demonstrated that the whole Gospel of Mark reveals a theological intent. The first thirteen verses are a veritable introduction to Mark's christology, that is the Good Tidings of Christ, Son of God. Lightfoot likewise studied the content and structure of the second Gospel discovering in it the theological aim of Mark present throughout. He illustrated how the choice and the arrangement of the materials, as well as the transitions show Mark's compositional activity.

II. Full Swing and Ring-leaders

After the war of 1945, three important works consecrated the RG as a method and as a stage in the history of exegetics.

1) In an article, of 1948, Gunther Bornkamm[2] studied the texts about the calmed storm, in Matthew 8:23-27, compared this with the account of Mark 4:35-41. He shows how Matthew interpreted the incident in a sense peculiar to him. In fact, he inserted the episode in the context of the summons to an apostolic life and of belief in the word of Jesus. This is why, in Matthew's account, the lesson of faith precedes the act of Jesus calming the storm. In Mark, on the contrary, the miracle precedes the rebukes addressed to the apostles. The compositional retouches by Matthew reveal his intention.

In a second article,[3] which appeared in 1954, Bornkamm studies the arrangement of the discourses of Jesus, on Matthew, and the ecclesiological interpretation which is to be taken from it. He emphasizes the importance, in Matthew's christology, of the relationship of Jesus to the Law. He studies in depth the meaning of the christological titles, as also the relationship of chistology to ecclesiology. The pupils of Bornkamm (notably G. Barth, H. Held, H.E. Todt and F. Hahn) followed the tracks of the master.

2) The first classic of RG is *Die Mitte der Zeit* by Conzelmann, which appeared in 1954. This work on the theology of Luke is to be compared, in importance, with that of Bultmann on the synoptic tradition or of Jeremias on the parables. Before Conzelmann, Luke was frequently considered as the first historian of Christianity. From then on he appears as a great theologian.

Starting from Mark and the Source, Conzelman studies the formally compositional activity of Luke. He endeavors to discover the theological approach which inspires and directs all his work, as well as the motives which justify retouches in detail. In this regard, Conzelmann sees in Luke 16:16 the key to his Gospel and to his concept of the history of salvation. "Until John, there was the law and the prophets; afterwards the Kingdom of God is announced." According to Conzelmann, Luke divides the history of salvation into three epochs: the times of Israel, until John the Baptizer; the times of Jesus or the "center" of times, until the ascension; finally, the times of the Church, until the parousia. For conceiving this third period, Luke compresses the eschatological expectation and makes of the times of the Church, not a simple prelude of the parousia, but an indefinite historical grandeur. The times of the Church are "expanded," but at the same time so too the times of the life of Jesus. This twofold "expansion" affects the position of the Church which thus becomes the times of salvation under the movement of the Spirit. These three epochs, intimately bound among themselves, have each their own character. This theological perspective of Luke affects his whole Gospel, down to the last details.

3) A third representative of RG is Willi Marxsen, in his study on Mark *(Der Evangelist Markus)* which appeared in 1956. The work begins with a comparison between the respective methods of FG and RG.

While FG considers the evangelists as compilers, RG envisages them as veritable authors. While FG is concerned first of all about the small units and the life environment where they rose up, RG is rather concerned about the great ensembles and seeks to discern the motives which explain them. Marxsen observes that FG does not give due credit to Mark who "created" the "Gospel" form. RG studies this new literary genre created by Mark, with the theology it implies, as well as the usage Matthew and Mark make of it. Finally, the works of RG from then on oblige criticism to distingusih clearly a triple *Sitz im Leben* of tradition: Jesus, the early Church, the evangelist.

Marxsen does not study the whole Gospel of Mark, but only four passages. These are the traditions concerning the Baptizer, the geographic framework of Mark and the concept of Gospel, Chapter 13. Let us illustrate the first study. In the eyes of Marxsen, the beginning of the second Gospel is a personal composition by Mark which clarifies for us his theology. Mark interprets the history of Jesus starting from the Baptizer. The Baptizer has a meaning, not in himself, but as *precursor* of Jesus. With him begins the history of Jesus, who is Christ and the Son of God. Such is the essential. Marxsen next studies the modification made by Matthew and Luke in the material received from Mark. These retouches show the theological concept peculiar to each one.

By his study, Marxsen thinks he can establish that the Gospel of Mark reflects the historical situation of Galilee around 66. If the study of the theology of a Gospel thus enables the determining of the historical moment of its composition in the Church, it must be concluded that RG opens up new perspectives on the history of early Christianity.

4) W. Trilling published, in 1959, *Das Wahre Israel,* a work on the theology of Matthew. The author studies the fundamental themes of Matthew and their influence on the composition of the first Gospel. Trilling analyzes most particularly Mt. 28:18-20, and three important sections: the crisis of Israel, the true Israel, the law of the true Israel. A typical example of his method is the analysis of the trial of Jesus before Pilate (Mt 27:15-26). Trilling shows how Matthew

directed the whole scene in the sense of the responsibility of the Jews.

These first essays help us the better to grasp the problem which RG in a research on the finding of Jesus through the Gospels. On uncovering to us the whole complexity of the compositional task of the evangelists, RG establishes a further "mediation" and, at the same time, increases the hermeneutical distance which separates us from the event Jesus. Thenceforth there is question of determining the degree of fidelity and of freedom the evangelist has in regard to prior tradition. To what extent does he feel bound by this tradition? To what extent can he feel free from it? Is his freedom of such a nature as to compromise his fidelity to history?

III. General description of the Task of RG

RG therefore, proposes to study the physiognomy proper to teach of the Gospels: the author's theological approach, the structurizing of the material chosen, his stylistic stamp. The Instruction of the Biblical Commission (1964) described, in its essential lines, this work of the evangelists. They made a *choice* of the material from tradition; they performed a work of *synthesis;* they adapted their Gospel to the needs of the local Churches.

1) The material was not originated, but found, under a written or oral form. In this material, the evangelists *chose,* leaving aside certain accounts or words. The fact of this selectiveness is clearly attested to by the Gospel of John, to the first as to the second conclusion (Jn 20:30; 21:25). It is equally manifest in the Gospel of Mark, above all narrational, which only relates two discourses: the parables (ch. 4) and the eschatological discourse (ch. 13). Luke omits Marks accounts, for example, the second multiplication of the loaves. The material thus laid aside is not less revelatory than what is preserved for us.

2) The material retained by the evangelists has been structured in such a way as to express their viewpoint. Typical

in this regard is the usage by Matthew and Luke of their main sources: Mark and the *Source*. Matthew structures his Gospel in five groups of deeds and words, in such a way as to symbolize the new Pentateuch of the new Moses for the new Israel. The sermon on the mount is a synthesis, partly compositional, of the *logia* pronounced by Jesus under various circumstances. The cycle of miracles (chs. 8-9) constitutes with this discourse (chs. 5-7) a synthesis which is intended to present Jesus as the Lawgiver and the *Thaumaturge* of the messianic times. This grand ensemble is "inclosed" between two summaries (Mt 4:23; 9:35) which sum up the twofold activity of Jesus in works and words. Luke, on his part, respects the quadripartite traditional structure of the ministry of Jesus (preaching of the Baptizer, Galilee, journey to Jerusalem, Jerusalem), but he has two incisions, of which the larger (Lk 9:51—18:14), inserted in the *Journey to Jerusalem*, signifies that Jerusalem is the center of the sacrifice and of the victory of Christ, and without doubt also that Christian life consists in following Jesus in suffering in order to enter with Him into glory.

3) Finally, the evangelists in their composition, took into account the diverse conditions and situations of their readers. Matthew writes for thhe Judeo-Christians, while Luke addresses himself to the Gentiles. Whence the respective orientation of their Gospel.

In the sermon on the mountain, Matthew wants to show the Jews that Christ did not come to abolish the Law, but to "perfect" it. So he proposes six examples which illustrate how the justice of the disciples of Christ must excel that of the scribes and Pharisees, the most faithful observes of the Law (Mt 5:20-47). Matthew shows, too, that Christian perfection forbids judging the neighbor (Mt 7:1), but commands we treat him as we ourselves want to be treated (Mt 7:12). Luke, on his part, has no special interest in showing the Christians, converts of paganism, how Jesus brought the Law to its perfection. So he develops the theme of charity, which is to be extended even to love of enemies (Lk 6, 27-36). Luke "concentrates," but retains what constitutes the essential of the Law and of the prophets, that is, charity (Mt 7:12).

Especially numerous are the examples of this adaptation to the conditions of local Churches, in the parables. Thus, the parable of the nuptial feast (Lk 14:16-24), becomes in Matthew (22:1-14), an allegory describing the tragic fate of the Jewish people. He was called to the Kingdom, but he refused to accept the invitation. He slew the prophets and persecuted the apostles. So he was rejected and chastised, while the Gentiles have taken his place.

IV. Diverse Types of Compositional Activity

Information on the general procedures used by the evangelists is not sufficient for answering the question posed above, namely, what is the degree of their fidelity and freedom? In order to appreciate the real extent of their compositional activity, and a fortiori to make a critical judgment, a detailed list of the various types of this activity seems necessary to us.[4] Here are the principal ones.

1) *Stylistic corrections.* A good number of the modifications introduced by Luke or Matthew are of a purely stylistic order. Therefore it is extreme to see in every modification of the text-source a theological intention. This must be proven in each historical case. This, when Luke uses the aorist instead of the present (the account of the calmed storm), or the subordination of propositons instead of juxtaposition, there is involoved purely stylistic retouches.

2) *Preciseness.* The evangelist, to help his reader, adds to the text-source at times a word which clarifies it. For instance:"tou Theou," in Lk 22:69, makes more precise "Dunamis" in Mk 14:62.

3) *Omissions.* In other cases, there is omission. Thus, in the account of the cure of the leper, Matthew and Luke omit the sentence on Mark 1:43: "Jesus gave him a stern warning and sent him on his way." Did Luke judge that this sounded too harsh to the ear of his reader or did he look on it as a later gloss?

4) *Adaptation of a metaphor.* In the parable of the house built on a rock, (Mt 7:24-27) there is seen a house of Palestinian

style, while Luke, clearly is thinking of a Grecian style house (Lk 6:47-49).

5) *Transposition of extracts.* Luke groups in one single account (Lk 3:1-20) two facts of the Baptizer's life, which, in the Gospel of Mark are found separate, that is, his preaching (Mk 1;1-8) and his imprisonment (Mk 6:17-19).

6) *Transposition within one and the same extract.* In the account of the triple temptation of Jesus in the desert, the second temptation which, in the Gospel of Matthew takes place in Jerusalem, in the Gospel of Luke becomes the third and last temptation. This is so, probably because, in the perspective of Luke, Jerusalem is the place of sacrifice and of the victory of Christ.

7) *Reduction of two moments of the narration to one.* In the account of the resurrection of the daughter of Jairus, Matthew does not mention the delegation of Jairus' servants who come to announce the death of his little daughter (Mk 5:35). Jairus is the only one to present himself before Jesus to tell him his daughter is dead (Mt 9:18).

8) *Addition of a "wandering" logion.* In the parable of the nuptial feast (Lk 14:16-24), Matthew adds a logion which, to all appearances, had its own peculiar and independent existence, on the guest who will be punished for not being properly dressed (Mt 22:11-14). In the parable of the workers sent to the vineyard, Matthew adds a verse: "Thus the last shall be first and the first shall be last." Now this same logion is found in Mt. 19:30 apropos of a rich young man; in Mk 10:31, apropos of the reward promised to detachment; and, finally, in Lk 11:30, apropos of the narrow gate for entering into the Kingdom of heaven. We are in the presence of a "wandering" logion which serves as the key of interpretation in different cases, for it admirably illustrates the change of perspective and mentality introduced by the Gospel. Another example: Luke adds to the parable of the Pharisee and the publican, the logion: "For everyone who exalts himself shall be humbled while he who humbles himself shall be exalted." (Lk 18:14). This same logion is found in Lk 14:11 apropos of the choice of seats, and in Matthew 23:12 apropos of the hypocrisy and

vanity of the scribes and Pharisees.

9) *Insertion of a traditional logion.* Mark introduces, between the parable of the sower (Mk 4:3-9) and its explanation (Mk 4:13-20), a logion of the Lord which not only serves for transition, but also reveals to us Mark's theology of the messianic secret.

10) *Addition of an account coming from another tradition.* Thus, Matthew, in the account of the trial of Jesus before Pilate (Mt 27:15-26), adds a verse (27:19) on the dream of Pilate's wife which, most likely, comes from another source.

11) *Abridgement of document-source.* Luke and Matthew often abridge Mark in narrative parts. Matthew, notably, only retains the essential of the accounts of miracles, to the point that his text often takes on a linear and hieratic character. Matthew's preocupations keep to the catechetical order, even when he is narrating. What interests him is the Lord's doctrine (Mt 8:28-34 and Mk 5:1-20; Mt 9:1-8 and Mk 2:1-12).

12) *Usage of Catch-words.* This procedure, frequently found in rabbinical literature, is equally found in our Gospels. It may bring us back to the oral stage of evangelical tradition, but it may also quite well reveal the compositional activity of the evangelist. Thus, in Mt 6:5-13, the expression "This is how you are to pray," serves to insert the Pater Noster in the framework of the sermon on the mount.

13) *Liaison of separated extracts.* While Mark is contented often to juxtapose pericopes, Luke and Mark are concerned about linking them with each other. These links, most often, have no other value than literary. Such expressions as "then," "at that time:," in Matthew and "after this," in Luke and John, are noted. At times, on the contrary, the transitions are intended and have value as an interpretation. Thus, after the temptation in the desert, Luke adds: "When the devil had finished all the tempting he left him, to await another opportunity."(Lk 4:13). Luke announces thus the future manifestation of the devil at the time of the passion (Lk 22:3; 22:53).

14) *Summaries.* They are the means of transition, but also constitute syntheses which define an aspect of the activity of

Jesus. These summaries, being personal compositions of the evangelist, are of capital importance for knowing his theology. Thus Mk 4:23 and 9:35, present Jesus as the Prophet and the *Thaumaturge* of messianic times.

15) *Geographical indications.* These are at times of a biographical nature, for instance, Nazareth, Philip's Cessea, Naim and Emmaus. Often too, they have a theological value. Thus, the place of the sermon on the "mount" in Matthew, is a "plateau" in Luke, for Matthew sees in Jesus the new Moses who promulgates the new Law on the mountain. In Luke, on the contrary, the mountain is the place of the solitary prayer of Jesus (Lk 6:12; 9:28). Equally classic is the meaning Luke attributes to Jerusalem, both geographical and mystical center of the history of salvation. This theological meaning is diffused throughout the accounts of the childhood, in the triple temptation in the desert, in the great journey toward Jerusalem, (hard to follow geographically, but easily understandable theologically), and in the first chapters of the Acts.

16) *Reference to the Old Testament.* The evangelists see in Christ the fulfilment of the Old Testament. The consciousness of the "fulfilment" so very alive in Matthew who addresses himself to the Judeo-Christians, is explicitly manifested in the formula which recurs like a *leitmotiv*: "All this happened to fulfill what the Lord had said through the prophet." (Mk 1:22; 2:5,15,17; 3:3; 4:14-16; 8:17; 12:7; 17:13, 35; 21:4; 27:9). Often it is "implicitly" presented in the interpretation or the orientation of an account (parable of the nuptial feast), or under the form of a simple allusion. Jesus is the first who gave the example of this reference to the Old Testament which the primitive Church, then the evangelists, took up later and deepened.

17) *Dramatization of a scene.* The quite sober account of the cure of Syrophenesian's daughter (Mk 7:25-30), becomes in Matthew an intensely dramatic scene (Mt 15:22-24). Likewise, the pericope in Mark on the Davidic origin of Jesus (Mk 12:35) becomes in Matthew a dialogue between Jesus and the Pharisees (Mt 22:41-46).

18) *Theological interpretation of tradition.* Thus, Mark

gives to the miracle of the multiplication of the loaves a christological meaning. He shows in Jesus the Messiah, Shepherd of His people, who teaches and feeds His own (Mk 6:34). In the account of the calling of Levi, only Luke adds: "leaving everything behind," in order to stress that one who decides to follow Jesus, must renounce everything (Lk 5:28; Mk 2:14). When Luke makes it very clear that we must bear our cross "each day" Lk 9:23; Mk 8:34), he doubtless wants to make it understood that abnegation is a reality which enters into all Christian existence.

19) *Addition of a logion of composition and theology.* It happens that the evangelist "composes" a text in which he openly reveals his theological aim. Thus, Luke introduces the account of Jesus going up to Jerusalem by a sentence which constitutes a veritable interpretation of the life of Christ: "As the time approached when He was to be taken from this world, he firmly resolved to proceed toward Jerusalem, and sent messengers ahead of him. (Lk 9:51). This going up of Jesus to the holy city, is in reality the beginning of His twofold elevation: on the cross and in glory.

V. Contribution of RG to research on Jesus

1) Let us note first that RG evolves within precise limits. It accepts the conclusion of FG on the formation of the evangelical tradition. On the other hand, it always assumes the validity of the theory of two sources. This is why it busies itself above all with the Synoptics. Its work is more conjectural when the exact sources conceal themselves as is the case for John and the Acts.

2) FG had shredded the documents of tradition and reduced the evangelists to the role of pure compilers. RG has "rehabilitated" them establishing that they are on the contrary guided by personal imperatives of a literary and theological order. A meticulous study of compositional phenomena has shed light of the physiognomy of each evangelist, as writer and as theologian. On the other hand, if it is true the RG has

contributed to "personalizing" the author, there must be added that this "profile of author" is to be conceived not as a passport picture but rather as the sum of the compositional and intentional facts which characterize a Gospel.

3) RG, as FG, runs the risks which it cannot always avoid. The main one is not having interest in the Gospels except for their theological value and practically ignoring their relationship to Jesus. This is Conzelmann's and Marxsen's defect. FG established a hiatus between the Church and Jesus. This time, the hiatus is made between the evangelist and Jesus. The theology of the evangelist is better known, but there is accepted distance in relation to Jesus Himself. Actually, when there is question of writers, it is not true that theological concern be the only thing dominant. Interest for the details of the life of Jesus is not absent from early preaching. Consequently, there is in the Gospels biographical details, thenceforth incorporated in tradition. For assuring the validity of its research, RG should then manifest a twofold sensitivity. This sensitivity of course is to be for the theological purpose of the writer, but also for the tradition of which he is the depository.

4) As a matter of fact, the examination into the compositional procedures carried on by the evangelist, shows that he is subjected to a veritable tension between his fidelity to tradition and his freedom of invention. His freedom is relative. It is first of all linked to the soundness of anterior source. These sources are the major ones identified by *Quellenkritik*, and material of lesser dimension identified by FG. It also depends on the weight of tradition of his purpose, and of the freedom he has, to be independent of this tradition and of the communities of which he is the mouthpiece.

5) RG enables us to measure, to "touch" we might say the degree of freedom and fidelity of the evangelists in relation to their sources. Their freedom of interpretation and composition is real, but "controllable." It appears discreet, motivated, and ever under the sign of fidelity. Luke, for instance, is remarkably faithful to his sources. The liberties he takes are explained, either because he is attentive to the condition of the Gentile, or

because he is anxious to present to his readers a harmoniously and literarily composed account, or because he wants to introduce in the traditional draft he received, some elements coming from sources which are peculiar to him, or finally, because he wants to stress the theological knowledge he has of the work of salvation accomplished in Jesus Christ.

Matthew follows the concerns of cathechesis. He makes a synthesis. He, for the sake of his readers, presents and arranges in a unified doctrinal body a subject matter which has long been preached in the Church. On the other hand, addressing himself to the Judeo-Christians, he explains the meaning of the coming of Jesus in the light of the history of Israel.

Finally, in the Gospel of Mark the compositional imprint is shown less in literary retouches, minor ones as a rule, than in the structure and economy of his work. In summary, the compositional activity of the evangelists manifests more fidelity than freedom. This freedom itself, since it is "verifiable," inspires confidence.

6) It is possible for us from now on, starting out from *literary* criteria to go back over the course of tradition to the earliest stage, to distinguish the most recent layers and the most ancient ones; to distinguish, on the one hand, what pertains to the compositional activity and to the theological interpretation of the evangelist, and, on the other hand what manifests the relevant intervention of the Church. We are ready to recognize the two "mediations" which separate us from Jesus and to appreciate their respective contribution. Yet recourse to literary criteria does not suffice. There remains still to establish that the message borne by these early literary forms is truly of Jesus. Actually, the study of FG and of RG lead to the obligation of studying the *historical content* of the literary forms identified. There is now question of establishing *criteria* of historicity properly so called, of value and critically proven, which enable the discovery of the isolation of the evangelical material which goes back to Jesus Himself. It is the *fourth* and final *critical verification* which remains for us to carry out. Then only, will it be possible to retrace the history of the Tradition (Traditionsgeschichte) and to show the continuity

which goes from Jesus to the present Gospel. The studies of FG and RG demand therefore to be completed by a criteriology of historicity.

Footnotes for Chapter XIV

1.   W. Marxsen, *Der Evangelist Markus* (Gottingen, 1956).
2.   G. Bornkamm, G. Barth, H.J. Held, *Tradition and Interpretation in Matthew* (London, 1963).
3.   W.D. Davies and D. Daube, ed. *The Background of the New Testament and its Eschatology. Studies in honor of C.H. Dodd* (Cambridge, 1954).
4.   Here we use largely the work of H. Zimmermann, *Neutestamentliche Methodenlehre* (Stuttgart, 1967).

Chapter XV

CRITERIA OF HISTORICAL AUTHENTICITY
OF THE GOSPELS

To establish the historical authenticity of the content of the Gospels, it is not enough to show that there was, from the very beginning, the possibility of active and faithful transmission of the words and actions of Jesus. Nor is it enough to show that there was, throughout the long course of the formation of tradition, concern for and the wish faithfully to transmit these words and actions of Jesus, not only on the part of the primitive Church, but also on the part of the evangelists. It still must be established that this fidelity belongs to *the order of facts* and is *verifiable*. In other terms, that writings and reality correspond. This *ultimate verification* is brought about by calling upon the criteria of historical authenticity, while literary criticism here gives way to historical criticism. Literary criticism, in fact, even if it reaches the most ancient forms of tradition, is not authorized, as such, to conclude there is historicity of content in an account or in a logion.

The study of the criteria of historicity is a recent undertaking which goes back to Kasemann, in 1954. Since then, interest did not cease to grow about the problems of criteriology. It is already shown in N.A. Dahl, R. Bultmann, F. Mussner, B. Rigaux, H. Schurmann, H. Conzelmann, W.

Trilling, X. Leon-Dufour, C. Martini, etc. Starting out from 1954, there are begun the first essays of systematization: attempts to define, to group and even to classify the criteria. To this second phase belong the works of H. K. McArthur, N. Perrin, I. de la Potterie, L. Cerfaux, M. Lehmann, J. Jeremias, R. Barbour, D.G.A. Calvert, J. Caba, N.J. McEleney, D. Luhrmann, E. Schillebeeckx, F. Lambiasi, F. Lentsen-Deis.

These authors, however, do not agree either about the number, or the nomenclature, or the classification, or the respective value of these criteria. Bultmann, for his part, only keeps two criteria; Perrin mentions three; de la Potterie and McArthur, four; Lehmann, eight; Calvert, eleven. As a whole, about fifteen criteria are thus enumerated.

Let us note immediately that the usage which may be made of these criteria, for qualifying as authentic or unauthentic the material studied, depends largely on the *Vorverstandnis* or the prior attitude adopted in regard to the Gospels.[1] Thus, A. Calvert observes that, with the help of the criteria, it is possible to come to an objective image of Jesus. He adds that the task is not without difficulty, "for there must constantly be made personal judgments on the nature of the evangelical material."[2] Dahl expresses his view in the same terms: "Here, generally the personal attitude of the researcher is decisive for appreciating the problem studied, and not the inverse."[3] We recognize that this difficulty affects as much radical criticism, typically represented by R. Bultmann and N. Perrin,[4] as it does Catholic criticism, naturally more optimistic. Without underestimating Radical Criticism, we must point out that it is losing ground. Among exegetes, there is coming about a more and more universal *consensus* in regard to certain criteria and their value. This *consensus*, as far from total distrust as it is from naive trust, represents a moderate criticism. Starting out from this *consensus* we shall proceed in the examination of the evangelical material and of the criteria of historical authenticity.

I. Signs and criteria, approaches and attitudes

However, it is important, before passing on to the study of the properly so called criteria, to make a certain number of critical distinctions and observations.

1) Let us distinguish first *signs* and *criteria*.[5] A sign may lead to a similitude, a probability, but not to a certain judgment of historical authenticity. Thus, the fact that the Gospels have preserved a certain number of pericopes, that are absolutely "neuter," that is, which do not show any visible theological intent (for example, Jesus sleeping on a cushion during the storm (Mk 4:38); or the curing of a blind man near *Jericho*, (Mt 10:46), constitutes a favorable sign, but not a criterion in the proper sense. Likewise the coloring and the vivaciousness of certain accounts, in Mark especially, invoked by Vincent Taylor[6] as a sign of a testimony by an eye witness, would not deserve the name of criterion. Of course such facts may show the faithfulness of tradition to the real event, but they may as well be indications of compositional activity. The proof of historicity is to be established. The same must be said of the "impression of truth" which the Gospels produce.[7] Well known is the reserve and even the distrust historians have as to this type of argument.

2) It is also important not to confuse the archaism of *forms* with the historical authenticity of their *content*. Thus, Bultmann esteemed that the study of the treatment to which the evangelical material was subjected on passing from Mark and from the *Quelle* to Matthew, Luke and John, and finally to the apocrypha, reveals the tendencies of tradition in the course of its transmission. Once the laws governing this transmission are known, it may be presumed they equally had a role in the case of Mark and of the *Quelle*. Thus it would be possible to find the early forms of tradition, or at the very least the purest forms.[8] McArthur points out some of these tendencies of tradition in development. He lists a) a tendency to modify the place, the time and the order of events; b) a modification of the beginning or of the end of an account, while the central portion remains unchanged; c) a tendency to make precise the accounts

by adding proper names; e) a tendency to slip in Aramaic words or phrases.[9]

Let us note that the application of this criterion rests on a solution of the synoptical problem which was given special concern from the start. Let us note too that the establishing of the "tendencies" or the "laws" of tradition is a fragile enterprise, exposed to all the risks of subjectivity. To conclude that the laws of tradition observed in Matthew, Luke and John, govern also the formation of Mark and the Quelle is even more hypothetical. Contemporary exegetics shows on the contrary that tradition ignores such laws and develops itself in most opposite directions. "It is at one and the same time longer and shorter, more detailed or less detailed, more Semitic or less Semitic."[10] If it is wished to speak of tendency of tradition, it will be necessary to furnish strict proofs and define the range of the phenomenon. Further, such a criterion, if it enables going back to the most ancient forms of tradition, is still set within the bounds of Literary Criticism. It is a criterion of archaism of the *forms*, but not of the historical authenticity of the *content* of the forms.

3) More correct is the approach and of more worth is the project of *Redaktionsgeschichte* which endeavors to find the compositional elements proper to each evangelist. When exegesis, indeed, came to find, in a logion or in an account, the compositional elements attributable to the evangelist or to the primitive Church, and when it finds itself faced with its most ancient form, we may presume that we have a serious sign of historicity, for we have reduced to the minimum the possibilities of deformation. Thus, in the pericope on the multiplication of the loaves (Mk 6:30-45), if we set aside the compositional elements of Mark and the traces of the re-reading of the event in liturgical catechesis, before Mark, we find the following nucleus which goes back to the oldest tradition we can reach. That is, an account of a miracle, in which it is related that Jesus had fed His disciples and a great multitude with a very small number of loaves and a very few fish. To research and thereby find the compositional elements of a pericope, and to come back to its oldest stage, is practically

to come back to its *Sitz im Leben*. Yet, strictly speaking, there is still not question of Historical Criticism but of *Literary Criticism*. There still remains to demonstrate the *historical reality* which underlies this account. It is then there enters in the properly so called criteria of historical authenticity. The results, however, of Literary Criticism, in certain cases, are so powerful, so compelling, they come close to the criterion of historicity. Proof that the frontier between a sign and a criterion, between a literary criterion and a historical criterion, is at times difficult to establish and that the passage of one to the other is imperceptible.

4) In a quite suggestive article,[11] McEleney observes that in the last analysis the *decisive* criterion is that of the "historical supposition," constantly used by historians. "There is accepted a statement on the word of the one who asserts it, until there is proof to the contrary."[12] Without this mutual trust, commerce between men becomes impossible. It must be supposed, as to the one who speaks, that he knows what he is talking about and intends to tell the truth. Unless there are serious reasons for distrust, it is taken on his word. So it would be very ungracious to refuse to make this presumption of veracity for the evangelists, and therefore of authenticity, which is freely granted to the human word and to every work of history. The criterion has so much the more weight in the case of the Gospels, that they belong to the literary genre "history" (on recognizing evidently the great part played by the interpretation they contain) and that we have no serious reason to doubt the good faith of the evangelists and of the primitive Church. Quite the contrary. Actually, McEleney concludes, exegetes and historians regularly call on this criterion.

We recognize the value of McEleney's observations, but it seems to us that the criterion he invokes expresses an *attitude* which precedes research or which *results* from it. In fact, the consideration of the literary genre "Gospel," the data of external criticism (notably testimony of the Churches of the 2nd century), the knowledge of the milieu in which was formed the evangelical tradition (pre-paschal community around Jesus, post-paschal community around the apostles), the manner of oral transmission in the Jewish milieu, authorize an over all confidence in regard to the Gospels, a favorable disposition, a "supposition of authenticity." The historian has no reason to approach the Gospels with a feeling of suspicion or aggressiveness. His supposition, however, not to remain vague and baseless, must submit the evangelical material to all the requirements of a critical and rigorous verification. Once this has been done, by recourse to the criteria of authenticity, its initial supposition, already globally founded, becomes a *certitude*, one that is *critically based*. The initial supposition is supported by external criteria. The certitude obtained at the end of the demonstration, is based rather on internal criteria. It seems to us therefore important not to confuse the criteria of authenticity with the *attitude* or the *state of mind* which brings about their application.

Likewise, there must be avoided confusing *criteria* and *proof*. Criteria are norms *applied* to the evangelical material, which enable us to prove the historical consistency of the accounts and to make a judgment of the authenticity or inauthenticity of their content. Their application enables the establishment of the *proof* or the *demonstration* of historical authenticity.

These observations once made, we may distinguish, among the properly so called criteria, the first or fundamental criteria, the second or derived criteria, and the mixed criteria.

II. First or fundamental criteria

By *fundamental* criteria we mean the criteria which have their own value, in themselves, and, consequently, authorize a certain judgment of historical authenticity. We do not say that these criteria must be employed in an exclusive manner, but we do say that they possess an intrinsic value sufficient for leading to certain and fruitful results. These criteria, acknowledged by even the most radical exegetes (except for the last criterion), are the following: the criterion of multiple attestation, the criterion of discontinuity, the criterion of coherence, the criterion of necessary explanation.

1) *The criterion of multiple attestation*

This criterion is proposed especially by Manson, Burkitt, Walker, Dodd, Downing, McArthur, Calvert, Perrin, Delorme, de la Potterie, Leon-Dufour, Zedda, Caba, Lambiasi, McEleney and Schillebeeckx. It is stated thus: "There may be considered as authentic an evangelical datum solidly attested to in all the sources (or most of them) of the Gospels (Mark, source of Matthew and of Luke; the Source, *Quelle,* source of Luke and of Matthew; the special sources of Matthew and of Luke and, eventually of Mark), and in the other writings of the New Testament, (especially the Acts the Gospel of John, the Epsitles of Paul, of Peter and of John, and the Epistle to the Hebrews." It is the criterion of most weight if the fact is found in diverse literary forms, attested to in many sources. Thus, the theme of sympathy and mercy of Jesus in regard to sinners, appears in all the sources of the Gospels and in the most varied literary forms (parable, Lk 15:11-32; controversies, Mt 21:28-32; accounts of miracles Mk 2:1-12; accounts of vocation, Mk 2:13-17).

This criterion is currently used in history. A concordant testimony, coming from diverse sources and not suspect of being intentionally linked among themselves, merits to be acknowledged as authentic. In an extreme case, Historian Criticism will say: "*Testis unus, testis nullus.*" The certitude obtained rests on the convergence and independence of the sources.[13]

The main difficulty the historian encounters in the application of this criterion to the Gospels concerns evidently the independence of source. In what measure is this independence assured, for, behind the *written* sources, there is the *oral* tradition, in the course of which the material studied might be introduced in the different sources, due to the role it had in the primitive Church.[14] This difficulty cannot be disregarded or minimized. This is why the conditions for the validity of this criterion need to be defined.

It is true that oral tradition and the primitive Church are the common source from which rose the evangelical tradition in its various written formulations. This assertion, however, must be nuanced and explained. Let us observe first that a *unique source* is not to be confused with a *unique attestation*. A source may represent a virtually large number of witnesses. Such is the case with 1Cor 15:3-9, which attests to the resurrection and the apparitions of Jesus. But what is even more important, in the case of the Gospels, is the quality of the *ecclesial milieu*. This is why the second critical verification of our demonstration has precisely as its object the study of this milieu. There results from this verification, the fact that the fundamental attitude of the primitive Church in regard to Jesus, is that of fidelity. This fidelity is guaranteed by the presence of eye witnesses, the apostles, and inscribed in the most frequently used words in the primitive kerygma (for instance, witnesses, tradition, ministry and ministers of the word, apostles, evangelists, teachers and preachers). We even know that the Churches of the 2nd century were convinced that the Gospels gave them true access to Jesus (His life and message), to the extent that the Gospels constituted for these Churches a norm of faith and of life even to the obligation of martyrdom. We likewise know the laws of oral transmission in the Judaism of the period, in which the teacher's word, and more so the word of Him whom the Church professed as her Lord, is the object of a sovereign respect. We know besides that the diversity and the regionalism of the ecclesial communities (diversity of language, mentality, culture) constitute a factor of independence which counterbalances the danger of uniformity. We may, finally, through the history of the composition, verify the degree of fidelity of written tradition in relation to oral tradition. The fidelity of the first enables us to conclude reasonably the fidelity of the second. These arguments authorize a *supposition*[15] (if not a certitude) in favor of the historicity of the evangelical material attested in many sources.

On this foundation of fidelity in the freedom, and of unity amid diversity of relevancies and interpretations, we can have trust in the criterion of multiple attestation and keep it as a fundamental criterion, especially when there is question of recognizing the essential characteristics of the figure, of the preaching, of the activity of Jesus. For example, the position He took in regard to the Law, to the poor, to sinners; His resistance to regal and political messianism; His activity as *thaumaturge* and His preaching in parables.

When there is question of logia or of particular facts, the criterion will as a rule have to be clarified by other criteria (for instance, discontinuity or coherence). In fact, it may happen that some evangelical material, present in many sources, may have been introduced before the sources were formed. Thus, Mark 8:34, on the necessity for the disciple of Jesus to bear His cross, is better explained in the context of the primitive preaching than in the context of the preaching of Jesus. The logion, though present in the triple tradition (Mt 16:24; Mk 8:34; Lk 9:23), reflects the post-paschal period. Yet the conformity of this logion with the whole of the message of Jesus on the necessity of dying to self in order to enter into the Kingdom, as well as the example of His own life and death, enable us to establish that it represents a faithful interpretation of Jesus. In other cases, the criterion suffices of itself to found a judgment of authenticity. Thus, the fact of the death of Jesus for the salvation of men is attested to in all the sources and beams on all the pericopes.

In summary, we may conclude that the criterion of multiple attestation is of value, and admitted to be so, when there is question of establishing the essential characteristics of the figure, the preaching and the activity of Jesus. When there is question of particular pericopes it is of value when it is supported by other criteria or when there is no serious reason for doubting the authenticity of the material attested.

2) *The criterion of discontinuity*

Agreement on this criterion is practically unanimous, even if the formulations presented concerning it vary. It is accepted by Bultmann, Kasemann, Conzelmann, Bornkamm, Jeremias, Perrin, McArthur, Dahl, Mussner, Trilling, Schurmann, Rigaux, Cerfaux, Leon-Dufour, Caba, Lentzen-Deis, de la Potterie, Calvert, Zedda, Lambiasi, McEleney and Schillebeeckx. It is formulated thus: "An evangelical datum (especially when there is question of the words and attitudes of Jesus) may be considered irreducible, whether to the concepts of Judaism, or to the concepts of the primitive Church.[16]

Before even envisaging the particular accounts, it may be said that the Gospels, as a whole, present themselves as an example of *discontinuity*, in the sense of forming something unique and original in relation to all other literature. The literary genre "Gospel" is in discontinuity with ancient Judaic literature as well as with later Christian literature. The Gospels are neither biographies, nor apologies, nor doctrinal speculations, but *testimonies* on the unique event of the coming of God into history, the tongue and the flesh of man. Their *content* is the person of Christ, a person who is not classified according to the categories of secular universal history, nor according to those of the history of religions. Jesus reveals Himself to the historian as an absolutely unique being.[17]

Examples of this discontinuity, at the level of pericopes, are innumerable, and deal with *form* as well as *content*. Here are some examples, first, of discontinuity with ancient Judaism. Jeremias studied, with particular attention, the instances of discontinuity which deal with *form*.[18] Thus, in the very frequent usage He makes of *antithetical* parallelism. Jesus, differing from the Old Testament, places the accent on the second part of the parallelism, rather than on the first (Mt 7:3-5). Likewise, differing from the Old Testament which makes use of the expression *Amen* for showing assent to a word already spoken, Jesus uses *Amen* (meaning in the Synoptics "verily"), or *Amen, amen* (in St. John), followed by "I say to you," "I tell you it," to introduce His own words. Analogous to that of the prophets, this manner of speaking shows the unique authority of Him who also said: "I am."

Discontinuity is still more significative on the level of *attitudes* and *content*. Thus, the expression *Abba* employed by Jesus to address God, shows an intimacy of relationship which is something unheard of in relation to ancient Judaism. Only Jesus may turn to God as to His Father, and only He can authorize His own to repeat with Him: "Our Father."[19] In the face of the *Law*, Jesus does not have the attitude of the Pharisees obsessed by the details of external observance. His attention as a whole is on the spirit of the law. His attitude, for instance, in regard to the sabbath and the legal purification represents an instance of a break with the rabbinical world. Likewise, His view of the *Kingdom* differs radically from that of the Jewish manner. This image joins the grandeur of the Davidic kingdom to the humility of the preaching to the poor, and the final glorification of the Son of man to the redemptive suffering of the Servant of Jahweh.

Let us now see some examples of discontinuity with the concepts of the primitive Church:

1) The baptism of Jesus counts Him among sinners. How could the primitive Church, which proclaims Jesus "Lord," invent a scene in such violent contrast with her faith? The same must be said about the triple temptation, the agony in the garden, and the death on the cross.

2) The command given the apostles not to preach to the Samaritans and to the Gentiles, no longer corresponds to the situation of a Church which is open to all nations.

3) The calling of the disciples *by* Jesus is in discontinuity with the rabbinical context, where it is the disciple who chooses his master, and with that of the primitive Church in which the expression "disciple" designates above all one who believes in Jesus.

4) All the passages of the Gospels, in which, despite the veneration of the primitive Church for the apostles, there is emphasized their lack of understanding, their faults and even their desertion (betrayal by Judas, denial by Peter) contrast with the post-paschal situation.

5) The Gospels have preserved the enigmas of the speech of Jesus, while the Church, thenceforth capable of understanding them, could be tempted to leave them out (Mt 11:11-12; Mk 9:31; 14:58; Lk 13:32; Mk4:11).

6) Keeping, by the Gospels, expressions such as "kingdom" "Son of man," represents an already anachronistic situation in relation to the more developed theology of St. Paul.

For Bultmann and Kasemann, the criterion of discontinuity is practically the only legitimate criterion. For others (the majority), this criterion is fundamental, but it must be used in connection with others, notably with the criterion of coherence.

Miss Hooker, in an article on N. Perrin's position,[20] rightly emphasizes the dangers of a too exclusive use of this criterion, which would tend to discard as unauthentic all which would be set in the line of Judaism or of the primitive Church. To reason thus, would be to make of Christ a being outside of time, cut off from His environment and His era. This would be to place Christ in a *vacuum*, without influence received from Judaism, and without influence exercised on the Church. Or, it would be to accept the supposition, unfounded, that the Church only deformed, or invented what concerns Jesus. The truth is that Christ, a Jew of His times, took on Himself the environment and the history of His people, along with their linguistic, social and religious traditions. On the other hand, the Acts show us how the Church remained attached to Judaism, and how painfully she succeeded in disengaging herself from it so as not to collapse with it.

We may conclude that the criterion of discontinuity provides us with an important minimum of historical data on Jesus. It is particularly valuable for knowing about certain words, certain events of His existence and certain essential topics of His preaching. But it would be illegitimate, on the basis of this sole criterion, to eliminate all that is in conformity with Judaic tradition or with ecclesial tradition.

3) *The criterion of coherence*

The criterion of coherence (or of *continuity* or of *conformity*) is proposed and accepted by authors as different as Bultmann, Bornkamm, Dahl, Mussner, Rigaux, Leon-Dufour, Trilling, Perrin, Calvert, Jeremias, de la Potterie, Lentsen-Deis, Zedda, Cerfaux, Caba, Schillebeeckx, Lambiasi. It is not, however, understood by all in the same way.

Thus, B. Rigaux, in an important article of the *Revue Biblique*,[21] gladly emphasizes the *coherence* of the evangelical accounts with the Palestinian and Jewish milieu of the period of Jesus, such as we know it through history, archeology and literature. In fact, the evangelical description of the human environment (work, habitation, professions), of the linguistic and cultural environment (patterns of thought, Aramaic substratum), of the social, economic, political and juridical environment, of the religious environment especially (with its rivalries between Pharisees and Sadducees, its religious preoccupations concerning the clean and the unclean, the law and the sabbath, demons and angels, the poor and the rich, the Kingdom of God and the end of time), the evangelical description of all this is remarkably *faithful* to the complex picture of Palestine at the time of Jesus. This conformity with the *unique* moment which represents the appearance of Jesus in Israel, constitutes, in the eyes of Rigaux, an indubitable sign of authenticity. In fact, it would not be possible to invent from all these pieces an ensemble so important and so complex, which effects the Gospels down to their ultimate particulars, like a web of woven straw. The sufficient reason of this fidelity is in reality itself.

Bultmann and Perrin consider as authentic only the materials admitted to be *conformed* to the materials obtained through the criterion of discontinuity. In other terms, once obtained, by means of the criterion of discontinuity, the authentic nucleus of the sayings and deeds of Jesus (especially His death on the cross and His preaching on the kingdom), all that is in conformity with these elements and with the image drawn from it, belong to the Jesus of history. Thus, the application of the criterion enables us to acknowledge as authentic the parables of the kingdom.

Widening and deepening this criterion, de la Potterie acknowledges as authentic all that is conformed to the central teaching of Jesus about the imminent coming of the Kingdom.[22] The subject of the Kingdom of God belongs in fact to the most ancient strata of the evangelical tradition. It is besides attested to by the criterion of discontinuity. Found omnipresent in the Synoptics, it has a resonance of eschatological urgency which distinguishes it as well from ancient Judaism as from the primitive preaching of the Church.[23]

Conformity with the environment, such as Rigaux understands it, seems to us a valid argument for proving the universal historicity of the Gospels. Indeed, when accounts so significant reflect an environment so faithfully, it may be said that there is therein a solid presumption of authenticity. The more so since the evangelical description flows from a source and does not show the least *post factum* attempt of reconstruction. Let us note, however, that such conformity does not lead directly to the historical Jesus, but to the *environment* in which He lived. It could not be sufficient of itself alone.

This is why we propose for the criterion of coherence the following definition, which includes the positions of Rigaux, Perrin and de la Potterie. "A saying or an act of Jesus may be considered as authentic when it is in strict conformity not only with the epoch and the environment of Jesus (the linguistic, geographic, social, political, religious environment), but also and above all closely coherent with the essential teaching, the heart of the message of Jesus, that is, the arrival and the instauration of the messianic Kingdom." In this regard, typical are the examples of the parables, all centered on the Kingdom and on the conditions of its development (analyzed by Jeremias), the example of the Beatitudes, originally the proclamation of the Good Tidings about the arrival of the messianic Ringdom (analyzed by Dupont), the example of the Pater Noster, originally and essentially a prayer for the restoration of the Kingdom (analyzed by H. Schurmann, J. Alonso Diaz, R.E. Brown, J. Jeremias), the example of miracles,[24] intimately connected with the subject of the Kingdom of God and to that of conversion, the example of the triple temptation (analyzed by Dupont and Jeremias). This is in conformity with the context of the life of Jesus and His concept of the kingdom: The Jews are insistently asking for a sign, a prodigy, Jesus constantly is refusing to give one. The Jews await a political and temporal Messiah, Jesus preaches about an interior Kingdom; the confrontation of the Kingdom of God and the Kingdom of Satan.

If we seek now to define the relationship which exists between the criterion of discontinuity and the criterion of coherence, we may say that both criteria are *different* from and *complementary* of each other at the same time.

It is conformity with the environment which enables placing Jesus in history and concluding that He is truly of His times, while the criterion of discontinuity shows Jesus as a unique and original phenomenon. He is at one and the same time attached to and detached from His times. It is also the criterion of discontinuity which enables the establishing of the essential characteristics of His personality and His teaching. On this limited but firm basis, the criterion of coherence also enlarges, amplifies, as from concentric circles, the zones of authenticity. The subject of the Kingdom, for instance, shines on the parables, the beatitudes, the miracles, the triple temptation, the Father. Finally, it is through the use of these two criteria that we come to establish what we shall later on call the *style* of Jesus. So there must be guarded against, in practice, isolating the two criteria, as absolutes. Valid of themselves, they are intended to clarify each other, to lend each other mutual support.

4) *The criterion of necessary explanation*

Although not known by most authors who are interested in the problem of evangelical criteriology, this criterion seems of capital importance to us. We even consider it as the most important of the fundamental criteria. We present the following formulation of it. "If, before a considerable collection of facts or of data, which require a coherent and sufficient explanation, there is offered an explanation which clarifies and brings together in harmony all these elements (which, otherwise, would remain enigmas), we may conclude that we are in the presence of an authentic datum (fact, deed, attitude, word of Jesus)."[25]

This criterion, evidently, puts in play a collection of observations which act by way of convergence, and whose totality demands an intelligible solution, that is, the reality of an initial fact. The exegete, who by profession toils rather on the level of particular pericopes, will be perhaps less sensitive to this class of criterion, habitually used however in history, in matters of law, in theology, and in most of the human science (sociology, anthropology).

This criterion, to tell the truth, is only the application, in the area of law, or of history of the principle of sufficient reason. Thus, when there is question of finding the author of a crime, the hypothesis which succeeds in clarifying the greatest number of facts is that which justice holds as the explanation of the crime. Likewise, Historical Criticism holds as acceptable the interpretation which renders an account of the greatest number of facts attested to by a rigorous documentation.[26] In the case of the Gospels, criticism has therefore a reason to hold as authentic an explanation which solves a great number of problems without causing even greater ones, or without causing even one to come about.

1) A great number of facts of the life of Jesus (for instance, His attitude in regard to legal ordinances, Jewish authorities, the Scriptures; the prerogatives He attributes to Himself; the language He adopts; the prestige He has and the charm He exercises on the disciples and on the people) have meaning only if we admit from the start the existence of a unique and transcendant personality. Such an explanation is more consistent than that of recourse to a primitive Church which invented the myth Jesus.

This criterion enables the setting up of the great lines of the career of Jesus: His initial success, His breaking away from Galilee, His activity in Jerusalem, His breaking away from the people, the attention he brought to and concentrated on His disciples.

3) In the case of miracles, we find ourselves before a dozen important facts, which the most severe criticism cannot challenge, and which require adequate explanation: the popular enthusiasm on the appearance of Jesus, the apostles' belief He is the Messiah, the place of miracles in the synoptic and Joannine tradition, the hatred of the high priests and of the Pharisees due to the prodigies worked by Jesus, the constant

link between the miracles and the message of Jesus about the decisive coming of the Kingdom, the place of miracles in the early kerygma, the close relationship between the claims of Jesus that He is the Son of the Father and the miracles as signs of His Might. All these facts demand an explanation, a sufficient reason.

Pushing still further our research, we think that this criterion of "necessary explanation" is of a nature to clarify some of the most acute problems of contemporaneous christology, notably those of messianic consciousness and of the divine filiation of Jesus. In fact, how to explain that, from the beginnings of Christianity, in the *Acts of the Apostles*, in the Epistles of Paul, in the oldest formulas of faith, in the liturgical hymns, in the predication and new behavior of the apostles, Jesus is ever presented as Christ, the Lord and the Son of God? We find ourselves in the presence of a unanimous agreement. To suppose that all this is but a spontaneous generation, a creation of a wild imagination, or the fruit of a faith without roots, is rather a *deus ex machina* than a true explanation. It is profitable and more coherent to think that this unanimous agreement of the primitive Church was due to its *raison d'etre* in the very existence of Jesus who, during His life, by His actions as by His speech, enabled the subject of His being the Messiah and the Son of God, to germinate, mature and fructify.[27] The faith of the Church is not a satellite without a launching pad.

Even if the field of privileged action of the criterion of necessary explanation is that of the major subjects of the Gospel, let us note that it is also applied as well to the particular pericopes, as I. de la Potterie has shown very well apropos of the multiplication of the loaves. In the case of this episode, there must be explained why subsequent to the event, Jesus was considered a great prophet, even the prophet expected by the nation, and why they wanted to make Him king. There must be explained the dangerous explosion of political messianism which the act of Jesus provoked. There must be explained why Jesus forced the disciples to re-embark without delay, as if they refused to abandon something to which they were enthusiastically devoted. There must be explained that the episode, at first not understood, was nevertheless for the disciples a decisive fact in their path to belief that Jesus was the Messiah. There must be explained why Mark brought out so strongly the christological import of the event and its value as a messianic revelation. There must be explained the fact, unique in kind, of the importance which the account takes on in the successive stages of tradition, first in liturgical catechesis, then in the composition of the Synoptics and of the Gospel of John, and finally, in the patristic tradition and in the iconography of the first centuries. All these facts brought together, some minimal, but most of great import, demand an explanation which is not farcical. If it is admitted that Jesus truly performed in wondrous-wise ways, this messianic feeding of the multitude in the desert, there is found in this initial fact the basis and sufficient reason of all the facts we have just mentioned.[28]

III. Second or derived criterion: the style of Jesus

There exists, in fact, in the speech as in the actions of Jesus, some characteristic traits, which constitute what may be called the style of Jesus, a unique and inimitable style. By *style*, we understand less the literary style than the *life style*.[29]

Jeremias in his studies on the Aramaic substratum of the Gospels endeavors to find the special modes of speech of Jesus.[30] Most assuredly, the study of the Aramaic and Semitic forms underlying the present text, enables us to go far back into tradition and reach the stage of the primitive Church and of oral tradition, but not necessarily the *ipsissima verba Jesu*. Let us repeat, the archaism of an expression or of a logion must not be confused with its historical authenticity. The influence of tradition can be enough to account for these linguistic phenomena. The study of the *literary* style will often be a solid indication of authenticity, but not a properly so called criterion. It must be said of this indication what we said above about the conformity of the Gospels with the Jewish environment, that is, there is question here of conformity with the linguistic milieu of the epoch.

More important and decisive seems to us what we call the *life or personal style* of Jesus. This time the style is the turn of thought which shapes speech; it is spirit, the movement of being which is imprinted not only on speech but on all attitudes and all behavior. It is this inimitable imprint of the person especially on all that is done and on all that is said. The components of this style, however, cannot be established save by starting out from the fundamental criteria of multiple attestation, of discontinuity, of conformity and of necessary explanation. So let us speak of a second or derived criterion. Once recognized a defined, style becomes in turn a criterion of authenticity.

A propos of the *speech* of Jesus, Schurmann has us note that it is characterized by a consciousness of self of a singular majesty, without parallel; by a note of solemnity, of elevation, of sacredness; by an accent of the same time of authority, of simplicity, of kindness, of eschatological urgency. Jesus inagurates in His person a new era.[31]

In His *conduct*, Trilling observes, there may be noted "an ever the same love of sinners, of pity for those who suffer, or are enslaved, an impitiable harshness toward every form of self-sufficiency, a holy wrath against lying and hypocrisy. And above all, a radical relation to God, Lord and Father."[32]

These characteristics are found in the actions as well as in the teaching of Jesus. There is, in His words, a tone of simplicity, of sweetness, and at the same time of sovereign authority. Thus, the same Jesus who proclaims Himself the servant of all, the good shepherd, the friend of the poor and the humble, is also He who declares: "I have come ..., I say to you ..., Verily, I tell you it ... Who builds on my word ... Go ... Come ... Follow me ... Stand ... March ..." His word has a tone of eschatological urgency: "Up to now it has been said to you ... From now on ... Then will be seen the Son of Man ... Heaven and earth shall pass, my words will never pass ... In those days, affliction will be such ..." Not only does Jesus inaugurate a new epoch, the decisive epoch announced and waited for the prophets, but it is He Himself, *in person*, who is the point of convergence with the Old testament and the beginning of the last end.

His actions show the same characteristics of simplicity and authority, and above all of kindness, of compassion toward sinners and all those who are suffering. Thus, the parable of Luke on the prodigal son describes the incomprehensible bounty of God toward sinners, but at the same time justifies the personal attitude of Jesus who frequents publicans and sinners, and eats at their tables. The same attitude is found in the parable of the lost sheep. It belongs to the *style* Jesus. The style of the miracles is identical with that of the teaching. It is made up of simplicity, of sobriety, of authority.[33]

IV. Mixed criteria

At times an important literary sign makes a compromise with one or more historical criteria. There is then involved a mixed criterion. We present here two particularly important forms of this criterion.

1) Internal intelligibility of the Account

When an evangelical datum is perfectly inserted in its immediate or mediate context, and, moreover, perfectly, coherent in its internal structure (in all the elements which compose it), it may be deemed there is question of an authentic datum. However of itself this ascertaining of the internal intelligibility of an account or of a group of pericopes, cannot constitute a criterion of historical authenticity. So we are again within the bounds of the literary sign. In order to be of validity on the historical level, the fact of internal intelligibility must be supported by one or many criteria, for instance, multiple attestation, discontinuity, coherence. The combination constitutes a *mixed* criterion.

Thus, the Synoptics, as St. John, attest that the true motive for the death of Jesus is the hostility of the leaders of Israel against Christ, and His claim to be Messiah and having equality with God (Jn 10:33; Mk 14:60-64). However, all recount the apparently political motive for His death and all recount the fact of the inscription on the Cross: "Jesus King of the Jews." There is an internal coherence between the trial, the attitude of the leaders of Israel before the Romans, and the inscription on the cross. This coherence of the account, *at the same time* as the multiple attestation of the fact (synoptic tradition, St. John, the Acts) and the contrast, the discontinuity between the evangelical account and the conviction of the primitive Church, constitute a mixed criterion and a sound guarantee of historicity.

Likewise, the fact of the burial of Jesus is attested to in the Synoptics, in St. John, in the First Epistle to the Corinthians (1 Cor 15:3), and in the Acts. Besides, in the account by Mark, we have a group of fully coherent findings. Thus, Pilate is surprised that Jesus is already dead. This is why he questions the centurion who was in charge about it. The request to bury Jesus was made by a member of the sanhedrin whose name was Joseph of Arimathia, a name verifiable by everyone. Jesus had to be buried at once since it was the eve of the sabbath. The women, frightened, only looked on. The body of Jesus was laid in a tomb near Calvary. Now a tomb is something which lasts and can be kept up. All these characteristics, multiple and coherent, constitute a literary sign which, with the criterion of multiple attestation, has value as a mixed criterion.

2) Diverse interpretation, agreement as to basis

Of itself, the diverse interpretation of a teaching or of a miracle is a phenomenon which comes from compositional activity. It testifies at the same time to the freedom of the writer and his respect for the sources. It brings us back to a most ancient tradition and, consequently, reduces to the minimum the mediations which separate us from Jesus, as well as from possibililities of deformation. But still it does not thereby constitute a criterion of historicity. Thus, the fact that Luke emphasized the social import of the beatitudes, while Matthew showed their moral import, enables J. Dupont to reconstruct the probable early form of the beatitudes in the oral tradition.

But it is by the application of the criteria of discontinuity and coherence that there is a passing from Literary Criticism to Historical Criticism. Once more, here we are in the presence of a *mixed* criterion. Agreement as to basis, despite the diversity of interpretations, however, constitutes a strong presumption of historical authenticity.

Thus, the parable of the feast, in Luke 14:16-24, signifies that the men are invited to the messianic joy, under the traditional figure of a banquet, but that they depreciate this promised felicity, due to their over worldly concerns. The places left free by those invited are offered to the poor. In Matthew 22:1-14, Matthew who writes for the Judeo-Christians, makes of the parable an allegory applied to the history of Israel. The Jews invited to the messianic Kingdom, rejected the invitation. They slew the prophets and persecuted the apostles. So the Roman soldiers destroyed Jerusalem, while the Gentiles took the place of the Jews in the Kingdom and came to faith. In Luke as in Matthew, the message is the same: more original in Luke, more relevant in Matthew. The invitation to the Kingdom through detachment and through belief, is, however, a subject which is attached to the fundamental teaching of Jesus. It belongs to Jesus. The criterion of coherence comes to the support of a literary sign.

A propos of the multiplication of loaves, John emphasizes more than Mark the sacramental symbolism of the miracle. Mark in turn emphasizes more than Luke the christological import of the miracle and presents Christ as the good Shepherd who has pity "on the sheep without a shepherd" (Mk 6:34). The Gospel of John contains many details which are peculiar to him: the place and the time of the miracle, the conversation with the disciples, the identification of Jesus by the people as the messianic prophet, the attempt to carry Him off and make Him king, the sermon on the bread of life, the division among the disciples before the demands of Jesus (Jn 6). There is ever question of the same fact, but interpreted and given depth. This literary sign is supported by the criterion of multiple attestation, for the fact is attested to by the synoptic tradition and the Joannine tradition. It is also supported by the criterion of coherence, for it is presented as a sign of the messianic and eschatological kingdom. Finally, it is supported by the criterion of necessary explanation, for without the actuality of the event, many facts remain without sufficient reason.

The cure of the epileptic child is attested to by the three synoptics, but interpreted in three different ways. *Luke* sees in the miracle an act of kindness by Jesus on behalf of the disconsolate father (Lk 9:42); *Mark*, in conformity with his overall perspective of his gospel sees in it first of all striking triumph of Jesus over Satan (Mk 9:14-27); *Matthew* finally, emphasizes the necessity of belief in the mission of Jesus (Mt 17:19). It is because they lacked this faith that the disciples could not exorcise the possessed. There is agreement on the fact, but diveristy of interpretations. Those interpretations have the very richness of the event, of an indefinite intelligility.

V. Conclusions

1) A first conclusion concerns the very usage to the criteria. The *proof* or demonstration of historical authenticity of the Gospels rests on the convergent usage of the criteria. Even if, in a particular case, such a criterion is found not to apply (for instance, the criterion of multiple attestation), in most of the episodes, there is convergence of many criteria. At the least one criterion, clearly valid, is found confirmed by one or many others. Further, when there is question of major themes of the Gospels (for example, of the Kingdom and of miracles), here is an application of all the criteria.[34]

2) A second conclusion concerns the extent and quality of the evangelical material as authentic by the application of the criterion of authenticity. Even upon adopting the position of moderate criticism (halfway between trust in principle and distrust of principle), there are astonishing results. Almost the totality of the evangelical material is thus recovered. These results concern:

a) the linguistic milieu, human, social, political, economic, cultural, juridical, religious (Rigaux).

b) The great lines of the ministry of Jesus: the beginnings

in Galilee, the enthusiasm of the people and of the apostles before the prodigies accomplished, the gradual lack of understanding, the ministry in Jerusalem, the political and religious trial, the condemnation and death (Trilling).

c) The great events of the life of Jesus: the baptism (de la Potterie), the temptations (Dupont), the transfiguration (Dupont), the teaching on the decisive coming of the Kingdom, the call to penitence and to conversion (Bultmann, Perrin), the teaching in parables, the parables of the Kingdom (Jeremias, Perrin), the Beatitudes (Dupont), the Father (Jeremias, Schurmann, Brown), the miracles and exorcisms as signs of the Kingdom (Mussner), the betrayal by Judas, the agony, the trial, the crucifixion, the burial, the resurrection (Trilling).

d) The controversies with the scribes and Pharisees on the regulations covering the sabbath, legal purity, divorce, taxes.

e) The contrasting attitudes of simplicity and authority, of absolute purity and of compassion for sinners, the poor, the ill, the oppressed, the attitude of service, even to the giving of life (Schurmann, Jeremias, Trilling).

f) The formulas of an obscure christology, at times enigmatic: sign of Jonas, sign of the Temple, Son of man.

g) The logia which belittle Jesus and constitute Him inferior to God.

h) The rejection of a political and temporal messianism, the preaching of a kingdom to be reached by way of penitence, conversion, faith.

i) The astonishing pretentions manifested in the antitheses of the sermon on the mount; in the attitudes in regard to the prescriptions of the law; in the usage of the term *Abba* to signify His relationship to God; in His assimilation with the Danielian Son of man and in the statements which will bring Him to death.

j) The calling and the mission of the apostles: their enthusiasm, then their lack of understanding; their betrayal and their desertion.

On each of the subjects enumerated, we can invoke the testimony of many exegetes. To the extent that researches go on, the material acknowledged as authentic grows ceaselessly until it covers the whole Gospel.

3) A third conclusion concerns the attitude of the historian in regard to the Gospels. After a rigorous application of the criteria of historical authenticity, it may no longer be said, as did Bultmann: "Of Jesus of Nazareth, nothing is known, or almost nothing." An assertion of this type is no longer tenable.

Further, the whole attitude in regard to the Gospels must be modified. During almost a century, there has prevailed a systematic prejudice of distrust toward the Gospels, the burden of proof ever falling on the Gospels. After recent studies carried on since 1950 on the criteria of historical authenticity, this attitude of the masters of distrust can no longer be maintained, for it is counter to the very evidence of history. The positions must be reversed and it should be said: *In dubiis stat traditio.* In other words, the burden of proof, is not on those who acknowledge Jesus at the source of the words and actions preserved in the Gospels, but on those who consider them as interpolations or as inventions of the early Church. The presupposition that the Gospels merit trust is founded, while the prejudice that the Gospels are not worthy of trust, is not.

This reversing of positions does not mean that criticism has gone back to an attitude of naive and a critical confidence. Confidence leaves room for an unlimited number of nuances. We only declare that the Gospels have now become creditable in the eyes of historical criticism. This change of attitude is attributable largely to recent researches on the criteria of authenticity.

Footnotes for Chapter XV

1. R. Brown, "After Bultmann, What? An Introduction to the Post-Bultmanians," *Catholic Biblical Quarterly*, XXVI (1964) p. 26.
2. A. Calvert, "An examination of the Criteria for distinguishing the Authentic Words of Jesus," *New Testament Studies* XVIII (1972), p. 219.
3. "Here, generally, the total perspective of the scholar is decisive for an evaluation of the case in point, and not vice-versa" (N.A. Dahl, Kerygma and History in;

240   FINDING JESUS THROUGH THE GOSPELS

H.K. McArthur, ed., *In Search of the Historical Jesus* (London, 1970) p. 133).
4. N. Perrin, *Rediscovering the Teaching of Jesus*, (London, 1967), p. 15.
5. Cf. the useful observations of F. Lambiasi, *L'autenticita storica dei Vangeli. Studio di Criteriologia* (Bologna, 1976) pp. 139-140.
6. V. Taylor, *The Gospel according to St. Mark*, (London, 1962), pp. 53, 82.
7. A. Dulles, *Apologetics and the Biblical Christ* (Westminster, 1964), pp. 37-41; J.-B. Phillips, *Ring of Truth* (London, 1967).
8. R. Bultmann, "The New Approach of the Synoptic Problem," *The Journal of Religion*, VI (1926) 337-362. Cf. S.M. Ogden, ed., *Existence and Faith: Shorter Writings of Rudolph Bultmann* (New York, 1960), pp. 35-54, esp. p. 41.
9. H.K. McArthur, "A Survey of Recent Gospel Research," *Interpretation* XVIII (1964), 49.
10. E.P. Sanders, *The Tendencies of the Synoptic Tradition* (Cambridge, 1969), p. 272.
11. N.J. McEleney, "Authenticating Criteria and Mark" 7:1-23, *Catholic Biblical Quarterly*, XXXIV (1972) 430-460, esp. 445-448.
12. *Ibid.*, 446.
13. H.I. Marrou, *De la connaisance historique* (Paris, 1966). pp. 128-132; G.J. Garraghan, *A Guide to Historical Method* (New York, 1946), p. 308; C.V. Langlois, & C. Seignobos, *Introduction aux études historiques* (Paris, 1897), p. 168.
14. N.J. McEleney, "Authenticating Criteria and Mark" 7:1-23, *Catholic Biblical Quarterly*, XXXIV (1972) p. 434.
15. Expression by N.J. McEleney.
16. In perspective of *Redaktionsgeschichte*, there may still be spoken of discontinuity or of "refractory traditions," in a sense which it is well to make clear. It being admitted that each evangelist has his point of view and his favorite subjects, all data which does not fit into the framework of this point of view may be considered authentic. The maintaining or the insertion of this data signifies at least that it has in the eyes of the primitive Church such importance that the evangelist would not be able to leave it out or interpret it otherwise. We know, for example, that Matthew and Mark differently regard the apostles: Mark emphasizes frequently their lack of understanding, while Matthew is more indulgent. The preservation of a passage which runs counter to a known attitude of Mark and of Matthew is a guarantee of authenticity.
17. E. Kasemann, *Essays on New Testament Themes* (London, 1964), pp. 46-47; J. Jeremias, *The Problem of the Historical Jesus* (Philadelphia, 1964); L. Cerfaux, *Jésus aux origines de la Tradition*, (Bruges, 1968), p. 62.
18. J. Jeremias, *Neutestamentliche Theologie*, Erster Teil: *Die Verkundigung Jesu* (Gottingen, 1971), ch. I.
19. *Ibid.*, ch.II.
20. Critique of the position of N. Perrin, *Rediscovering the Teaching of Jesus* (London, 1967) by M.D. Hooker, "Christology and Methodology," *New Testament Studies* XVII (1970-1971), pp. 480-487.
21. B. Rigaux, "L'historicite de Jesus devant l'exégese recente," *Revue Biblique*, LXVIII (1958), 518-520.
22. I. de la Potterie, "Come impostare il problema del Gesu storico?", *La Civilta Cattolica*, CXX (1969) qu. 2855, 447-463; cf also; H. Schurmann, "Die Sprache des Christus," *Biblische Zeitschrift*, II (1958), 55.
23. J. Jeremias, *Neutestamentliche Theologie*, Erster Teil. ch. I, N. Perrin, *Jesus and*

and the Language of the Kingdom, (London, 1976).

24. R. Latourelle, "Authenticite historique des miracles de Jesus. Essai de criteriologie," *Gregorianum* LIV (1973), 225-262.

25. The facts which are the subject of explanation may be of a very diverse nature and involve external as well as internal criticism. For instance, charm of Jesus, the enthusiasm of the throngs, the hatred by Jewish authorities, the fecundity and diffusion of Christian faith. The essential is the attestation and accumulation of facts which demand a satisfactory explanation.

26. "The only possible explanation why so many bits of evidence point to the same alleged fact, is that the fact is objectively true" (Cf. J. Garraghan, *A Guide to Historical Method,* p. 305).

27. A. Dulles, rightly distrustful of an apologetic which would intend to isolate the event from its interpretation, has recourse, in his own exposition, to the criterion of necessary explanation. He emphasizes that Christianity presents a certain number of facts which require a sufficient reason. These facts are: 1) the unique image of Christ, underlying the diversity of perspectives and approaches of the New Testament; 2) the invincible assurance of witnesses of Christ founded on an irrefutable experience; 3) the wholly new character, unheard of, of the message of the Gospel; 4) the radical transformation of the apostles and the pervasive fire of their hope and charity; 5) the fecundity of a message which regenerated a decadent world and which lost nothing of its power of transformation. The heart of this message, is the person of Christ, endowed with contrasting and transcendant characteristics.

After this exposition, A. Dulles concludes: "The rational inquirer must seek to give some explanation for the genesis of the extraordinary faith and the unique religious society depicted for us in the New Testament. One answer is that given by the New Testament writers themselves. If we accept that explanation, we can readily account for all the attributes we have just noted in the message and in the witness of the primitive Church. If it be false, the faith of the first Christians is an enigma." (A. Dulles, *Apologetics and the Biblical Christ,* pp. 37-41). All the facts enumerated by Dulles can be the object of observation on the part of an honest researcher. One principle if sufficient enables the making of a conclusion on a reality of which it renders an account.

28. I. de la Potterie, "Le sens primitif de la multiplication des pains," in J. Dupont, ed. *Aux origines de la christologie* (Gembloux, 1975), pp. 323-324.

29. Cf. G. Bornkamm, *Jesus of Nazareth* (London, 1960), pp. 59-66; F. Lambias, *L'autenticita storica dei Vangeli,* pp. 178-181.

30. J. Jeremias, *Neutestamentiche Theologie,* Erster Teil, ch. I.

31. H. Schurmann, "Die Sprache des Christus," *Biblische Zeitschrift* II (1958), 54-84.

32. W. Trilling, *Jésus devant l'histoire* (Paris, 1968), p. 59.

33. R. Latourelle, "Authenticité historique des miracles de Jésus. Essai de criteriologie," *Gregarianum,* LIV, (1973), 251-255.

34. *Ibid.,* 260.

Conclusion

SUMMARY AND EVALUATION OF OUR STUDY

On terminating our study, the results obtained we think may be summed up under three heads: the type of demonstration developed, the ways of approach implied, the itinerary thus opened up for finding Jesus. This chapter as a conclusion synthesizes the elements of the analysis, but at the same time shows how the convergence of the proofs gives new weight to the demonstration and to the certitude on which it is based.

I. A demonstration

A first conclusion concerns the nature of the undertaking. It is not an introduction to the Gospels, nor a history of evangelical criticism, nor a presentation of recent methods of exegesis applied to the Gospels. It is above all an endeavor to solve a problem, and a demonstration, of which all the stages are articulated and linked, in view of a conclusion, qualified itself by the validity of the proofs brought out and by their convergent usage.

The problem is that of the relationship existing between the Christ of the Gospels, professed as Messiah, Lord and Son of God, and Jesus of Nazareth, the prophet followed by enthusiastic throngs, then rejected and condemned by the leaders of His nation. If it is true that we have access to Jesus only through the testimonies of the primitive Christian communities, is it equally true that the Jesus presented by the Gospels corresponds substantially to the historical reality of Jesus of Nazareth? Is it possible to establish that the ecclesial interpretation of Jesus is faithful to the meaning Jesus put into and manifested in His existence? What paths must we traverse, starting out from the texts, to meet with the message, the actions and the person of Jesus? If Christianity cannot be defined in its relationship to Jesus, as the seat of the decisive intervention of God in history, the discourse of faith is vain and threatened by ideology.

In an early period, we have followed the evolution of evangelical criticism. After a period of increasing radicalization, which extends from Reimarus to Bultmann, criticism ushers in a movement of reaction, which unfolds in three succesive waves. Bultmann saw a total breach between the Christ of the kerygma and the prophet of Nazareth. To be sure, chronological continuity, but real theological discontinuity. Furthermore, the Gospels, pervaded by legend, deprive us of the true Jesus. Kasemann establishes, refuting Bultmann, that the inherent discontinuity had by every historical process, does not prevent speaking of true continuity. If this were not so, history must be abolished. The truth is that the kerygma was already "in germ"(as implicit relative to explicit) in the sayings and deeds of Jesus. Without a constant going back to Jesus, the kerygma itself is dissolved, and Christ becomes a myth or a gnosis. The New Hermeneutic holds that the faith of Jesus, being the sole authentic interpretation of human existence, historical research on the prophet of Nazareth is a necessary undertaking for discovering the authentic faith of Him who is the norm and foundation of ours. This evolution of Protestant criticism "ties in" with the present day generation of theologians (Pannenberg, Moltmann), who reaffirm the unbreakable bond between faith and history, between Jesus and Christ. Christology has its origins and its foundation in the existence and the undertaking of Jesus of Nazareth.

This evolution of criticism even now is one piece of

evidence in the record. If, in fact, in the trial of the Gospels, the jury made up of the body of Catholic and Protestant exegetes, declares that a historical access to Jesus of Nazareth is an enterprise necessary and possible, it may be presumed that the truth lies in this direction. This authoritative proof has meaning and weight.

In the second section, which serves as a transition between the history of criticism and properly so called systematic reflection, we have taken up a problem of method. Indeed it was important, before engaging in a discussion which involves the question of the historical authenticity of the Gospels, that we first determine whether they truly depend on the historical process. Now a careful examination of the literary genre "Gospel" and of the characteristics which define it, shows clearly that, without being biographies or memoirs, the Gospels relate to us the acts, sayings and the project of a historical person for whom they vouch. Thenceforth, the Gospels cannot avoid "questioning," nor avoid the criteria of history, even if these could not wholly support them. Hence a chapter on the nature and limits of historical research for determining whether the objective of the Gospels, far from being counter to the interests of history, is consistent with its principal aim.

The third section enumerates, classifying them, the arguments of properly so called proof. All these arguments are interlinked.

1) Even if internal criteria are from now on at the first level of evangelical criticism, the data of external criticism could not be neglected. In this regard, the testimony of the Churches of the 2nd and 3rd centuries, remain irreplaceable for informing us about essential points: the authors of the Gospels, their authority in the Church, the attitude of the Church toward the apocrypha and the gnostic writings.

2) Internal criticism has as its first objective to determine to what extent the twofold mediation of the evangelists and of the primitive Church maintains or breaches the continuity which comes from Jesus (or at least from the most ancient traditions about Jesus) down to us. The endeavors of RG

enable us from now on to portray a true profile of each evangelist. The freedom of interpretation and of composition of each one is real, but controllable. As a rule, it appears as discreet, motivated and ever under the sign of fidelity to the tradition received.

3) The study of the milieu in which this *tradition* was formed has been taken over by FG. The great merit of the school was the providing of a strict method of analysis of the texts and a means for reaching the environments which saw it arise. Thenceforth we know the *milieu* and the milieux of the primitive Church: prayer, worship, ministerial and catechetical effort, difficulties in relation to the surrounding world, development in diverse religious and cultural spheres. Exegesis is now ready to find the original context of numerous pericopes and to discern the first results of the Church's efforts to make relevant and to interpret the original data. The progress realized by FG has, nonetheless had its counterpart. The radical positions of the School often brought up serious problems, thereby obliging criticism to make important verifications.

4) In regard to the past, FG exaggerated the hiatus between Jesus and Christ, between the pre-paschal and the post-paschal communities. Consequently, criticism must make precise the nature and the degree of continuity which links these two communities. On the other hand, upon exaggerating the creative force of the primitive community, FG brought upon the Church a grave suspicion as to her fidelity to Jesus. It is here, we think, that a study on the speech and attitudes of the primitive ecclesial milieu, such as can be pursued starting out from the vocabulary most used, that is, key-words, enables us to have access to the most profound zones of the consciousness and subconsciousness of the Church. Now this basic vocabulary indubitably manifests that the primitive Church evolved under the sign of fidelity to Jesus. From the Church to Jesus, there is not only continuity, but also constant will for continuity. Thereby is exorcised the phantom of a deformative and mythisizing ecclesial milieu.

5) In the last phase, there is involved the verifying of *the*

fact of this fidelity by recourse to the criteria of historical authenticity. Indeed, it is not sufficient through the use of literary criteria to go back to the most ancient phase of tradition. There must also be established that the message borne by these primitive literary forms, is attributable to Jesus. So there is question of establishing properly so called criteria of historicity, valid and critically proven, which enable us to discern and set apart the evangelical material which goes back to Jesus Himself. There is to be found the authentic Jesus and His authentic message.

We do not think this demonstration evades any of the major difficulties posed by the initial problem. It takes into consideration the resources of external and internal criticism. It studies the nature of the two mediations which separate Jesus from the modern reader. It proceeds to the verifications imposed by these two mediations, as well as by the difficulties coming from FG and RG themselves, in their attempts to clarify these two mediations. Once these verifications have been carried out, there results a current of fidelity throughout the whole of tradition. From the origins, in Jesus, down to the last composition of the Gospels, there may be observed a concern for and an actuality of faithful transmission of the words and deeds of Jesus. There is no hiatus between Jesus and the Christ of the Gospels, but a vital and organic continuity. Tradition, however, is not simple repetition, but relevance and deepening. Criticism, on the other hand, is capable of discerning the traces of this process and to grasp its orientation.

The legitimate conclusion is that it is truly possible, by means of the Gospels, to find Jesus, to hear His message, to know His project of existence, to identify the major events activity among us. The certitude acquired by this procedure is *firm*. On certain points (for instance the passion and crucifixion of Jesus), it reaches the evident. On others, on the contrary, it is susceptible of progress, following the rhythm of researches, but it already is sufficient for motivating the confidence of contemporaneous criticism. In fact there exists a certitude proper to the respective domains of mathematics, metaphysics, history, psychology and sense perception. Our demonstration moves on the level of history and ends up with a certitude of the same order which besides is highly elevated.[1]

II. A convergence of approaches and arguments

In the demonstration we have presented, there is not only a linear linkage of the arguments, but also convergence of *approaches* and of arguments.

Indeed, the demonstration develops at different levels: on the literary level (tasks of RG and FG); on the historical level (history of evangelical criticism, research of historical science itself in order the better to define data of the history of religions, recent tasks of Historical Criticism applied to the Gospels); on the philosophical level (reflection on the nature of speech and on the historicity of man); on the sociological level (analysis of the pre-paschal community and the environments of the primitive Church; on the psychological level (analysis of the knowledge of the Church by way of semantics); on the theological level (among representatives of the New Hermeneutic and with theologians specializing with the problems of christology). All these approaches, conducted starting out from very diverse disciplines, lead to one and the same conclusion: finding Jesus through the Gospels is a feasible and fertile enterprise.

The arguments taken from these approaches are themselves grouped along convergent lines of one and the same circle, all directed toward the same center: Jesus.

1) *The development of criticism.* From its previous radicalism, criticism develops more and more in the direction of moderation and shows a return to trust in the Gospels as a source of knowledge of Jesus.[2] Typical of this "turn about" of attitude is the phenomenon of the marked interest for Jesus and the life of Jesus. We think, for example, of the works of G. Bornkamm, O. Cullmann, W. Grundmann, N. Perrin, D. Flussner, H. Braun, K. Niederwimmer, J. Blank, H. Zimmer-

mann, J. Dupont, P. E. Langevin, S. Nisin, J. Klaussner, H. Zahrnt, G. Vermes, R. Aron, L. Sabourin, J. Guillet, E. Stauffer, etc. Numerous christologies of the last few years testify to the same interest (Ch. Duquoc, W. Kasper, K. Rahner, L. Boff, E. Schillebeeckx, U. von Balthasar, J. M. Moltmann, etc.

2) *Reflection on history.* A positivist concept of history sets the Gospels in an unfavorable situation. Their freedom seems like treason. Most fortunately, the efforts of G. Dulthey, H.I. Marrou, R. Aron, H.G. Gadamer, P. Ricoeur, on the meaning and the real import of history, rehabilitated the Gospels. In fact, historical knowledge conceived as a recreative interpretation of the project-realization of real history, shows that the evangelists upon intending to interpret the project of the existence of Jesus, that is His voluntary offering to the Father for the salvation of humanity, bring out more profoundly the design of history than a material fidelity to the development of His life. Upon introducing us to the profound meaning of the life of Jesus, that is, the giving of Himself for the salvation of all, the Gospels place themselves at the very heart of history.

3) *The literary genre "Gospel."* This specially Christian invention unites us with history. The Gospel, in fact, is the joyous proclamation of the decisive Event of salvation, in the historical person of Jesus. The *Arche* of the Gospel of Mark emphasizes the dynamism, under the sign of the temporality, of the establishment of the Kingdom. This *debut* (preaching of the Baptizer and the baptism of Jesus) calls for a *development* (ministry in Galilee and in Judea) and an *accomplishment* (death and resurrection). This debut, which marks the presence of Jesus, is something absolutely new, (like the first creation) which will not be understood until the end. On adopting the narrative genre of history, in respect to temporal planes, the evangelists show their intention to introduce us to the movement of an existence involved in the condition of man. Going over the routes and stages, following a rhythm of project-realization, Christ brought about our salvation. History can retrace these stages and find again this rhythm.

4) *Contribution of external criticism.* Without constituting the most decisive contribution of the demonstration, external criticism has its weight, for it expresses the attitude of the Church of the 2nd and 3rd centuries and enables us to know what the text of our Gospels presents to her eyes. Now this attitude is that of absolute respect due to an indisputable authority; the fact is attested to by the usage of the Gospels as liturgical texts and as an irrefutable argument in the polemics against heretics. Furthermore, the local Churches clearly express their persuasion that through the Gospels, they truly meet with Jesus of Nazareth and His vital message, a spontaneous, acritical, but an incoercible argument.

5) *Knowledge of the pre-paschal milieu.* It is possible, through the very techniques of FG, to establish that tradition has its origins in the group of Jesus and His disciples. The inaugurator of the tradition is Jesus Himself. In fact, the circle of Jesus and His own is a stable community characterized by the intimacy of life with the Master, principle of attraction and of cohesion of the group. In this community, the personality of Jesus, prevails, His word is authoritative. Such a context suffices to explain the interest in the words of Jesus, as well as the interest to preserve them. Criticism can equally establish that Jesus while living sent His disciples on a mission and that He prepared them to preach about the essential themes of His message. In a milieu of oral culture, where memories are trained, an enterprise of this class favors tradition.

6) *Speech and attitudes of the primitive Church.* By means of semantics, we have access to the knowledge of the primitive Church. The study, as a matter of fact, of the basic vocabulary, in use in the Epistles of Paul and in the Acts of the Apostles, betrays the first reactions, the fundamental reflections, the "instinctive" attitudes of the Church in regard to Jesus. Now the key words of this vocabulary (for instance: tradition, witness, testimony, apostle, servant and ministry of the word, Gospel, evangelize, teach) express all of them—one and the same preoccupation: the primitive ecclesial milieu wants to be faithful to Jesus.

7) *The contribution of criteriology.* Although of recent

date, this contribution is not lesser. It is in fact what authorizes the passage from Literary Criticism to properly so called Historical Criticism. Better and better defined and qualified, these criteria enable us to verify the faithfulness of the content of the Gospels to the reality of Jesus of Nazareth. The application of these criteria (multiple attestation, discontinuity, coherence, necessary explanation, style of Jesus, internal intelligibility, accord of base and diversity of interpretation) has enabled the greater and greater understanding of the field of evangelical material recognized as authentic, to the point of recovering little by little the whole of the Gospels.

8) *Techniques of control of the history of Tradition.* After the labors of RG and FG and of historical research in criteriology, we are ready to discern, in a number of cases, the compositional activity of the evangelist, the first efforts to make relevant and of interpretation by the Church and, finally, by the application of the criteria of authenticity, what is most probably the original message of Jesus, His deeds and his procedures. This verification of the respective contributions of each element of tradition, enables us to discern the organic, vital continuity, and at the same time the deepening of tradition. Now, this verification, made on a great number of pericopes, reveals, at the heart of tradition, a fundamental attitude of fidelity to Jesus. We are no longer on the level of a priori, nor of hypotheses, but on the level of critical verifications.

All these arguments show a *convergence*. No matter what the approach, no matter what the argument, the Gospels ever send us back to Jesus. They are not a film of His life, nor a register of His words, but a re-reading of His existence, in the light of the resurrection, of the Old Testament and of ecclesial experience. They are also, on the part of the evangelists, a *re-writing* of tradition in a formal theological perspective. In this twofold operation, the sayings and deeds of Jesus have been better understood, deepened, and also made relevant according to the needs, the language, the mentality, the culture of the local Churches. However the convergence of the arguments we have just enumerated, establishes that the Gospels give us access to Jesus: to His authentic message and to the major facts of His earthly existence. This certitude rests on the detail as on the convergence of the approaches and of the arguments.

III. An itinerary

A third result of our study concerns the itinerary to be followed for coming to Jesus. This procedure, it seems to us, should be *fundamentally* retrogressive and *complementarily* progressive.

It must first, and necessarily, be retrogressive. Our aim, in fact, is to know Jesus of Nazareth, as He manifested Himself while alive, such as his first witnesses saw Him, and such as He can be perceived today by the exegete working with the means of history. Now, we insist on it the historian has as documents only difficult texts. Our Gospels present complex superstructures, in which the Jesus of witnesses is as it were "hidden" by the Christ of faith. Faith in the Lord has as it were "hieratized" the earthly Jesus. On the other hand, the evangelists attest to a desire and a real need of rooting faith in history. We can and must then make use of their texts for "jumping back."

1) *A retrogressive procedure*

a) The point of departure is the present text. While the tradition of the 2nd century considers the Gospels as a *whole*, that is, the four forms of the unique Good Tidings, *Redaktionsgeschichte*, through the minute examination of the texts, seeks to find what is manifestly an addition, an explanation or an interpretation of the evangelist himself. Without doubt the essential of what he relates comes to him from the anterior tradition; but there is in his text a part of composition, of formulation, of literary and theological elaboration, which is *his very own*. *Redaktionsgeschichte* seeks to find equally the elements which do not fit in with his theological perspective, that is, the "refractory traditions." The maintenance and insertion of these elements signify that they are vested in the eyes of the primitive Church with such an importance that the evangelist could not omit them or interpret them otherwise. We know, for instance, that Mark emphasizes often the lack of understanding of the apostles, while Matthew is more indulgent. The preservation of an element which goes counter to the recognized attitude of Mark and of Matthew, is a guarantee of authenticity. This task is an application of the criterion of discontinuity, but on the level of RG.

b) In a second stage (level of FG), there is question of discerning what is attributable to the first Christian community, before the composition of the Gospels. There is question of seeing how the environments (Catechetical, liturgical, polemic, ministerial) and the concerns of the Church which preaches the Gospel, have been able to give to such a word or such an event, a new resonance, a relevant interpretation. Thus, on the level of the Christian community, the account of the multiplication of the loaves reveals a liturgical milieu and a eucharistic interpretation. Thus there comes to be found the most primitive stage, the most ancient literary form of tradition. This research is again placed on the level of literary criticism.

c) In the third stage (the level of historical criticism), there must be found what belongs to Jesus: it is the research of the event itself, with the meaning it takes on in its original context. There is involved the knowing in what measure the lost archaic literary form introduces us to the reality Jesus. It is at this moment there is carried out the passing from the primitive kerygma to the *real Jesus*. This is done by recourse to the criteria of historicity, applied by means of complemetarity and convergence. On this level, criticism will find, for instance, that the miracle of the multiplication of the loaves is presented as a manifestation of the *Agape* of God, with a messianic and eschatological meaning. Jesus is the new Moses who repeats the prodigy of the manna in the desert, the awaited prophet, in whom is accomplished the messianic hope.

2) *A progressive procedure*

If an itinerary, going backwards, that is, retrogressive, is imposed on us by the very nature of our sources, nonetheless it requires it be completed by a "progressive" procedure. Indeed, during the decades which came after the resurrection, the Jesus of history, in a sense, *becomes* the Christ, the Lord, without ever ceasing to be Jesus. There is tradition and change, remembrance and prophecy, continuity and further investigation. So it is not enough to go back to the source. There must also be known what the events and words of Jesus could and should signify to each one of these three stages of tradition, how there is fidelity, but also maturation and fructification of the same initial data.

a) In a *first* stage, there is grouping the data we have collected, in the retrogressive process, on the first community of Jesus and His disciples. First of all, what was the first image of Jesus: that of the eschatological prophet who announces the imminent coming of the Kingdom and calls to conversion; that of the teacher who teaches with authority and who sends His own on a mission. There is also the effort made, starting out from our present knowledge about Palestine of that period, to know the impact caused by the presence of Jesus, by His statements and His attitudes in the face of Judaic institutions. It is of importance at this moment to make precise the attitude of the disciples in regard to Jesus. Even if the scandal of His death shocked the apostles, this shock did not erase the image of the pre-paschal Jesus. The apostles remained deeply obsessed by their memories of Him. The fact that He, risen, appeared to those who knew him in His pre-paschal condition, underlines even further continuity with remembrance of the earthly Jesus.

b) In a *second* stage, there is the effort to make clear the christology of the primitive preaching. This christology attributes to Jesus titles which identify Him in His person and in His mission. But the outline of the primitive kerygma always evokes the career of Jesus of Nazareth, from the baptism to the ascension (Ac 1:21-22). It is also the time of the first attempts to make it relevant, under the influence of various milieux.

c) In a *third* stage, there can be studied the christology of the Gospels. Even though it be agreed they had full liberty of composition and of interpretation, they manifestly represent going back to the past. They adopt the narrative genre and develop the elements of the kerygma to illuminate the rooting of faith in the earthly existence of Jesus.

The perception of continuity of tradition is the fruit of this procedure of a progressive or diachronic nature. It enables the grasping of the interior progress of the Church which gradually assimilates the Event Jesus: makes it its own; understands it, formulates it, deepends it, and also makes it relevant for the first believers. One of the dominant traits of contemporaneous exegesis is precisely reflection on the profound relations which link the Gospel and the Church of the first hour. A "diachronic" reading of the Gospels introduces us gradually into the current of tradition.

3) *Historical Criticism*

The two procedures, as is seen, are complementary. In both cases, however, the fidelity of the Gospels to the true reality of Jesus, is verified by recourse to the criteria of history.

The criterion of discontinuity (contrast between the glory of the risen and the brutal humiliation of death on the cross) enables us to establish the fundamental meaning of the project of life of Jesus, that is, His passion and His death as an act of abandonment to the Father for the salvation of men. The criterion of discontinuity, the criterion of necessary explanation and the criterion of multiple attestation enable us to reconstruct the central nucleus of he life of Jesus: outside of the fact of death, all the sayings and deeds of Jesus inexplicable in a Jewish environment. These are: expressions such as "Abba," "Verily, verily," the acts of compassion in regard to sinners, lepers, the weak, the oppressed, the enigmas of His message, the temptation in the desert, the baptism which places Jesus among sinners, the failure of His task, the constant use of expressions as "Kingdom," "Son of man" and the preaching on the imminent instauration of the messianic Kingdom.

The criterion of coherence enables the establishing of the historical authenticity of a certain number of logia and of facts connected with this central nucleus. For instance, antecedents of the putting to death of Jesus (declarations on Himself and on His mission, controversies with the leaders of the nation);

10

likewise His teaching and His actions concerning the Kingdom (the parables, the beatitudes, the miracles, the triple temptation, the Father). The use of the criteria of discontinuity and of coherence enable in turn what we have called the style of Jesus, to be defined.

To take thus as a point of departure the death on the cross of Jesus, is not an arbitrary choice, but a datam provided by primitive predication itself (Ac 2:23; 1Cor 2:2). The passion and death of Jesus is the nucleus of the kerygma as of the Gospels.

IV. Faith and History

At the conclusion of this study, it seems important to us to make precise a number of points concerning the relations of faith to history.

1) It should be clear that our effort to reach Jesus by way of historical research, is not a subtle return to the perspective of the *Leben-Jesu-Forschung*. To think so would be to have failed in understanding our project. There is no intention to subject faith to historical research. None to reduce Christ to the man Jesus in order to propose Him then as the religious ideal of humanity. None to make void the christological interpretations of the kerygma and of the councils in order to retain only a Jesus immunized against all ulterior interpretation. Rather our project aims at coming to Jesus of Nazareth, who was identified as Christ and Lord, on the basis precisely of what he said and did, really and truly, during His earthly passage among us. The *Leben-Jesu-Forschung*, at bottom, is satisfied with research of the event; our research, on the contrary, never separates the event from its meaning. If Jesus never stopped supporting the reflection of the Church, it is that He was God already among us, not identified but in process of identification.

2) A historical and critical inquiry on Jesus evidently does not govern faith, but it renders it eminent services. It can furnish faith a concrete content. It can show that an access to

the authentic Jesus and to His authentic message is a possible and feasible enterprise. It can show that the ecclesial interpretation of Jesus is coherent with the historical life and message of Jesus. This is an important contribution, for whatever is pronounced about Jesus is of importance. After all, faith refers to Jesus of Nazareth, such as He was, for it is in Him that God manifested Himself. Historical research can also establish that the call to the decision of faith belongs to the original message of Jesus. It can even, upon enlightening us on this message, dispose us in regard to it and manifest to us its credibility. It can, however, not impose the decision of faith, nor force us to acknowledge in Him who speaks the living Son of God. Historical research does not impose faith, but it renders it possible; it gives access to the authentic Gospel of the authentic Jesus. It still remains for us to let ourselves be called by Christ and abandon ourselves to the Spirit who speaks from within and makes us perceive as a living word, addressed personally to us, the living message of Jesus.

3) To the believer, historical research also renders a priceless service. It establishes first that the multicentry confidence of the Church in the Gospels as source of knowledge of Jesus, rests on solid proofs, which stand up against the blows of criticism. It teaches him also to read the Gospels correctly. In fact when we are faced with the Gospels, there is not a matter of simply asking what they tell us today, but rather of asking them what meaning there is for us *today* what Jesus, read and understood by the Church and the evangelist, *said and did yesterday*. If not, the Gospel risks being a simple doctrine, or an ideology, detached from its author, a message without a messenger. A supreme risk, in the present case, for the message here has as its object the messenger Himself.

Footnotes for the Conclusion

1. The possession of the proofs which support this certitude is collegial fact, that is, a possession of the Church inasmuch as a social body. Just as a doctor could not possess by himself medical science in its entirety, so no theologian could exhaust the intelligibility of the proofs which found the historical authenticity of the Gospels. The faithful in varying degrees, following their preparation and their culture, share in this collective science of the Church.

2. W.G. Kummel, Ein Jahrzehnt Jesusforschung (1965-1975), *Theologische Rundschau* NF XLI (1976) 197-258, 295-363.

CHAPTER BIBLIOGRAPHY

CHAPTER I

BORNKAMM G., *Qui est Jésus de Nazareth?*, Paris, 1973, pp. 19-33.
BOUTTIER M., *Du Christ de l'histoire au Jésus des Évangiles*, Paris, 1969.
CABA J., *De los evangelios al Jesús histórico*, Madrid, 1970.
DELORME J., *Des Évangiles à Jésus*, Paris, 1972.
DESCAMPS A., « Portée christologique de la recherche historique sur Jésus », in : J. DUPONT, éd., *Jésus aux origines de la christologie*, Gembloux, 1975, pp. 23-45.
GRECH P., « Jesus Christ in History and Dogma », in : *A New Catholic Commentary on Holy Scripture*, London, 1969, pp. 822-837.
KERTELGE K., hrsg., *Rückfrage nach Jesus*, « Quaestiones disputatae » 63, Freiburg, 1974.
LAMBIASI F., *L'autenticità storica dei Vangeli*, Bologna, 1976.
LÉON-DUFOUR X., *Les Évangiles et l'histoire de Jésus*, Paris, 1963.
MALEVEZ L., « Jésus de l'histoire et interprétation du kérygme », *Nouvelle Revue théologique*, 91 (1969) 786-808.
POTTERIE I. de la, éd., *De Jésus aux Évangiles*, Paris 1967; ID., « Come impostare il problema del Gesù storico? », *La Civiltà Cattolica*, 120 (1969) 447-463.
RICŒUR P., « Préface » à R. BULTMANN, *Jésus. Mythologie et démythologisation*, Paris, 1968, pp. 9-28.

RISTOW H. und MATTHIAE K., hrsg., *Der historische Jesus und der kerygmatische Christus*, Berlin, 1961. Contributions de : J. JEREMIAS, pp. 12-25; R. MARLÉ, pp. 26-38; W. G. KÜMMEL, pp. 39-53; J. DE FRAINE, pp. 121-135; H. DIEM, pp. 219-232; R. BULTMANN, pp. 233-235; O. CULLMANN, pp. 266-280; G. BORNKAMM, pp. 281-288; H. RIESENFELD, pp. 331-341; H. SCHÜRMANN, pp. 342-370. Recueil important, non seulement à cause de la valeur des contributions, mais aussi en raison du vaste éventail des positions qu'il représente.

SCHILLEBEECKX E., *L'approccio a Gesù di Nazaret*, Brescia, 1972.

TRILLING W., *Fragen zur Geschichtlichkeit Jesu*, Düsseldorf, 1966. Traduction française : *Jésus devant l'histoire*, Paris, 1968.

WEBER J.-J., « Les Évangiles méritent-ils notre confiance? », in : WEBER J.- J. et SCHMITT J., éd., *Où en sont les études bibliques*, Paris, 1968, pp. 185-212.

ZAHRNT H., *Es begann mit Jesus von Nazareth*, Stuttgart-Berlin, 1964[5].

ZEDDA S., *I Vangeli e la critica oggi, II : Il Gesù della storia*, Treviso, 1970.

CHAPTER II

BOUTTIER M., *Du Christ de l'histoire au Jésus des Évangiles*, Paris, 1969.

BULTMANN R., *Jésus*, Paris, 1968; ID., *Das Verhältnis der urchristlichen Christusbotschaft zum historischen Jesus*, Heidelberg, 1960; ID., *L'interprétation du Nouveau Testament*, recueil de contributions de R. Bultmann, traduction de O. LAFFOUCRIÈRE, éd., Paris, 1955; ID., *Die Geschichte der synoptischen Tradition*, Göttingen, 1961[5].

FLORKOWSKI J., *La théologie de la foi chez Bultmann*, Paris, 1971.

GRECH P., « Jesus Christ in History and Dogma », in : *A New Catholic Commentary on Holy Scripture*, London, 1969, pp. 822-837.

HOFFMANN J. G. H., *Les vies de Jésus et l'histoire de Jésus*, Paris, 1947.

HOLTZMANN H. J., *Die synoptischen Evangelien. Ihr Ursprung und ihr geschichtlicher Charakter*, Leipzig, 1863.

KÜMMEL W. G., *Das Neue Testament. Geschichte der Erforschung seiner Probleme*, München, 1958. Traduction anglaise : *The New Testament : The History of the Investigation of its Problems*, New York, 1970.

MALET A., *La pensée de R. Bultmann. Mythos et Logos*, Genève, 1962.

MALEVEZ L., « Jésus de l'histoire et interprétation du kérygme », *Nouvelle revue théologique*, 91 (1969) 785-808; ID., *Le message chrétien et le mythe. La théologie de R. Bultmann*, Bruxelles, 1954.

MARLÉ R., *Bultmann et l'interprétation du Nouveau Testament*, Paris, 1966[2].

NEIL S., *The Interpretation of the New Testament (1861-1961)*, New York-Toronto, 1966.

SCHWEITZER A., *Geschichte der Leben-Jesu-Forschung*, München, 1906.

SLENCZKA R., *Geschichtlichkeit und Personsein Jesu Christi. Studien zur christologischen Problematik der historischen Jesusfrage*, Göttingen, 1967.

CHAPTER III

BORNKAMM G., *Jesus von Nazareth*, Stuttgart, 1956. Traduction anglaise : *Jesus of Nazareth*, New York, 1960. Traduction française : *Qui est Jésus de Nazareth?*, Paris, 1973.

BOUTTIER M., *Du Christ de l'histoire au Jésus des Évangiles*, Paris, 1969.

BROWN A., « After Bultmann, what? — An Introduction to the Post-Bultmanians », *Catholic Biblical Quarterly*, 26 (1964) 1-30.

CAHILL J., « Rudolf Bultmann and Post-Bultmann Tendencies », *Catholic Biblical Quarterly*, 26 (1964) 153-178.

GISEL P., « Ernst Käsemann ou la solidarité conflictuelle de l'histoire et de la vérité », *Études théologiques et religieuses*, 51 (1976) 21-37; ID., *Vérité et Histoire. La théologie dans la modernité : Ernst Käsemann*, Paris et Genève, 1977.

KÄSEMANN E., « Das Problem des historischen Jesus », *Zeitschrift für Theologie und Kirche*, 51 (1954) 125-153; ID., « Sackgassen im Streit um den historischen Jesus », in : *Exegetische Versuche und Besinnungen II*, Göttingen, 1965, pp. 31-68.

CHAPTER IV

ACHTEMEIER P. J., *An Introduction to the New Hermeneutic*, Philadelphia, 1969.

BARTHES R., BEAUCHAMP P. (et collaborateurs), *Exégèse et Herméneutique*, Paris, 1971.

BULTMANN R., *Glauben und Verstehen*, I (1933), II (1952), III (1960), IV (1965).

COUTURIER F., *Monde et Être chez Heidegger*, Montréal, 1971.

DE WAELHENS A., *La Philosophie de Martin Heidegger*, Louvain[4], 1955.

EBELING G., *Das Wesen des christlichen Glaubens*, Tübingen, 1959; ID., *Wort und Glaube*, I (1960), II (1970); ID., *Theologie und Verkündigung*, Tübingen, 1962.

FUCHS E., *Hermeneutik*, Bad Cannstatt, 1954 und 1958; ID., *Zum hermeneutischen Problem in der Theologie*, Tübingen, 1960; ID., *Zur Frage nach dem historischen Jesus*, Tübingen, 1960; ID., *Marburger Hermeneutik*, Tübingen, 1968; ID., *Glaube und Erfahrung*, Tübingen, 1965.

GADAMER H.-G., *Wahrheit und Methode. Grundzüge einer philosophischen Hermeneutik*, Tübingen, 1952.

GRECH P., « La Nuova Ermeneutica : Fuchs ed Ebeling », in : *Esegesi ed Ermeneutica*, Atti della XXI Settimana biblica dell'Associazione biblica italiana, Brescia, 1972, pp. 35-69. Article reproduit dans : *Augustinianum*, 12 (1972) 227-296.

GRELOT P., « Que penser de l'interprétation existentiale? », *Ephemerides Theologicae Lovanienses*, 43 (1967) 421-443.

HEIDEGGER M., *Sein und Zeit*, Tübingen, 1927; ID., *Unterwegs zur Sprache*, Pfullingen, 1959.

LAPOINTE R., *Les trois dimensions de l'herméneutique*, Paris, 1967; ID., « Panorama de l'herméneutique actuelle », *Bulletin de théologie biblique*, 2 (1972) 107-156.

MALET A., *Mythos et Logos. La pensée de Rudolf Bultmann*, Genève, 1962. Surtout, pp. 277-311.

MALEVEZ L., *Le message chrétien et le mythe*, Bruxelles-Bruges-Paris, 1954.

MARLE R., *Bultmann et l'interprétation du Nouveau Testament*, Paris, 1956; ID., *Le problème théologique de l'herméneutique*, Paris, 1963; ID., *Parler de Dieu aujourd'hui. La théologie herméneutique de G. Ebeling*, Paris, 1975.

MUSSNER F., *Histoire de l'herméneutique*, in : *Histoire des Dogmes*, T. I. : *Les fondements de la foi*, fascicule 3c, Paris, 1972.

PALMER R. E., *Hermeneutics. Introduction Theory in Schleiermacher, Dilthey, Heidegger and Gadamer*, Evanston, 1969.

PÖGGELER O., *La pensée de Heidegger*, Paris, 1967.

RANDELLINI R., « L'Ermeneutica esistenziale di Bultmann », in : *Esegesi ed Ermeneutica*, Atti della XXI Settimana biblica dell'Associazione biblica italiana, Brescia, 1972, pp. 35-69.

ROBINSON JAMES M., *A New Quest of the Historical Jesus*, London, 1959.

ROBINSON JAMES M. and COBB J. B., ed., *The New Hermeneutic*, New York, 1964.

STACHEL G., *Die neue Hermeneutik : Ein Ueberblick*, München, 1968.

CHAPTER V

DUQUOC C., *Christologie*, 2 vol., Paris, 1968 et 1972.

KASPER W., *Jesus der Christus*, Mainz, 1974. Traduction française : *Jésus le Christ*, Paris, 1976.

KÜNG H., *Christ sein*, München, 1974.

MOLTMANN J., *Der gekreuzigte Gott*, München, 1972. Traduction française : *Le Dieu crucifié*, Paris, 1974.

PANNENBERG W., *Grundzüge der Christologie*, Gütersloh, 1964. Traduction française : *Esquisse d'une christologie*, Paris, 1971.

SCHILLEBEECKX E., *Jezus, het verhaal van een levende*, Bloemendaal, 1974.

SESBOUÉ B., « Bulletin de théologie dogmatique. Christologie », *Recherches de Science Religieuse*, 61 (1973) 423-465.

CHAPTER VI

BOUTTIER M., *Du Christ de l'histoire au Jésus des Évangiles*, Paris, 1969.

CABA J., *De los Evangelios al Jesús histórico*, Madrid, 1971.

COMMISSIO BIBLICA, *Instructio de historica Evangeliorum veritate*, AAS 56 (1964) 712-718.

DESCAMPS A., « Progrès et continuité dans la critique des Évangiles et des Actes », *Revue théologique de Louvain*, I (1970) 5-44.

DUPONT J., éd., *Jésus aux origines de la christologie*, Gembloux, 1975.

FITZMYER J. A., « The Biblical Commission's Instruction on the Historical Truth of the Gospels », *Theological Studies*, 25 (1964) 386-408.

KERTELGE K., hrsg., *Rückfrage nach Jesus*, « Quaestiones disputatae » 63, Freiburg, 1974.

LÉON-DUFOUR X., *Les Évangiles et l'histoire de Jésus*, Paris, 1963.

POTTERIE I. de la, « Come impostare il problema del Gesù storico? », *La Civiltà Cattolica*, 120 (1969), qu. 2855, pp. 447-463; ID., « Le sens primitif de la multiplication des pains », in : J. DUPONT, éd., *Aux origines de la christologie*, Gembloux, 1975, pp. 303-329.

WAMBACQ B. N., « Instructio de historica Evangeliorum veritate », *Catholic Biblical Quarterly*, 26 (1964) 299-312.

CHAPTER VII

BLAESER P., « Évangile », in : H. FRIES, éd., *Encyclopédie de la foi*, II, Paris, 1965, pp. 87-95.

BORNKAMM D. G., *Bibel : Das Neue Testament. Eine Einführung in seine Schriften im Rahmen der Geschichte des Urchristentums*, 1971.

DELORME J., « Aspects doctrinaux du second Évangile », in : I. de la POTTERIE, éd., *De Jésus aux Évangiles*, Gembloux et Paris, 1967, pp. 74-99.

DODEWAARD J. A. EVAN, « Jésus s'est-il servi lui-même du mot Évangile? », *Biblica*, 35 (1954) 160-173.

FRIEDRICH G., « Euaggelizomai, euaggelion », TWzNT II (1935) 705-735.

GABOURY A., *La structure des Évangiles Synoptiques. La structure-type à l'origine des Évangiles*, Leiden, 1970.

GRAYSTONE G., « The Forms of New Testament Literature », in : *A New Catholic Commentary on Holy Scripture*, col. 641-642.

KÄSEMANN E., « Sackgassen im Streit um den historischen Jesus », in : *Exegetische Versuche und Besinnungen*, II, Göttingen, 1964, pp. 31-68.

LAMARCHE P., *Révélation de Dieu chez Marc*, « Le Point théologique » 20, Paris, 1976.

LAMBRECHT J., « Qu'est-ce qu'un Évangile? », *Revue du Clergé africain*, 22 (1967) 6-14.

LÉON-DUFOUR X., *Les Évangiles et l'histoire de Jésus*, Paris, 1963.

MARXSEN W., *Mark the Evangelist*, New York, 1969, pp. 117-150.

MOLLAT D., « Évangile », in : *Dictionnaire de Spiritualité*, 4 : 1745-1765.

MUSSNER F., « Évangile » et « Centre de l'Évangile », in : R. SCHNACKENBURG, A. VÖGTLE, H. SCHÜRMANN, F. MUSSNER, H. FRIES, H. SCHLIER, *Le message de Jésus et l'interprétation moderne*, Paris, 1969, pp. 151-176.

PERRIN N., « The Literary Gattung Gospel », *The Expository Times*, vol. 82, oct. 1970, n. 1, pp. 4-7.

PESCH R., « Anfang des Evangeliums Jesu Christi. Eine Studie zum Prolog des Markusevangeliums », in : *Die Zeit Christi*, Festschrift H. SCHLIER, Freiburg i. Br., 1970, pp. 108-144.

ROBINSON J. M., *The Problem of History in Mark*, 1957.

SCHNACKENBURG R., « Das Evangelium im Verständnis des ältesten Evangelisten », in : HOFFMANN, hrsg., *Orientierung an Jesus*, Freiburg, Basel, Wien, 1973, pp. 309-323.

TALBERT CH. H., *Luke and the Gnostics*, New York, 1966.

TREVIJANO R., *Comienzo del Evangelio. Estudio sobre el prólogo de Marcos*, Burgos 1971.

VÖGTLE A., « Formazione e Struttura dei Vangeli », in : *Discussione sulla Bibbia*, « Giornale di Teologia » 1, Brescia, 1967³, pp. 82-123.

ZIMMERMANN H., *Neutestamentliche Methodenlehre*, Stuttgart, 1967.

CHAPTER VIII

ARON R., *Introduction à la philosophie de l'histoire*, Paris, 1948.

FRUCHON P., *Existence humaine et Révélation. Essais d'herméneutique*, Paris, 1976.

GADAMER H.-G., *Wahrheit und Methode*, Tübingen, 1960. Traduction française : *Vérité et méthode*, Paris, 1976; ID., *Le problème de la conscience historique*, Louvain, 1963.

HOURS J., *Valeur de l'histoire*, Paris, 1954.

LAPOINTE R., *Les trois dimensions de l'herméneutique*, Paris, 1967.

LÉON-DUFOUR X., *Les Évangiles et l'histoire de Jésus*, Paris, 1963.

MARROU H.-I., *De la connaissance historique*, Paris, 1954; ID., *Théologie de l'histoire*, Paris, 1968.

MELCHIORRE V., *Il sapere storico*, Brescia, 1963.

MÜLLER M., *Expérience et histoire*, Louvain, 1959.

RICŒUR P., *Histoire et vérité*, Paris, 1966.

SALMON P., *Histoire et critique*, Bruxelles, 1969.

RIZZI A., *Cristo verità dell'uomo*, Roma, 1972.

CHAPTER IX

BENOÎT A., « Die Überlieferung des Evangeliums in den ersten Jahrhunderten », in : V. VAJTA, hrsg., *Evangelium als Geschichte*, Göttingen, 1974, pp. 161-186.

CABA J., *De los Evangelios al Jesús histórico*, Madrid, 1971.

CERFAUX L., *La voix vivante de l'Évangile au début de l'Église*, Tournai et Paris, 1958.

DESCAMPS A., « Progrès et continuité dans la critique des Évangiles et des Actes », *Revue théologique de Louvain*, 1 (1970) 5-44. Surtout 6-20.

LATOURELLE R., *De veritate historica Evangeliorum* (ad usum privatum), Romae, 1968.

LÉON-DUFOUR X., *Les Évangiles et l'histoire de Jésus*, Paris, 1963.

VAGANAY L., *La question synoptique. Une hypothèse de travail*, Paris, 1954.

VAN DEN EYNDE D., *Les normes de l'enseignement chrétien dans la littérature patristique des trois premiers siècles*, Gembloux, 1933.

ZEDDA S., *I Vangeli e la critica oggi, I : I Vangeli*, Treviso, 1965².

CHAPTER X

ALBERTZ M., *Die synoptischen Streitgespräche*, Berlin, 1921.

BENOIT P., « Réflexions sur la formgeschichtliche Methode », *Revue Biblique*, 53 (1946) 481-512; ID., *Exégèse et théologie*, vol. I, Paris, 1961, pp. 25-61.

BERTRAM G., *Die Leidensgeschichte und der Christuskult*, Göttingen, 1922.

BRAUN F. M., « École de la Formgeschichte », in : *Dictionnaire de la Bible, Supplément*, 3 : 312-317.

BULTMANN R., *Die Geschichte der synoptischen Tradition*, Göttingen, 1921; ID., *Erforschung der synoptischen Evangelien*, Giessen, 1925.

CULLMANN O., « Les récentes études sur la formation de la tradition évangélique », *Revue d'histoire et de philosophie religieuses*, 5 (1925) 459-477, 564-579.

DESCAMPS A., « Progrès et continuité dans la critique des Évangiles et des Actes », *Revue théologique de Louvain*, 1 (1970) 5-44.

DIBELIUS M., *Die Formgeschichte des Evangeliums*, Tübingen, 1919.

DONLON S. E., « The Form-Critics, the Gospels and St. Paul », *Catholic Biblical Quarterly*, 6 (1944) 159-179, 306-325.

FASCHER E., *Die formgeschichtliche Methode. Eine Darstellung und Kritik*, Giessen, 1924.

FLORIT E., « La storia delle forme nei Vangeli in rapporto alla dottrina cattolica », *Biblica*, 14 (1933) 212-248; ID., *Il metodo della storia delle forme e sua applicazione al racconto della Passione*, Roma, 1935.

GROBEL K., *Formgeschichte und synoptische Quellenanalyse*, Göttingen, 1937.

GÜTTGEMANS E., *Offene Fragen zur Formgeschichte des Evangeliums*, München, 1970.

HANSON A., ed., *Vindications. Essays on the historical basis of Christianity*, London, 1966.

HEUSCHEN E., éd., *La formation des Évangiles. Problème synoptique et Formgeschichte*, « Recherches bibliques » 2, Bruges-Bruxelles-Paris, 1957.

IBER G., « Zur Formgeschichte der Evangelien », *Theologische Rundschau*, NF 24, (1956-1957) 283-338.

KOCK K., *Was ist Formgeschichte?*, Neukirchen, 1964.

KÖHLER L., *Das formgeschichtliche Problem des Neuen Testaments*, Tübingen, 1927.

LÉON-DUFOUR X., « Formgeschichte et Redaktionsgeschichte des Évangiles Synoptiques », *Recherches de science religieuse*, 46 (1958) 237-269.

McGINLEY L. J., *Form Criticism of the Synoptic Healing Narratives*, Woodstock, 1944.

REDLICH E. B., *Form Criticism*, London, 1931.

SCHICK E., *Formgeschichte und Synoptikerexegese*, Münster, 1940.

SCHMIDT K. L., *Der Rahmen der Geschichte Jesu*, Berlin, 1919.

SCHNACKENBURG R., « Formgeschichtliche Methode », in : *Lexikon für Theologie und Kirche*, 4 : 211-213; ID., « Zur formgeschichtlichen Methode in der Evangelienforschung », *Zeitschrift für Katholische Theologie*, 85 (1963) 16-32.

SOLAGES B. de, *Critique des Évangiles et méthode historique. L'exégèse des Synoptiques selon Bultmann*, Toulouse, 1973.

TAYLOR V., *The Formation of the Gospel Tradition*, London, 1933.

ZIMMERMANN H., *Neutestamentliche Methodenlehre*, Stuttgart, 1967.

CHAPTER XI

CERFAUX L., *Jésus aux origines de la Tradition*, Bruges, 1968.

DESCAMPS A., « Aux origines du ministère. La pensée de Jésus », *Revue théologique de Louvain*, 2 (1971) 3-45.

HENGEL M., *Nachfolge und Charisma. Eine exegetisch-religionsgeschichtliche Studie zu Mtt. 8, 21f und Jesu Ruf in die Nachfolge* (Berlin, 1968).

PERRIN N., *Jesus and the Language of the Kingdom*, London, 1976.

SCHÜRMANN H., « Die vorösterlichen Anfänge der Logientradition. Versuch eines formgeschichtlichen Zugangs zum Leben Jesu », in : H. RISTOW und K. MATTHIAE, hrsg., *Der historische Jesus und der kerygmatische Christus*, Berlin, 1962, pp. 342-370; ID., « Le groupe des disciples de Jésus prototype de la vie selon les conseils », *Christus*, 13 (1966) 184-209.

CHAPTER XII

BOMAN T., *Die Jesusüberlieferung im Lichte der neueren Volkskunde*, Göttingen, 1967.

DAVIES W. D., « Reflections on a Scandinavian Approach to the Gospel Tradition », in : *Neotestamentica et Patristica*, Festschrift O. Cullmann, 1962, pp. 14-34.

GEDEN A. S., « Inspiration (Hindu) », in : *Encyclopedia of Religion and Ethics*, col. 352-354.

GERHARDSSON B., *Memory and Manuscript. Oral Tradition and Written Transmission in Rabbinic Judaism and Early Christianity*, Uppsala, 1961.

JOUSSE M., *Le style oral et mnémotechnique chez les verbo-moteurs. Études de psychologie linguistique*, Paris, 1925.

LENGSFELD P., *Tradition, Écriture et Église dans le dialogue œcuménique*, Paris, 1964.

LORD A., *The Singers of Tales*, Cambridge, USA, 1964.

RIESENFELD H., « The Gospel Tradition and its Beginnings », in : *Studia Evangelica*, vol. I, Berlin, 1959, pp. 43-65. Texte reproduit dans : *The Gospel Tradition*, Oxford, 1970, pp. 1-30.

SMITH M., « A Comparison of Early Christian and Early Rabbinic Tradition », *Journal of Biblical Literature*, 82 (1963) 169-176.

VANSINA J., *De la Tradition orale. Essai de méthode historique*, Tervuren, 1961.

CHAPTER XIII

On Witness and Testimony

BROX N., *Zeuge und Märtyrer*, München, 1961; ID., « Testimonianza », in : *Dizionario teologico*, Brescia, 1969, pp. 492-502.

CERFAUX L., « Témoins du Christ d'après le Livre des Actes », in : *Recueil L. Cerfaux*, 2 vol., Gembloux, 1954, t. 2 : 157-174.

JAEGER H., « Parrèsia et fiducia », in : *Studia Patristica*, vol. I, TU 63, Berlin, 1957, pp. 221-239.

LATOURELLE R., *Théologie de la Révélation*, Bruges-Paris, 1969³, pp. 51-60, 75-84; ID., *Le témoignage chrétien*, Tournai et Montréal, 1971, pp. 18-22; ID., « Évangélisation et témoignage », in : *Evangelisation*, « Documenta missionalia » 9, Roma, 1975, pp. 77-110.

MENOUD Ph.-H. « Jésus et ses témoins », *Église et Théologie*, juin 1969, pp. 1-14.

RÉTIF A., *Foi au Christ et mission*, Paris, 1953.

SCHMITT J., *Jésus ressuscité dans la prédication apostolique*, Paris, 1949.

STRATHMANN H., « martus, martureô, marturia », in : TWzNT 4 : 492-514.

On Apostle

AGNEW F., « On the Origin of the term Apostolos », *Catholic Biblical Quarterly*, 38 (1976) 49-53.

CERFAUX L., « Pour l'histoire du titre Apostolos dans le Nouveau Testament », in : *Recueil L. Cerfaux*, t. 3, Gembloux, 1962, pp. 185-200.

DESCAMPS A., « Aux origines du ministère. La pensée de Jésus », *Revue théologique de Louvain*, 2 (1971) 3-45.

DUPONT J., « Le nom d'apôtres a-t-il été donné aux Douze par Jésus? », *L'Orient syrien*, 1 (1956) 267-290, 425-444.

GIBLET J., « Les Douze, histoire et théologie », in : A. DESCAMPS, éd., *Le prêtre, foi et contestation*, Gembloux-Paris, 1969.

JAUBERT A., « L'élection de Matthias et le tirage au sort », in : *Studia Evangelica*, vol. VI, TU 112, Berlin, 1973, pp. 267-280.

LEMAIRE A., *Les ministères aux origines de l'Église*, Paris, 1971.

RENGSTORF K. H., « Apostolos », in : TWzNT 1 : 406-448.

RIGAUX B., « Les Douze apôtres », *Concilium*, n. 34 (1968) 11-18, avec bibliographie.

ROLOFF J., *Apostolat, Verkündigung, Kirche*, Gütersloh, 1965.

SCHELKLE K. H., *Jüngerschaft und Apostelamt*, Freiburg, 1961.

On Diakonos and Diakonia

BEYER W., « diakonos, diakonia », in : TWzNT 2 : 87-93.

GERHARDSSON B., *Memory and Manuscript*, Uppsala, 1961.

LEMAIRE A., *Les ministères aux origines de l'Église*, Paris, 1971.

RIESENFELD H., « The Gospel Tradition and its Beginnings », in : *The Gospel Tradition*, Oxford, 1970, pp. 1-30.

CHAPTER XIV

PERRIN N., *What is Redaction Criticism?*, London, 1970.

POTTERIE I. de la, éd., *De Jésus aux Évangiles*, Gembloux, 1967.

ROHDE I., *Die redaktionsgeschichtliche Methode*, Hamburg, 1958².

STEIN R. H., « What is Redaktionsgeschichte? », *Journal of Biblical Literature*, 88 (1969) 45-46.

ZIMMERMANN H., *Neutestamentliche Methodenlehre*, Stuttgart, 1967.

On Matthew

BORNKAMM G., BARTH G., HELD H. J., *Ueberlieferung und Auslegung im Matthäus-Evangelium*, Neukirchen, 1959.

DIDIER M. et collaborateurs, *L'Évangile selon Matthieu : rédaction et théologie*, Gembloux, 1972.

HUMMEL R., *Die Auseinandersetzung zwischen Kirche und Judentum im Matthäus-Evangelium*, München, 1963.

RIGAUX B., *Témoignage de l'Évangile de Matthieu*, Bruxelles, 1967.

SABOURIN L., *Il Vangelo di Matteo*, Marino, 1975; ID., *Il Discorso della montagna nel Vangelo di Matteo*, Marino, 1976.

STRECKER G., *Der Weg der Gerechtigkeit*, Göttingen, 1962.

TRILLING W., *Das Wahre Israel. Studium zur Theologie des Matthäus-Evangeliums*, München, 1964.

On Mark

MARXSEN W., *Der Evangelist Markus. Studien zur Redaktionsgeschichte des Evangeliums*, Göttingen, 1956.

MINETTE DE TILLESSE G., *Le secret messianique dans l'Évangile de Marc*, Paris, 1968.

RADERMAKERS J., *La Bonne Nouvelle de Jésus selon Saint Marc*, Bruxelles, 1974.

ROBINSON J. M., *The Problem of History in Mark*, London, 1957.

RIGAUX B., *Témoignage de l'Évangile de Marc*, Bruxelles, 1965.

SABBE M. et collaborateurs, *L'Évangile selon Marc : Tradition et rédaction*, Gembloux, 1974.

On Luke

CONZELMANN H., *Die Mitte der Zeit*, Tübingen, 1954.

FLENDER H., *Heil und Geschichte in der Theologie des Lukas*, München, 1965.

KECK L. E., MARTYN J. L., *Studies in Luke-Acts*, London, 1968.

LOHSE E., *Lukas als Theologe der Heilsgeschichte*, Bruxelles, 1970.

NEIRYNCK F., *L'Évangile de Luc : problèmes littéraires et théologiques*, Gembloux, 1973.

PAPA B., *La cristologia dei Sinottici e degli Atti degli Apostoli*, Bari, 1972.

RASCO E., *La teología de Lucas : Origen, Desarrollo, Orientaciones*, Roma, 1976.

VOSS G., *Die Christologie der lukanischen Schriften in Grundzügen*, Paris, 1965.

On Others

LÜHRMANN D., *Die Redaktion der Logienquelle*, Neukirchen-Vluyn, 1971.

SCHULZ S., *Q-Die Spruchquelle der Evangelisten*, Zürich, 1972.

GNILKA J., *Die Verstockung Israels. Is. 6, 9-10 in der Theologie der Synoptiker*, München, 1961.

CHAPTER XV

BARBOUR R. S., *Traditio-historical Criticism of the Gospels*, London, 1972.

BULTMANN R., *Die Geschichte der synoptischen Tradition*, Ergänzungsheft, bearbeitet von G. THEISEN und P. VIELHAUER, Göttingen, 1971, pp. 9-12.

CABA J., *De los Evangelios al Jesús histórico*, Madrid, 1971, pp. 391-403.

CALVERT D. G. A., « An Examination of the Criteria for distinguishing the authentic Words of Jesus », *New Testament Studies*, 18 (1972) 209-218.

CARLSTON C. E., « A positive Criterion of Authenticity? », *Biblical Research*, 7 (1962) 33-44.

CERFAUX L., *Jésus aux origines de la Tradition*, Bruges, 1968.

CONZELMANN H., « Jesus Christus », in : *Religion in Geschichte und Gegenwart* III, Tübingen, 1959³, pp. 619-653. Spécialement : pp. 648-651.

DAHL N. A., « Der historische Jesus als geschichtswissenschaftliches und theologisches Problem », *Kerygma und Dogma*, 1 (1955) 104-132. Spécialement, pp. 114-122.

DELORME J., « Pour une approche méthodique des Évangiles », *Foi et Vie*, 4 (1968) 3-71.

DOWNING F. Y., *The Church and Jesus*, London, 1968, pp. 96-117.

DULLES A., *Apologetics and the Biblical Christ*, Westminster, 1964, pp. 36-43.

FITZMYER J. A., *Essays on the Semitic Background of the New Testament*, London, 1971; ID., « The Languages of the Palestine in the first Century A.D. », *Catholic Biblical Quarterly*, 32 (1970) 501-531.

FULLER R., *Critical Introduction to the New Testament*, London, 1966, pp. 96-97.

HOOKER M. D., « Christology and Methodology », *New Testament Studies*, 17 (1972) 480-487.

JEREMIAS J., *Neutestamentliche Theologie, I : Die Verkündigung Jesu*, Göttingen, 1971.

KÄSEMANN E., « Das Problem des historischen Jesus », *Zeitschrift für Theologie und Kirche*, 51 (1954) 125-153.

LAMBIASI F., *L'autenticità storica dei Vangeli. Studio di criteriologia*, Bologna, 1976.

LATOURELLE R., « Authenticité historique des miracles de Jésus. Essai de critériologie », *Gregorianum*, 54 (1973) 225-262; ID., « Critères d'authenticité historique des Évangiles », *Gregorianum*, 55 (1974 609-638.

LEHMANN M., « Synoptische Quellenanalyse und die Frage nach dem historischen Jesus », *Beihefte zur Zeitschrift für die neutestamentliche Wissenschaft*, 38 (1970) 63-205.

LENTZEN-DEIS F., « Die Wunder Jesu », *Theologie und Philosophie*, 43 (1968) 392-402; ID., « Kriterien für die Beurteilung der Jesusüberlieferung in den

Evangelien », in : K. KERTELGE, hrsg., *Rückfrage nach Jesus*, Freiburg, 1974, pp. 78-117.

LÉON-DUFOUR X., *Les Évangiles et l'histoire de Jésus*, Paris, 1963.

LÜHRMANN D., « Liebet eure Feinde (Lk 6, 27-36; Mtt. 5, 39-48 », *Zeitschrift für Theologie und Kirche*, 69 (1972) 412-438; ID., « Die Frage nach Kriterien für ursprüngliche Jesusworte — eine Problemskizze », in : J. DUPONT, éd., *Jésus aux origines de la christologie*, Gembloux, 1975, pp. 59-72.

MARTINI C. M., « La storicità dei Vangeli sinottici », in : *Il Messaggio della Salvezza* IV, Torino, 1968, pp. 127-145.

McARTHUR H. K., « A Survey of Recent Gospel Research », *Interpretation*, 18, (1964) 39-55.

McELENEY N. J., « Authenticating Criteria and Mark 7, 1-23 », *Catholic Biblical Quarterly*, 34 (1972) 430-460.

MUSSNER F., « Der historische Jesus und der Christus des Glaubens », *Biblische Zeitschrift*, 1 (1957) 224-252.

PERRIN N., *Rediscovering the Teaching of Jesus*, London, 1967, pp. 38-49.

POTTERIE I. de la, « Come impostare oggi il problema del Gesù storico? », *La Civiltà Cattolica*, 120 (1969), qu. 2855, pp. 447-463.

RIGAUX B., « L'historicité de Jésus devant l'exégèse récente », *Revue Biblique*, 68 (1958) 481-522.

SCHILLEBEECKX E., *Jesus, het verhaal van een levende*, Bloemendaal, 1974.

SCHÜRMANN H., « Die Sprache des Christus. Sprachliche Beobachtungen an den synoptischen Herrenworten », *Biblische Zeitschrift*, 2 (1958) 54-84.

TRILLING W., *Fragen zur Geschichtlichkeit Jesu*, Düsseldorf, 1966.

WALKER W. O., « The Quest for the Historical Jesus », *Anglican Theological Review*, 51 (1969) 38-56.

ZEDDA S., *I Vangeli e la critica oggi, II: Il Gesù della storia*, Treviso, 1970, pp. 37-44; I.D., « Criteri letterari e criteri reali nella ricerca del Gesù storico », *Rivista Biblica*, 21 (1973) 329-336.

GENERAL BIBLIOGRAPHY

The literature concerning historical access to Jesus through the Gospels in the course of the last few decades has taken on considerable proportions. Without intending to be complete, the present bibliography covers the whole of the subject.

AUDET, L.,
D'ARAGON, J.L. et collaborateurs, *Jésus. De l'histoire a la foi*, "Héritage et Projet" 9, Montréal, 1974.

BALDENSPERGER, G., "l'historicité de Jésus. A propos des récits évangéliques de la passion et de la résurrection", *Revue d'histoire et de philosophie religieuses*, 15 (1935) 193-209.

BARR, A., "Recurrent Questions in the historical Study of the Gospels," in: *Historicity and Chronology in the New Testament*, "Theological Collections" 6. London, 1965, 19-27.

BAUER, J. B., "Evangelium und Geschichtlichkeit," in: *Evangelienforschung*, Graz, (1968) 9-32.

BEA, A., *La storicita dei Vangeli*, Brescia, 1964.

BEILNER, W., "Die Geschichtlichkeit der Evangelien," *Bibel und Liturgie*, 40 (1967) 159-176; *Die Frage nach dem historischen Jesus*, Salzburg-Munchen, 1968.

BERTEN, I.,   "Christologie et recherche historique sur Jésus,"
Revue des Sciences philosophiques et théologiques, 53
(1969), 233-244. "Le retour de la question historique de
Jésus," *ibid.*, 54 (1970), 128-165.

BIEHL, P.,   "Zur Frage nach dem historischen Jesus,"
Theologische Rundschau, 24 (1957-1958), 54-76.

BORNKANN, G., *Jesus von Nazareth*, Stuttgart, 1957.

BOURKE, J.,   "Le Jésus historique et le Christ kérygmatique,"
Concilium, no. 11 (1966), 27-43.

BOUTTIER, M., *Du Christ de l'histoire au Jésus des Evangiles*, Paris,
1969.

BOWMAN, J.W.,"The Quest of the Historical Jesus," *Interpretation*, 3
(1949), 184-190.

BRAATEN, C.E. AND
HARRISVILLE, R.A., ED.,*Kerygma and History*, New York, 1962, "The
historical Jesus and the kerygmatic Christ," *Essays on
the New Quest of the historical Jesus*, New York, 1964.

BROWN, R.E.,   "The Problem of Historicity in John," *Catholic
Biblical Quarterly*, 24 (1962), 1-14, *New Testament
Essays*, Milwaukee, 1965.

BULTMANN, R.,   *Die Geschichte der synoptischen Tradition*, Gottingen, 1957, *Jesus*, Tubingen, 1926, *Das Verhaltnis
der urchristlichen Christusbotschaft zum historischen
Jesus*, Heidelberg, 1960.

CABA, J.,   *De los Evangelios al Jesús histórico*, Madrid, 1970.

CADOUX, C.J., "The Historical Jesus: A Study of Schweitzer and
After," *Expository Times*, 46 (1934-1935), 406-410.

CAMBIER, J.,   "Historicité des Evangiles Synoptiques et
Formgeschichte," in: Heuschen E., éd., *La formation
des Evangiles*, Bruges-Bruxelles-Paris, 1957, 195-212.

CERFAUX, L.,   "La probité des souvenirs évangéliques," *Ephemerides Theologicae Lovanienses*, 4 (1927), 13-28, *La voix vivante de l'Evangile au début de l'Eglise.*, Tournai, 1946, *Jésus aux origines de la Tradition*, Bruges-Bruxelles-Paris, 1968.

CLAVIER, H.,   "Recherche du Jésus de l'histoire," *Revue d'histoire et de philosophie religieuses*, 44 (1964), 236-244.

CLOGG, F.B.,   "The Trustworthiness of the Marcan Outline," *Expository Times*, 46 (1934-1935), 534-538.

CROSS, F.L.,   ed., *Studia Evangelica*, "Texte und Untersuchungen" (TU): vol. I, TU 73, Berlin, 1959; vol. II, TU 87, 1964; vol. III, TU 88, 1964; vol. IV, TU 102, 1968; vol. V, TU 103, 1968; vol. VI, TU 112, 1973. Vol. I, TU 73: Riesenfeld, H., "The Gospel Tradition and its Beginnings," pp. 43-65; Ramsey, A.M., "The Gospel and the Gospels," 35-42.
Vol. II, TU 87: Dunstone, A.S., "Ipsissima verba Christi," 57-64; Radermachers J., "Mission et apostolat dans l'Evangile johannique," 100-121.
Vol. III, TU 88: Bornkamm, G., "The Problem of the Historical Jesus and the kerygmatic Christ," 33-44.
Vol. IV, TU 102: Ramsey, A.M., "History and the Gospel," 75-85.
Vol. VI, TU 112: Fuller, R.H., "The Choice of Matthias," 140-146.

DAHL, N.A.,   "Der historische Jesus als geschichtswissenschaftliches und theologisches Problem," *Kerygma und Dogma*, 1 (1955), 104-132.

DELLING, G.,   "Der historische Jesus und der kerygmatische Christus," *Wort und Gemeinde*, Berlin, 1967, 19-42. "Gepragte Jesus-Tradition im Urchristentum," *Studien zum N.T. und zum hellenistischen Judentum*, Gottingen, 1970, 160-175.

DELORME, J.,   *Des Evangiles a Jésus*, Paris, 1972

DESCAMPS, A., "L'approche des Synoptiques comme documents historiques," *Ephemerides Theologicae Lovanienses*, 46 (1970) 5-16. "Progres et continuité dans la critique des Evangiles et des Actes," *Revue théologique de Louvain*, 1 (1970) 5-44. "Portée christologique de la recherche historique sur Jésus," J. Dupont, ed., *Jésus aux origines du christianisme*, Gembloux, 1975, 23-45.

DODD, C.H., *History and the Gospels*, London, (1938); ID., *The Founder of Christianity*, London, (1971). "The Gospel as History: a Reconsideration," *The Bulletin of the John Rylands Library*, 22 (1938), 122-143.

DULLES, A., "Jesus of History and Christ of Faith," *Commonweal*, 87 (1967) 225-232. *Apologetics and the Biblical Christ*, Westminster, 1964

DUPONT, J., ed., *Jésus aux origines de la christologie*, Gembloux, 1975.

EBELING, G., "Die Frage nach dem historischen Jesus und das Problem der Christologie," *Wort und Glaube I*, Tubingen, 1967, pp. 300-318.

ENSLIN, M.S., "The Meaning of the Historical Jesus for Faith," *The Journal of Bible and Religion*, 30 (1962), 219-223.

FARMER., W.R., MOULE, C.F.D.,
NIEBUHR, R.R., ed., *Christian History and Interpretation*, Cambridge, 1967.

FUCHS, E., *Zur Frage nach dem historischen Jesus*, Tubingen, 1960, "La question du Jésus historique dans la théologie contemporaine," *Bulletin du Centre protestant d'études*, 22, 6s, Geneve, 1970, pp. 5-17.

GABOURY, A., *La structure des Evangiles Synoptiques. La structure-type a l'origine des Synoptiques*, Leiden, 1970.

GEISELMANN, J.R., "Der Glaube an Jesus Christus. Mythos oder Geschichte?," *Theologische Quartalschrift*, 129 (1949),

257-277, 418-439. *Jesus der Christus, I: Die Frage nach dem historischen Jesus*, Stuttgart, 1951.

GERHARDSSON, B., *Memory and Manuscript*, Lund, 1961.

GRAESSER., E., "Christologie und historischer Jesus. Kritische Anmerkungen zu Herbert Brauns Christologieverstandnis," *Zeitschrift fur Theologie und Kirche*, 70 (1973), 404-419.

GRECH, P., "Jesus Christ in History and Kerygma," *A New Catholic Commentary on Holy Scripture*, London, 1969, 822-837; "From Bultmann to the New Hermeneutic," *Biblical Theology Bulletin*, 1 (1971) 190-213; "La Nuova Ermeneutica: Fuchs e Ebeling," *Augustinianum*, 12 (1972), 227-296.

HAHN, F., "Die Frage nach dem historischen Jesus," *Trierer Theologische Zeitschrift*, 82 (1973), 193-205.

HANSON, A., ed., *Vindications. Essays on the historical basis of Christianity*, London, 1966.

HENGEL, M., "Kerygma oder Geschichte?," *Theologische Quartalschrift*, 151 (1971), 323-336.

HENRY, CARL F.H. ed., *Jesus of Nazareth: Saviour and Lord*, Grand Rapids, 1966. Contributions of Martin R., "The New Quest of the Historical Jesus," 23-45; Gerhardsson B., "The Authenticity and Authority of Revelation," 47-59; Bruce F.F., "History and the Gospel," 87-107; Van Elderen B., "The Teaching of Jesus and the Gospel Records," 109-119.

HOFFMAN., J.G.H., *Les vies de Jésus et le Jésus de l'histoire*, Paris, 1947.

HUBY, J., *L'Evangiles*, Paris, 1954.

JELLOUSCHEK, H., "Zur christologischen Bedeutung der Frage nach dem historischen Jesus," *Theologische Quartalschrift*, 152 (1972), 112-123.

JEREMIAS, J., "Kennzeichen der ipsissima verba Jesu," *Synoptischen Studien*, Munchen, 1953, 86-93. "The Present Position in the Controversy concerning the Problem of the Historical Jesus," *Expository Times*, 69 (1957-1958), 333-339, *Das Problem des historischen Jesus*, 1960; *Le message central du Nouveau Testament*, Paris, 1966, *Théologie du Nouveau Testament, I: La prédication de Jésus*, Paris, 1973.

KAHLER, M., *Der sogenannte historische Jesus und der geschichtliche, biblische Christus*, 1892.

KASEMANN, E., "Das Problem des historischen Jesus," *Zeitschrift fur Theologie und Kirche*, 51 (1954), 125-153, "Sackgassen im Streit um den historischen Jesus," *Exegestische Versuche und Besinnungen II*, Gottingen, 1964, 31-68, "Die neue Jesus-Frage," J. Dupont, ed., *Jésus aux origines de la christologie*, Gemblous, 1975, 47-57.

KEE, H.C., *Jesus in History*, New York, 1970.

KERTELGE, K., ed., *Ruckfrage nach Jesus*, "Quaestiones disputatae" 63, Freiburg, 1974. Contributions of: Hahn F., 11-77; Lentzen-Deis F., 78-117; Mussner F., 118-147; Schnackenburg R., 194-220.

KRECK, W., "Die Frage nach dem historischen Jesus als dogmatisches Problem," *Evangelische Theologie*, 22 (1962), 460-478.

KREMER, J., "Die methoden der historisch-kritischen Evangelienforschung und die Frage nach Jesus von Nazareth," *Bibel und Liturgie*, 46 (1973), 83-91.

KUMMEL, W.G., *Das Neue Testament: Geschichte der Erforschung seiner Probleme*, Munchen, 1958, "Das Problem des historischen Jesus in der Gegenwartigen Diskussion," *Deutsches Pfarrerblatt*, 61 (1961) 573-578, "Jesusforschung seit 1950," *Theologische Rundschau*, 31 (1965-1966) 15-46, 289-315; ID., "Ein Jahrzehnt

Jesusforschung (1965-1975)," *Theologische Rundschau*, NF 41 (1976) 197-258, 295-363.

LAMBIASI, F., *L'autenticita storica dei Vangeli. Studio di criteriologia*, Bologna, 1976.

LATOURELLE, R., "Authenticité historique des miracles de Jésus. Essai de critériologie," *Gregorianum*, 54 (1973), 225-262, "Criteres d'authenticité historique des Evangiles," *Gregorianum*, 55 (1974), 609-638.

LEAL, J., *Valor histórico de los Evangelios*, Granada, 1956, *Nuestra confianza en los Evangelios*, Madrid, 1965.

LÉON-DUFOUR, X., *Les Evangiles et l'histoire de Jésus*, Paris, 1963, *Etudes d'Evangile*, Paris, 1965.

LOHSE, E., "Die Frage nach dem historischen Jesus in der gegenwartigen neutestamentlichen Forschung," *Theologische Literaturzeitung*, 87 (1962), 161-174.

MAGNANI, G., *Introduzione alla cristologia fondamentale*, for private use, Rome, 1976.

MALEVE, L., "Jésus de l'histoire et interprétation du kérygme," *Nouvelle Revue théologique*, 91 (1969), 786-808, "Jésus de l'histoire, dondement de la foi," *Nouvelle Revue théologique*, 99 (1967) 785-799, *Le message chrétien et le mythel La théologie de R. Bultmann*, Bruxelles, 1954.

MANSON, T.W., "The Life of Jesus: a study of the available materials,' *The Bulletin of the John Rylands Library*, 27 (1942-1943) 323-337.

MARLÉ, R., "Le Christ de la foi et le Jésus de l'histoire," *Etudes*, 302 (1959), 65-76. "Le probleme de Jésus et les Evangiles," *Recherches de science religieuse*, 48 (1960) 466-489. *Parler de Dieu aujourd'hui. La théologie herméneutique de Gerhard Ebeling*, Paris, 1975.

MARTINI, C   "La storicita dei Vangeli Sinottici," *Il Messaggio della salvezza*, IV, Torino, 1968, 127-145. "Adumbratur quomodo complenda videatur argumentatio pro historicitate Evangeliorum synopticorum," *Verbum Domini*, 41 (1963), 3-10.

MARXSEN, W., "Zur Frage nach dem historischen Jesus," *Theologische Literaturzeitung*, 87 (1962), 575-580.

MC ARTHUR, H.K., "The Burden of Proof in Historical Jesus Research," *Expository Times*, 82 (1970-1971), 116-119. *In Search of the Historical Jesus*, London, 1970.

MC COOL, F.J., "The Preacher and the historical Witness of the Gospels," *Theological Studies*, 21 (1960), 517-543.

MOREAU, J.L   "The Historical Value of the Gospel Materials," *Biblical Research*, 5 (1960), 22-43.

MOULE, C.F.D., "The intention of the Evangelists," HIGGINS, A.J.B., ed., *New Testament Essays*. Studies in Memory of T.W. Manson, Manchester, 1959, 165-177.

MUSSNER, F., "Der historische Jesus und der Christus des Glaubens," *Biblische Zeitschrift*, 1 (1957), 224-252. "Der historische Jesus," *Trierer theologische Zeitschrift*, 69 (1960) 321-337. "Leben-Jesu-Forschung," *Lexikon fur Theologie und Kirche*, 6 859-864. *Le langage de Jean et le Jésus de l'histoire*, Bruges-Bruxelles-Paris, 1969.

NEIL, S.,   *The Interpretation of the New Testament 1861-1961*, New York and Toronto, 1966. *What we know about Jesus*, Grand Rapids, 1972.

NINEHAM, D.E., "Some Reflections on the present Position with regard to the Jesus of History," *Historicity and Chronology in the New Testament*, 6, London, 1965, 1-18.

OGDEN, M.,   "Wie neu ist die neue Frage nach dem historischen

Jesus," *Zeitschrift fur Theologie und Kirche*, 59 (1962), 46-87. "Bultmann and the New Quest," *Journal of Bible and Religion*, 30 (1962), 209-218.

PERRIN, N., *Rediscovering the Teaching of Jesus*, London, 1967, 207-248. *Jesus and the Language of the Kingdom*, London, 1976.

PESCH, R., *Jesu ureigene Taten?* "Quaestiones disputatae" 52, Freiburg, 1970.

PESCH, W., hrsg., *Jesus in den Evangelien*, "Stuttgarter Bibelstudien" 45, Stuttgart, 1970.

PONTIFICIA COMMISSIO DE RE BIBLICA,
"Instructio de historica Evangeliorum veritate," *Verbum Domini*, 42 (1964), 113-120

POTTERIE, I. DE LA,ed., *De Jésus aux Évangiles*, Paris, 1967. "Come impostare oggi il problema del Gesu storico?," *La Civilta Cattolica*, 120 (1969), qu. 2855, 447-463.

RANDELLINI, R., "Possiamo ricostruire una biografia di Gesu?," *Bibbia e Oriente*, 1 (1959), 82-88.

REICKE, B., "Incarnation and Exaltation. The historic Jesus and the kerygmatic Christ," *Interpretation*, 16 (1962) 156-168.

RIESENFELD, H.,*The Gospel Tradition*, Oxford, 1970

RIGAUX, B., "L'historicité de Jésus devant l'exégese récente," *Revue Biblique*, 68 (1958) 481-522.

RISTOW, H. and MATTHIAE, K., eds., *Der historische Jesus und der kerygmatische Christus*, Berlin, 1961.

RIZZI, A., *Christo verita dell'uomo*, Roma, 1972.

ROBINSON, J.M., *The New Quest of the Historical Jesus*, London, 1959. "The Recent Debate on the New Quest," *Journal of Bible and Religion*, 30 (1962), 198-208. "Kerygma and History in the New Testament," Hyatt J.P., ed, *The Bible in Modern Scholarship*, New York, 1965, 114-150.

ROLOFF, J., *Das Kerygma und der irdische Jesus. Historische Motive in den Jesus-Erzahlungen der Evangelien*, Gottingen, 1970, 9-50. "Die Geschichtlichkeit der Schrift und die Bezeugung des einen Evangeliums," VATJA, V., ed., *Evangelium als Geschichte*, Gottingen, 1974, 126-159.

ROWLINGSON, D.T.,"The Gospel-Perspective and the Quest of the Historical Jesus," *Journal of Bible and Religion*, 33 (1965), 329-336.

SCHEIFLER, J.R., *Asi nacieron los Evangelios*, Bilbao, 1967.

SCHILLEBEECKX, E., *L'approccio a Gesu di Nazareth*, Brescia, 972.

SCHMITT, J., "Le kérygme et l'histoire de Jésus," Weber, J.J. et Schmitt, J., ed., *Ou en sont les études bibliques*, Paris, 1968, 213-233.

SCHNACKENBURG, R.,Jesusforschung und Christusglaube," *Catholica*, 13 (1959), 1-17. "La christologie du Nouveau Testament," *Mysterium salutis*, vol. 10, Paris, 1974, 12-234, wt al., *Le message de Jésus et l'interprétation moderne* Paris, 1969.

SCHUBERT, K.,"Das Problem des historischen Jesus," *Bibel und Liturgie*, 38 (1964-195) 369-378; ID., hrsg., *Der historische Jesus und der Christus unseres Glaubens*, Wien, 1962.

SCHWEITZER, A., *Geschichte der Leben-Jesu-Forschung*, Tubingen, 1906.

SCHWEIZER, E., "Mark's Contribution to the Quest of the Historical Jesus," *New Testament Studies*, 10 (1963-1964), 421-432.

SLENCZKA, R., *Geschichtlichkeit und Personsein Jesu Christi*, Gottingen, 1967.

STOCK, H., "Das Verhaltnis der Christusbotschaft der synoptischen Evangelien zum historischen Jesus als Problem des biblischen Unterrichts in der Schule," Dinkler, E., ed., *Zeit und Geschichte*, Tubingen, 1964, 703-717.

STRECKER, G., "Die historische und die tehologische Problematik der Jesusfrage," *Evangelische Theologie*, 29 (1969) 453-476, ed.,*Jesus Christus in Historie und Theologie*, Tubingen, 1975.

STRUBE, G., hrsg., *Wer war Jesus von Nazareth? Die Erforschung einer historischen Gestalt*, Munchen, 1972.

TAYLOR, V., *The Formation of the Gospel Tradition*, London, 1935.

TRILLING, W., *Fragen zur Geschichtlichkeit Jesu*, Dusseldorf, 1966

TURNER, H.E.W., *Jesus, Master and Lord. A Study in the Historical Truth of the Gospels*, London, 1953, *Historicity and the Gospels. A Sketch of Historical Method and its application to the Gospels*, London, 1963.

VANHENGEL, M., PETERS, J.,"Ce Jésus-ci, Jésus connu par l'Evangile et par la foi," *Concilium*, no. 20 (1966), 141-150.

VOGTLE, A., "Die historische und theologische Tragweite der heutigen Evangelienforschung," *Zeitschrift fur Theologie und Kirche*, 86 (1964) 385-417. *Formazione e Struttura dei Vangeli*, Brescia, 1967. "Die hermeneutisch Relevanz des geschichtlichen Charakters des Christusoffenbarung," Thils G. and Brown R.E., ed., *Exégèse et théologie. Les Saintes Ecritures et leur interprétation théologique*, Paris, 1968, 191-208. *Das Evangelium und die Evangelien*, Dusseldorf, 1971.

WALKER, W.O., "The Quest for the Historical Jesus," *Anglican*

Theological Review, 51 (1969), 38-56.

WEBER, J.J.,   "Les Evangiles méritent-ils notre confiance?," Weber, J.J. and Schmitt, J., ed., Ou en sont les études bibliques, Paris, 1968, 185-212.

WILKENS, U.,   "Tradition et kérygme du Christ," Revue d'histoire et de philosophie religieuses, 47 (1967), 1-20.

ZAHRNT, H.,   Es begann mit Jesus von Nazareth, Stuttgart-Berlin, 1960

ZEDDA, S.,   I Vangeli e la critica oggi, II: Il Gesu della storia, Treviso, 1970. "Il problema del Gesu storico nella luce del Vaticano II," La Civilta Cattolica, 2 (1968, 334-357. "Gesu storico alle origini della cristologia del Nuovo Testamento," Sacra Doctrina, 16 (1971), 433-448.

ZIMMERMANN, H.,   Neutestamentliche Methodenlehre, Stuttgart, 1967.